Abandoned in Search of Rainbows

A. K. DRIGGS

BOOK PUBLISHERS NETWORK
Changing the World One Book at a Time

Book Publishers Network
P.O. Box 2256
Bothell • WA • 98041
PH • 425-483-3040
www.bookpublishersnetwork.com

A portion of proceeds from the sale of this book and all music goes to various animal, ocean, marine, and land conservation causes in the United States and globally.

All songs by A. K. Driggs can be found at:
www.AbandonedInSearchOfRainbows.com.

10 9 8 7 6 5 4 3 2 1

Printed in the United States of America

LCCN   2015946830
ISBN   978-1-940598-77-2

Editor: Julie Scandora
Cover designer: Laura Zugzda
Typographer: Melissa Vail Coffman
Production: Scott Book

Your talent is God's gift to you; what you do with it is your gift to God.

– Leo Buscaglia

CONTENTS

Acknowledgments vii
Preface ix

Act I

On the Road with Mom *1*
1   In the Beginning 3
2   Moving Up 15
3   Always Have Health Insurance 25
4   Betty and Bob 33
5   The Sensitive One 41
6   Play Time 53
7   The Dark Side 59
8   Defining Myself 71

Act II

On the Road with Mom *89*
9   A Date, a Friend, and Inklings of Love . . 91
10   Moving Up . . . and Out 99
11   College Quitter 109
12   London for Longer 123
13   Beginnings of True Independence . . . 139
14   Following My Music Muse 151

15   Shaky New Start 169
16   New Career. 177
17   Good-byes 199
18   Opening New Doors 207

Act III
   On the Road with Mom *219*
19   Viva Las Vegas. 221
20   My One and Only 235
21   Downers 245
22   Life Is Too Precious 257
23   Filling the Last Holes 277
24   Outflowing to All Living Creatures . . . 289

A Note from the Author **293**

Acknowledgments

The mere willingness to reconstruct the dramatic journey from where I began to where I am now called for a huge commitment and at times an overwhelming one. I needed guidance. So I phoned a dear friend, Gail Provost Stockwell (a.k.a. Nushka), a published author but also co-founder of a nationally known writer's program, the Writers Retreat Workshop. After I told her a shortened version of my story, without hesitation, she agreed it needed to be told, that I could do it, and that she'd coach me. Thanks to her guidance and mentoring, not only have I managed to bring this project to fruition, but I have also learned to focus on you, my reader. Nushka, you are an angel to me, and I am eternally grateful for all you have given me throughout this journey.

Thank you, Dr. Tappen, whose soul resides in heaven now. Without your guidance and belief in me, I might never have stepped out on that high school stage. You were and are with me always.

Hailie, my beloved heart-adopted child, my little pumpkin, you are such an inspiration to me and a huge reason why I decided to write this book. Your precious comments so often struck me as uncannily in sync with whatever topic I was writing about on that particular day. You couldn't have known—and yet you did. I no longer question our extraordinary soul connection. I simply accept the blessing and thank Spirit for sending you into my life.

I also count as blessings my *hanai ohana* family and friends across the pond from coast to coast and here in Kona. You have all supported me and cheered me on, and your enthusiasm has energized me more than you may realize.

Thank you to Mom and Dad for their undying love in taking in an emotionally broken child and loving me as if they had created me. They gave me the strength, love, and support to pursue my dreams and instilled in me the work ethic and professional integrity that has stayed with me my entire life. Without their love, I might never have made it. I miss you both every day.

Jae, you are my best friend, my spouse, and my love. You have been my rock, as you unwaveringly stood by me throughout this process, enduring each emotional challenge with either a smile and encouragement or a good ol' kick in the pants to show your tough love. It is your strength that's given me the courage to see this project through, despite all the tears and fears. Had you not come into my life back in 1994, this story could never have been written. It's just that simple. My true love, I thank you.

PREFACE

For the last forty years, my closest family of friends have been pushing me to write my story. Each time I declined. I didn't understand then what I do now, that my ego was in control of my reaction. After all, I wasn't a professional writer. But then, in the fall of 2012 while I was dreaming, I heard a voice as clear as any I'd ever heard: "Kim, you have to tell your story."

Upon awakening, I agreed the time had come, despite my ego's fear of ridicule. I had to just plain *do it!* But how? And when?

My clients, my company, and tending to their needs—they could not be abandoned because they were and would always be my highest priority. So, with miraculously acquired additional energy, I became the one doing the pushing. I spent Saturdays and Sundays from seven in the morning until three or so in the afternoon hiding out in what became my little writing room, just doing it, getting the memories down on paper.

And so my beloved readers, here is my story. I hope it reaches into each of your souls and finds a place that resonates with you.

ACT I

On the Road with Mom

Naples, Florida is behind us now. It's the summer before my fortieth birthday, and Mom and I are driving cross-country in her car with the stuff she chose to keep with her rather than send along with the moving van. We're heading to the Vegas condo I found for her in The Lakes, only ten minutes away from the rental house I share with Shannon and Kyle.

It's a busy time for Avatar, my company, but I'm not concerned about being away from it. One thing I know for sure about myself is that the busier I become, the more I can take on. And right now, what matters most to me is that I convinced Mom to make this move. I need to watch over her, be there for her. God knows she's always been there for me. Well, except for that one time. I look over at her and take in her sadness, her aches and pains.

I want so much for her to be happy. And because I'm in the driver's seat right now, I'm working some magic. We're singing together. I glance over and catch a little sparkle gleaming from her baby blues that once upon a time dazzled every beholder. To see her smile like that still takes my breath away.

Mom reaches over to my arm and suddenly asks, "You still have it? The article?"

"Not on me," I tell her. "But I still have it. At home." I decide not to mention that I also still have it in my head. Without realizing it, I had memorized effortlessly every word of it. I know where Mom's going with this, and it makes sense. Mom wants to talk now, not sing. She wants to go down memory lane while we're on this trip.

"Go ahead, honey," she says. "You start."

I look over and see she's tearing up. "Okay if we start at the beginning again?" That's usually where we start because the truth is we both know I can never hear her tell these stories often enough, even though by now I know all of them not only by heart but also backwards and forwards.

Mom leans against the passenger window, closing her eyes. "My God, Kim," she says, and though I'm passing a truck, I can hear her smile. Mom continues. "I'll never forget that moment," she says, "the moment I turned the page, and there was your precious little face. And I'll never forget what happened after that, every step of the way."

❈ ❈ ❈ CHAPTER 1 ❈ ❈ ❈

In the Beginning

January 25, 1954, in upstate New York was another gloomy and frigid winter day. In downtown Rochester, piles of icy snow, filthy from automobile exhaust, road salt, and sand, lined the sidewalks.

As Mrs. Slora, owner of Saeger's Grill, the neighborhood bar and restaurant located at 218 Clinton Avenue North, tended to her chores inside, she saw a young woman enter through the bar's side door. Dressed in a long, black coat and a flowered kerchief tied around her head, she appeared very tired. As the young woman headed directly toward the restroom, Mrs. Slora noticed that she was carrying a brown paper bag.

After several minutes had passed, Mrs. Slora realized she'd not seen the woman come out of the restroom. Thinking there might be a problem, Mrs. Slora hurried over to find out if she could help. But when she opened the restroom door, the woman was not to be found.

What she did find, however, was the paper sack the woman had been carrying. It had been placed on the lid of the toilet seat. Mrs. Slora walked over and peered inside the bag. To her utter dismay, she saw a tiny infant, sleeping peacefully.

Bits of dark brown hair flared out from beneath the blanket in which the child had been wrapped. As gently as possible, Mrs. Slora removed the tiny bundle, unwrapped the blanket, and saw that the abandoned infant was a baby girl.

⌗ ⌗ ⌗

The police came quickly after Mrs. Slora's phone call. Detective James Martin immediately sent the foundling to Genesee Hospital. Nurses took over. The baby, they reported, appeared to be in good health. In a few days, they would turn her over to the Society for the Prevention of Cruelty to Children. Soon, SPCC director, Guy D. Harris, reported that his agency would be joining in the police investigation to find the foundling's mother.

Although not front-page news, the abandoned baby rated high in human interest and ran in the following day's paper.

⌗ ⌗ ⌗

While reading the January 26, morning edition of the *Democrat and Chronicle* newspaper over breakfast, Betty blurted out, "Bob, look, here in the paper." She pointed with enthusiasm to an article. "Now there's a little girl that needs a home. Why can't we have her?"

Bob leaned over his eggs and toast and quickly read the article showing a photo of an infant girl with dark brown hair resting in the arms of a nurse. Somewhat emotionless, he replied, "Why, that is quite a story. Honey, I don't know why we can't have her." And he went back to reading the business section.

Betty looked at him with frustration. Was that it? He had nothing more to say on the matter? She was distraught and pulled the paper back to her chest. She sat in silence staring at the little face of the baby being fed a bottle by a nurse. Betty's heart sank as she thought of herself. *Will I ever have a little girl of my own?* And she felt sad for the little girl. *Who would abandon such a beautiful child?*

She continued drinking her black coffee and turned the page to read an article that the Supreme Court had ruled that race-based segregation in schools is unconstitutional. That was the only thing that pleased Betty that morning.

⌗ ⌗ ⌗

The article said the infant had been crying "lustily." The caption of the photo of the baby being fed read: "WHOSE? Foundling girl, abandoned in rest room, finds solace in bottle offered by Nurse Ruth Lyon in Genesee Hospital. Investigators seek baby's mother."

At the hospital, doctors identified Mediterranean traits and ordered numerous blood tests to see if they could verify the baby's nationality. The results were inconclusive. The authorities determined that the female baby was approximately two to four days old, so when they created her birth certificate, they dated it January 23, 1954. They named the foundling Jane Churchill.

❋ ❋ ❋

So there it is, my entrance into society! Oh, but wasn't I one lucky babe! I had a birth mother who so clearly wanted me to be found. I shudder to think of all the unwanted babies who in those days would be discovered in a trash barrel or, if that was not despicable enough, weighted down by a rock at the bottom of a body of water.

Not only had I been found alive and sleeping peacefully in a dry, warm place, but also, the authorities had blessed me with quite a distinguished last name. (I later learned that the great Sir Winston Churchill, UK's prime minister at the time, turned eighty years old the same year I was born. It's interesting to me that he died exactly ten years later on January 24, 1965.)

I assume the children's welfare authorities chose the name hoping it might be an asset to counter some of the negative issues associated with me, which came to light once I was placed with the SPCC for foster care and eventual adoption. For one thing, a mysterious rash developed all over my body, and it would not go away.

For another, I had two visibly unappealing red birthmarks. One showed from my left temple across my left cheek and over my nose to my right cheek and then all the way down to the bottom of my chin. The second, a thick, dark birthmark, rose about a quarter of an inch off my left shoulder.

These visual factors along with the auditory ones—the fact that I cried not only "lustily" but also most of the time—were defects they believed only a mother could love in her own child. They deemed me unadoptable.

Oh, and as for the search to find my birth mother? Well, that trail just ran icy cold.

❊ ❊ ❊

Betty and Bob Driggs of Rochester had always loved children. For years, they had tried to have their own, but after several heartbreaking miscarriages, they decided to adopt. Embracing their Plan B, the prospect thrilled them. They'd adopt first a baby boy and then a baby girl.

In 1947, six years and four months before I was born, they found their first child—a six-month-old baby boy, whom they named Robert Parker Driggs II (after Bob) but nicknamed "Chip," as in chip off the old block.

Unfortunately for the Driggs, the trial period that began the adoption process was indeed a *trial*. Because Chip was such an adorable baby, his birth mother had difficulty deciding whether or not to keep him for herself. She'd put him up for adoption and then, during the trial period, change her mind and take him back. Finally, when this happened one time too many, the authorities at the adoption agency had had enough of her shenanigans. She was told that this was her last chance and that if she changed her mind again they were going ahead with the adoption. The baby would belong to the Driggs, permanently.

Devastated, Bob and Betty Driggs could not fathom that she'd let him go again, not under these final terms. Now they believed they would never see their little boy again.

At this time, Chip had begun to say a few words. The one word he repeated again and again came out sounding like "jig," and so his birth mother was sure he was saying "Driggs" because he had bonded with them. Guilt set in, and she knew he'd be better off with them, and so, she decided to let her baby go.

The adoption went through. And now Chip was permanently with Bob and Betty Driggs . . . and their pet, Jiggy, a funny little cocker spaniel that Chip absolutely adored.

❊ ❊ ❊

By 1954, when Chip was in second grade, Bob and Betty were ready to find their baby girl. Betty contacted the Monroe County Children's Services, inquiring about a baby girl to adopt. She was told no, there were no baby girls for her to see. So she waited a few months before calling again. Again she was told no. Every six months, she called, and every six months she was told the same thing: no girls for her to see.

The wait was becoming agonizing not only for Bob and Betty but now also for their son, Chip, who was impatient for the little sister he'd been promised.

One afternoon, about fifteen months later, Chip walked into the kitchen, loaded down with shopping bags. They'd just come back from town. It had been a rare, beautiful, fifty-degree day, blue skies and sunshine. For early April, spring was definitely in the air that day, and like everyone else, they were eager for winter to end. While Chip unpacked the bags, Betty put the groceries away listening to Chip rattle on about the upcoming baseball season and how he could hardly wait to find out who his Little League coach would be this year.

Then the telephone rang.

Chip, closest to the wall phone, picked it up quickly. Betty noticed his eyes widen. "It's Mr. Hanson," he said, holding the phone out toward his mother, "from Monroe County Children's Services."

Betty closed the fridge and for just a moment leaned against it. Dare she believe this would be the call she'd been praying for, for so long? Then, with her heart pounding, she walked over to take the phone. "Hello?"

"Elizabeth," Dave Hanson said, "I'm happy to say that we have a little girl for you to look at, but . . ."

❋ ❋ ❋

The next afternoon, the weather returned to cold and cloudy. Betty had arranged for Chip to go to a friend's house after school and for Bob to leave the office early for their three o'clock appointment to meet their little girl.

When they arrived right on schedule, Dave was there to greet them. He ushered Betty and Bob upstairs and into a wood-paneled room with four large windows that let in little light due to the dark cloud cover outside.

There was something cold and unsettling about the moment. Most chilling of all were the heart-wrenching sounds of a child's misery that was emanating from a crib at the back of the room.

My mother's recollection of that moment is that she saw Dave roll his eyes and nod as if to say, *Yup. That's the baby! That's the one you've come to see.* He then motioned for them to go ahead, saying, "See for yourself."

Bob took Betty's hand, and as they approached the crib in the far corner under the window, they saw me, a fifteen-month-old baby girl, lying on her back, rubbing her eyes, and shrieking to beat the band. They had dressed me in a simple, off-white dress. I had on one pink bootie but had already kicked off the other.

"Oh the poor darling," Betty whispered as tears dripped from her eyes.

Bob took charge and immediately tried to calm me down by removing his wristwatch and swinging it in front of me. But it didn't work. I wailed even louder.

From behind them, Dave proclaimed, "I told you."

Betty spun around. "Please!" she snapped. "Don't talk like that!"

"Well, I tried to warn you on the phone."

"Yes you did, and I told you we don't care about all of that. We *want* her. She's our little girl, and we don't care where she came from or that she doesn't look like us or anything else!" Then Betty turned her attention to me again. "It's okay, honey," she said. "We're here now. You don't need to cry."

So then Dave backed away, and even though I was still kicking and screaming, Bob lifted me from the crib, and before handing me over to Betty, he planted gentle kisses all over my birthmarks. When I was nestled in Betty's arms, she began to sing a lullaby.

I was still bawling my eyes out at first, but as she continued to sing and to sway me from side to side in a nice wide arc, my sobbing lessened, and then, when I was merely whimpering, I finally opened my big brown eyes and looked up at her. When our eyes locked, the crying abruptly stopped. Just like that! And, just like that, I gave her a great big smile.

In that magical moment between mother and child, Betty and I forged a bond that was nothing short of unbreakable, the kind of bond that simply had to last for . . . *ever.*

※ ※ ※

As is always the case, a mandated trial period took place before the official adoption could occur. This trial for Betty and Bob was going well, unlike the period with Chip. Betty was elated to be at home with me, and Bob was always itching to get home from the office to spend as much time as possible with his children. It was a bonus too that Chip acted so protective of me—his soon-to-be little sister. I apparently idolized Chip because the moment he came home from school, I followed him everywhere.

Soon after the trial period had commenced, my rash began improving. Even so, Betty and Bob complied with the instructions to have me get steroid shots and be fed primarily orange foods, and they included the details of both in their regular weekly and monthly progress reports to the authorities, as they'd done during Chip's trial period.

Poor Betty had to take me for my shots, and each time, even before we'd leave the house, my fears set in, and I'd be crying. By the time we were at the pediatrician's office, I'd be screaming in abject terror at the mere sight of a lab coat, never mind the needle.

It didn't take Betty and Bob terribly long to become convinced of three things. One, the amount of steroids I was getting couldn't possibly be good for me. Two, all those orange foods my previous captors had me on were doing nothing but causing the bizarre orange darkening of my skin. I guess they thought all that beta-carotene would clear up the unsightly phantom rash. And three, the only medicine that would truly benefit me was their unconditional love and the security that being with them would provide. And so, the shots were soon suspended, a decision made by Bob and Betty, and I was put on a normal healthy diet. That diet did include orange foods—but only within reason.

Week after week, month after month, my issues were getting better and better. In fact, everything was getting better because we were getting closer to the trial period being over.

❋ ❋ ❋

August 30, 1956, arrived a steamy hot day with intermittent rain, drizzle, fog, and thunder, and it couldn't have been more beautiful. I'd been with the Driggs family since I was about fifteen months old.

Although now only a two-and-a-half-year-old child, I could fully grasp the monumental importance of this day.

Betty and Bob had bought me a special outfit, a pretty pink dress with matching socks and patent-leather shoes. And they too were all dressed up because it was so special an occasion.

After we piled into Bob's car, he turned on the windshield wipers, and Betty turned on the radio. Doris Day was singing her new hit song, "Que Sera Sera," and they both happily sang along with her. By the time we pulled into the parking lot next to the county courthouse, I had learned the song and was chiming in.

When we first walked into Judge Fritch's office at the county courthouse, Betty and Bob couldn't hold me back. I dashed over to him, exclaiming, "Hi, Judge! Hi, Judge! I'm getting adopted!"

He was such a warm, friendly man. While Betty set aside her umbrella and Chip and Dad took seats, the judge led me over to his big swivel chair behind his desk.

He invited me to sit on his big chair behind his big desk while he gathered up papers for Bob and Betty to sign. Mom told me I was jumping up and down on his chair, chanting, "I'm getting adopted, I'm getting adopted!"

The judge looked over at Bob and Betty. "Guess I already know how Jane feels about this topic."

"Oh, yes. We're all so happy, Judge Fritch," Betty said. "Finally, we have our little girl!"

Bob was beaming. "She's everything we dreamed of," he said, "and more."

Betty called me over to sit on her lap as soon as the conversation turned to the documents to be read and then signed. The reading went on for quite a while. Of course, to me it all sounded like gobbledegook, but still I tried to tune in every now and then. Mostly, I just loved cuddling up to Betty. I remember smiling at her the whole time and looking into her dancing blue eyes.

> In the Matter of the Adoption of Jane Churchill
> . . . upon reading and filing the petition . . . duly
> acknowledged Agreement . . . written report of the
> investigation . . . and it appearing that the . . . interests

of said child, Jane Churchill, born January 23, 1954, in Rochester, New York, will be prompted by said adoption . . . are in all respects satisfactory and proper persons to adopt said child and that no objections exist thereto . . . ordered, adjudged and decreed that the said Jane Churchill shall be raised and treated in all respects . . . lawful child of Robert P. Driggs and Elizabeth L. Driggs, his wife, and shall henceforth be known . . . Ann Kimberly Driggs.

"So," the judge finally was asking, "everything seem in order?"

"Perfect," Bob and Betty agreed.

I watched Bob—now my official daddy—place his copy into his briefcase, handling it as though it were an injured bird. Then he looked over at me with raised eyebrows. When he reached for his hat and umbrella, he looked over at me. "Kimmy," he said, "thank the judge now."

I bounded over to the judge and then raised my arm to shake hands with him, though I'd never done that with anyone before. "Thanks, Judge," I said. He held onto my little hand and gave me a good, firm handshake.

With true joy in his voice he said, "You are most welcome, Miss Kimberly Driggs. Most welcome."

"You too," I said, and they all laughed.

Once we were outside again, it was only drizzling. I remember skipping along between my parents and holding their hands, with Chip marching ahead of us. In a singsong sort of way, I kept repeating, "I am adopted, and you're my mom and dad!" How I must have adored the sound of those words.

As I was about to get into the car after Chip, the clouds above were just then parting, letting in some sunshine. Daddy and I both looked up. He knelt beside me and pointed to a tall building one street behind the courthouse.

"Look, Kimmy. See that big building?"

"Uh huh."

"Now look up, up in the sky. Do you see those colors, honey? That's a rainbow. That's a rainbow."

"A rainbow!" Mom said, happily.

"A rainbow," I whispered to myself. "A rainbow."

❋ ❋ ❋

I learned quickly that by being an adopted child I had been chosen. Although I didn't comprehend the distinction from how Chip and I were chosen but other children were not, I sure loved the sound of that word, "chosen," especially the way my mom said it.

One night shortly after the adoption when Mom tucked me into bed, she recited a poem to me.

> *Not from my womb*
> *Nor bone of my bone,*
> *But still, miraculously, my own.*
> *Don't forget for a single minute,*
> *You didn't grow under my heart, but in it.*

As she said the words, she moved her hands to touch either her heart or tummy. It was then that I came to understand the true meaning of the word "chosen."

The original poem, I have since discovered, began with the words, "*Not flesh of my flesh*," and its author is Fleur Conkling Heyliger. But for me the words and phrasing as my mother recited the poem are what feels right. To this day, I recite it the same way in my mind when feelings of insecurity begin to sneak up on me, threatening to set off ye olde phantom rash.

Betty and Kim, ca. 1956.

Dad holding Kim during trial period, 1956.

CHAPTER 2

MOVING UP

During the trial period for my adoption, Mom had experienced a few unnerving experiences with strangers who had recognized me when she'd be taking me for a walk in my stroller. The final straw had come one day when a woman we were passing on the sidewalk had blurted out, "Hey, wait a minute. Stop! I know that kid!"

Without losing a beat, Mom had called over her shoulder, "Sorry, but you're mistaken. This is my daughter." She had continued pushing me forward with no further drama.

Later that day, though, when Dad had come home from work, she had urged him to hurry along the process of finding a house away from the city. So they had begun their search in earnest.

A few months after the adoption was official, my dad came home with a carload of old flattened cartons, which he'd been collecting for weeks. And at supper that day, my parents informed my brother and me that we were going to move out of our small ranch house in Rochester to a small colonial house they'd found in the suburbs.

We were moving because of my father's latest promotion at the R. T. French Company (maker of French's mustard) where, from the time my brother was about a year old, Dad had begun in their advertising department. In no time at all, he had been promoted to assistant advertising manager, then to sales promotion manager, and then to group marketing manager. I believe my dad was promoted so rapidly because of his high standards and work ethic as much as his big personality and talent.

Now, Dad was being promoted to marketing director for the company and was expected to maintain a certain lifestyle, one unlike what we had been used to. This meant socializing with the upper middle class and living in a more upscale neighborhood where my parents could belong to a country club, play bridge, and most important, play golf with other members of the club.

The up-and-coming town of Pittsford—a charming colonial village along the Erie Canal with the requisite country club and golf courses—seemed to perfectly fit all the requirements.

The Little Singer

During the entire period of packing up all our stuff, the actual move, and then the unpacking of everything, my mother and I engaged in a new and favorite activity. She taught me new songs. My favorites at the time were "How Much Is That Doggie in the Window?" and "Frère Jacques."

I may have sung those two songs to death, I think, because about then my mother purposely set down her freshly brewed cup of black coffee, took me by the hand out of the kitchen and into the living room of our cute two-story house, and asked me to sit on the sofa and to be still. As she struggled with a few unopened cartons, looking for something in particular, I could barely wait to see what it was. Soon she had kitchen shears in her hand to cut through the packing tape of two of the cartons. I ran over and discovered piles of record albums.

Dad and Chip had already set up the stereo system the day before, so now Mom chose a few albums, removed the records from their paper sleeves, and stacked them carefully on the record player. She told me to go back to the couch and to stay there and listen to the music while she continued putting things away.

I heard a variety of recording artists—Frank Sinatra, Nat King Cole, Ella Fitzgerald, Johnny Mathis, Tony Bennett, Andy Williams— each with his or her unique sound and style. When the last record was ending, Mom waltzed back into the room—she loved to dance—turned the records over, and restacked them into the player.

Day after day, this would be part of our routine. I would listen to a stack of albums and memorize the words and tunes, so on the next go-round, I'd be able to sing along. Mom wasn't surprised with how quickly I learned the melodies and lyrics because even Dave Hanson had reported I'd been a fast learner. What surprised her was my perfect pitch and ability to recall each singer's phrasing, dynamics, and register. But what really blew her mind was that even at my tender age—I was only about three years old—I intuitively had begun to harmonize.

I could see all this in my mother's eyes. Whenever I sang, her baby blues sparkled, her gorgeous smile widened, and because she loved to dance, she always swayed and twirled around the room. Boy, oh boy, did I love seeing my mom happy like that. Nothing meant more to me.

And to ensure her happiness, I learned, all I needed to do was what I loved to do anyway—sing. I'd sing; she'd be happy. I'd see her happy; I'd be happy. It was that simple. Or so I thought.

❈ ❈ ❈

Whenever we were in the car on our way to visit Grandma Flossie and Grandpa Joe, I'd wonder if Grandma would serve burnt pork chops again for dinner. Then I'd wonder what song I'd sing that day because I always would perform for them after jumping out from behind their musty living room drapes. "Ta da!" I'd shout. "I'm going to be a singer!"

Around the time I turned seven, though, that all changed. I'd only agree to sing for them if they promised not to look at me. So, at my grandparents' house, I did my singing from behind their curtains. At home and at Uncle Earl and Uncle Bud's place, I'd sing only from behind their sofa.

One day when I was twelve years old, Uncle Bud stopped me in the middle of singing, "Leaving on a Jet Plane." "Hold it right there!" he said, leaning over the couch and looking at me. "You wanna be a singer, kiddo? Ya gotta get out from behind the couch!"

"But I don't want people to look at me."

"Sorry, kid, but ya gotta let them. That's just the way it is. C'mon. Out front. Let's go."

"Fine! I'm coming . . . but I'm not singing."

"Suit yourself," he said taking my hand as though we were dancing. "Sooner or later, you're going to have to do it, Kimbo," his nickname for me. "Think about it at least, okay?"

I said I would, but I didn't mean it. At the time, I already had too many other things to worry about, two of them dealing with speaking.

For one thing, I had developed a stuttering problem that embarrassed me greatly. Mom suggested a few coping strategies. For example, if I answered our telephone and had trouble getting out the word "hello," she recommended I just laugh at myself and say something like, "Please wait a second. Let me try that again."

She assured me the day would come when I'd be able to say whatever I wanted without stuttering, that my stuttering problem would eventually end. As it turned out, stuttering in terms of a serious problem did end but not until I was in my junior year of high school. To this day, a stutter here or there might take me by surprise but only if I'm extremely fatigued or if I try to get too many thoughts out at one time.

Also, I had a difficult time overcoming a speech impediment, mostly with the letter *s*. Mom and Dad hired a speech therapist to work with me, and surprise, surprise, I had to practice the tongue-twister you probably said just for the fun of it. Well, try repeating "Sally sells seashells down by the seashore" or "Betty's blue beach bag" a zillion-katrillion-bazillion times, and see how much fun that is for you. No matter what, though, if you do it, you'll probably learn what I did: Practice makes perfect.

Dad's Ethics

My father's responsibilities at work continued to increase, and soon the company added business trips to his already crammed schedule. As it was, because of his diligent work ethic, exceptional management style, and high standards, he tended to be the first person to get to work in the morning and the last to leave at the end of the day.

One night after he had finally returned to Pittsford after having been away on a three-week business trip, he was supposed to be in my room tucking me in for the night. But he wasn't.

"I know you're disappointed, honey," my mother said as she smoothed out my comforter. "Your daddy'd be here if he could. You know that, don't you?"

"But why can't he be? He said he would."

"I already told you that he had no choice. He had to stay late again because his team counts on him to straighten things out when they go wrong."

"Yes, but so do I."

Mom touched my face. "What's going on at work is an emergency, Kimmy. What's going on here in this room isn't."

"What's 'emergency'?"

"That's when something needs to be done right away to fix something that's happened. Maybe something doesn't work anymore, or something broke, or someone got hurt. If nothing's done right away, the problem will continue to get worse."

"Oh, like when I cut my finger."

"That's exactly right."

"But—"

"Look, Kimberly, your daddy wishes he could be in two places at one time, but that's just not possible, is it?"

"Well . . . maybe he could."

"Aw c'mon now, you're just being silly."

"But, Mom, I want him to see what I got!"

"I know you do, and you know what? I bet you'll get to show it to him tomorrow night. Know why?"

"Why?"

"Because Daddy's project *must* be finished by noontime tomorrow to meet the deadline."

"What's that?"

"That's when time's up, ready or not." She reached under my chin and tickled me. "Get it?"

For those giggling moments before Mom kissed me goodnight, I actually forgot about all the birthday presents, cards, bows, and ribbons that I'd kept neatly piled at the foot of my bed for weeks.

❊ ❊ ❊

From as far back as I can remember, Dad gave us kids three pieces of advice: "Always do your best, always be honest, and always have health insurance." He taught me to give 100-percent effort to whatever I was doing and to tell the truth. But, as a little kid, that last part about health insurance? I could never understand what in the world that had to do with the two other pieces of advice, so whenever I'd hear him say that, I'd just laugh myself silly, certain he was just kidding around.

It never occurred to me—me, the big questioner, the big wonderer—to ask the question, *Why? Why always have health insurance?*

❊ ❊ ❊

In some ways, though, even in those first few years in Pittsford, I worried that Daddy was being stretched in too many different directions at the same time. Work, all day long. Us kids in the evening. So much stuff to do on the weekends. So much this, so much that.

Both of my parents now were leading an active social life. On weekends, if they weren't entertaining other couples at our house, my parents were being entertained at someone else's home. Or they were having dinner out at a restaurant. Or they were at the country club. Or playing bridge. Or playing golf. Or playing golf. Or playing golf. And a lot of booze was being poured and consumed. A lot of cigarettes were being purchased and smoked.

Somehow, as much as I hated the stench of that cigarette smoke, I got used to it. In time, the swirling smoky veil in every room became invisible. Although I never said a word about their smoking—and almost all their friends smoked as well—I thought my wrinkled up nose and flailing arms would tell them for me.

No such luck.

Connecting to Nature

By the time Elvis Presley had appeared on *The Ed Sullivan Show* for the third time, I was singing along with "Don't Be Cruel." My rash continued to lessen. The ugly reddish birthmark was fading. Even the bumpy birthmark on my shoulder was beginning to shrink. With the love and security of my parents and my big brother, I was in the right place, in more ways than one. The 1950s was a great time to be a kid growing up in Pittsford, especially in such a friendly, safe neighborhood.

Our house was situated at the corner of Rand Place and Jefferson Road. Gorgeous, big old elm and maple trees lined both sides of Rand Place, whereas Jefferson Road was actually a major thoroughfare. I wasn't allowed to go out onto Rand Place by myself when I was little. So, I watched the older kids swoosh past our house on their bikes and then screech to a halt at the corner of Rand and Jefferson.

The girls tended to ride by more slowly, and when they reached the corner, they would either get off their bikes and turn them around or make a wide, slow turn before heading back in the direction they'd come from. The point of all this, I learned, was that Rand Place was safe, just as long as you knew enough to steer clear of Jefferson Road. I guess you could say it was an unwritten law.

The neighborhood itself was safe, though. Back then, neighbors left their doors unlocked, and when they said, "Please drop by," they meant it. In many ways, our neighborhood was more than just safe. It was like one big, happy family.

During the day, which Chip spent at school and Dad, at work, Mom and I enjoyed many lively mornings or afternoons visiting with neighbors either at our house or theirs. In those days, with no shortage of stay-at-home moms, I had plenty of friends to play with. Loneliness was never a problem. That is, as long as my mom was within eyesight or within range of my voice. If that were true, I felt like the happiest kid on the planet.

With each new person I met in Pittsford—child or adult—I proudly announced, "I'm adopted!" Not that anyone had asked me and not that anyone seemed to care about that one way or the other.

On separate occasions, though, I heard a few of my mother's new friends ask her if I'd been foreign-born. She always answered by saying, "No." That was all, just, "No."

The truth of the matter was that being adopted was on no one's radar. And before long, it was not even on my own.

The one thing I had trouble adjusting to in our new home was falling asleep at night. The trucks on Jefferson Road were terribly noisy. Finally, I stopped seeing in my mind's eye what was out there, those eighteen-wheelers speeding along the asphalt highway on their way up state and down state. Instead, I saw something magical in my private eye: the ocean. And the thunderous noise I was hearing was the ocean's waves coming in and going out and crashing against slick, giant boulders.

And it worked.

※ ※ ※

While Mom and Dad had their jobs, I seemed to have my own. I liked giving 100 percent effort to my job: being happy. It was easy, living on Rand Place. I loved our house, inside and out. Becoming bored was not one of my many issues.

Outdoors, all I had to do to be amused was look closely. I'd find amazing things happening right under my nose. Another world existed that I otherwise would never think about. The little creatures scampering, crawling, hopping around our house, entertained me to no end. Chipmunks, squirrels, caterpillars, worms, ladybugs, ants, grasshoppers, fireflies . . . birds! Birdsongs.

One day after spotting a yellow bird in one of the cherry trees at the side of our house, I thought instead of the bird singing to me, I would sing to it.

"I left my heart in San Fran . . . ," I sang, but darn it, I didn't even get through the first line before that bird flew away. That was one of mom's favorite songs; she'd play it all the time. With hurt feelings, I ran to my house, but by the time I got inside, I was wondering what would have happened if I'd sung a different song.

For such a little girl, I was a great big wonderer. That's what my mother always said about me.

※ ※ ※

Our backyard sloped down to a little creek that wiggled its way through other backyards and neighborhoods on its way down to the Erie Canal. Some days, Mom would dress me in dungaree overalls so I could explore down by the creek to my heart's content without her worrying about getting out stains from my good clothes.

If I were lucky—which I always seemed to be, especially after a good rainfall—I'd find a slew of pollywogs. Mom would allow me to keep them in jars of water so we could observe their evolution.

The most fun I had after a rain was spotting a frog and chasing it. I knew that if I could catch it, I'd be able to keep it for a pet. But only for a few days. After that, I'd have to let it go. Mom explained that frogs couldn't be happy if they were cooped up. They needed to be free.

Even only a few days of having a frog for a pet was worth the effort. While that frog was mine, I sang to him all the time so I knew he was happy before I let him go off to be on his own.

I think I loved catching frogs almost as much as singing because whenever I caught one I'd turn around to show it to my mom. She would always be smiling proudly.

Whether she'd be there beside me down at the creek or watching me from the kitchen window, I always knew she was there.

Chip teaching Kim baseball on Rand Place, Pittsford, 1959.

⊞ ⊞ ⊞ CHAPTER 3 ⊞ ⊞ ⊞

ALWAYS HAVE
HEALTH INSURANCE

I was three and a half years old the day Dad rushed home from work early. He snatched some of my toys, grabbed my hand, and rushed me over to a neighbor's house. At the door I heard him say to Mrs. Pitkin, "Sorry to trouble you, Nora. Can you watch Kimberly? I have to take Betty to the hospital."

"Of course," she said. "Whatever you need, Bob. Whatever you need! Go! She'll be fine with me."

It had all happened so fast. Mom hadn't been feeling well all morning, and then by the time Chip got home from school, she was doubled over in agony. It was the scariest thing I'd ever seen. I couldn't stop crying. I didn't know what to do, but Chip knew to call Dad. Now, here he was, obviously upset beyond belief yet speaking calmly and trying his best to keep things together for my sake, but at the time, I certainly wasn't thinking about that. I wasn't thinking about him.

Through my tears, I begged him not to leave me at Mrs. Pitkin's house. But he did. It was like a nightmare, watching my daddy run back to our house where Chip was in the car waiting with Mom. The car sped away. Mrs. Pitkin took me by the hand into her kitchen. That's about all I remember.

It wasn't until many years later that my father shared what had happened at the emergency room. Because Mom was writhing in pain, the nurses whisked her off in a wheelchair to be examined by the doctors. A doctor came out to talk to Dad and gave him the horrifying news: His true love, his one and only, was in critical condition. They needed to operate on her. Immediately.

After my father and Chip were left in the emergency waiting room to absorb what was happening to my mother, Dad led my brother over to a quiet corner. He asked Chip to pray with him. He said they had to pray during her surgery because there was nothing else they could do. They had to pray for the woman they adored, for the operation to go well, for her to get through it, for her to be well again, and for her to come home to them. And, of course, to me.

"Your sister needs her even more than we do, Chip. She won't survive without Mom, you know?"

And with that, the two actually knelt and prayed, which was extremely difficult for me to visualize because Dad had never been a religious man before that day or afterwards.

The doctor informed him that an ovarian cyst had ruptured. Peritonitis had set in, and the poison had spread throughout his wife's female organs. During the surgery, she had flat-lined for several minutes before they were able to resuscitate her. In order to save her life, they performed a radical hysterectomy, and that meant that all of Betty's female organs, including her cervix, had to be removed.

"I'm sorry to say that your wife's recovery period will take some time. Months," the doctor said. "Perhaps years."

"I see," Dad said.

"And there will also be serious side effects after that."

"Side effects?"

"Severe mood swings, for example," the doctor said. "Menopause." He reached out and touched my father's arm. "I'm sorry," he said. "She's so young. But there was no other choice. I hope you understand."

※ ※ ※

After my mother's hysterectomy, she had to stay in the hospital for weeks. So, Dad, Chip, and I stuck to a routine. Each morning after Dad got Chip off to school, Daddy would walk me to Mrs. Pitkin's house, kiss me good-bye, and say to have fun. Then he'd go on to the office, and I would stay all day long and play with Jeannie Pitkin, who was three years older than I was. After school, my brother would go there, too. And then, at some point Dad would come to take us home.

Each day, all day, I wished with all my might that when Daddy came back to pick us up I'd hear him announce that Mom was coming home.

Whatever happened between when Dad dropped me off and when he came back to get me is still a blur. I remember only that each day and each night that passed without him saying those magic words I grew more and more terrified that my mother might never come home again. The thought always made me feel sick to my stomach.

During that third week, when Dad still hadn't said the magic words, my miserable phantom rash returned with a vengeance. Each day while I pretended to be having fun on the outside, inside, it was as though I were numb in one way and on fire in another.

At night, when Dad tucked me in, I tried really hard to be brave. But I usually cried myself to sleep.

One late afternoon during that third week, Dad came into the Pitkins' house with the biggest surprise I'd ever had.

"Guess what, children!" he said. "Your mother's home!"

"Already?"

"Now?"

"Yes, she is!" he said, smiling brightly for the first time in weeks.

Right then and there, I started jumping up and down like a little maniac, and Chip ran to the back room to gather up all his homework and baseball stuff.

Dad reached down to hold me still. "Kimmy," he said, "I want you to listen to me."

"What, Dad?"

He explained that Mom was at home in bed, that she would need plenty of rest, and that it was up to the three of us to help her with her recuperation.

"What's recuperation, Dad?"

"That's the time it will take for her to feel all better."

"Oh."

He knelt down and took my face in his hands, turning it so he could look me in the eye. "Kimmy," he said, "when you cut your finger, remember how much it hurt and how the doctor fixed you up but then how long it took to heal?"

"Uh huh."

"Well, that was for just a little finger. Mom's operation was really big, wasn't it?"

"Inside her whole tummy."

"Right. So that's where Mom still is very, very sore."

"Still?"

"Yes, so we have to be extremely careful around her. Gentle. Okay?"

"Okay. I will be."

His strong hands held me in place when I turned to leave. "So, Kimmy, there's to be no jumping when you're with Mom."

"Okay."

"You understand?"

"Uh huh."

He gave me a hug. "That's my big girl!"

So then, we thanked the Pitkin family for all their help, Dad held my hand tightly, and my brother led the way across the street, around our house, to our back door, and into the breakfast room. Chip and I dropped our stuff right there on the linoleum floor, expecting to see Mom watching for us through the doorway of their bedroom. But the door was closed. I was about to jump out of my skin and tried to break away from my father's grasp, but he held me back.

"Not so fast," he said quietly. "If she's fallen asleep, we don't want to wake her. Let's check and see."

We tiptoed around the table. Dad placed his free hand on the doorknob and turned it slowly.

There she was. That one peek at Mom sitting propped up with pillows all around her was all it took for me to yank my hand free, shove the door all the way open, and cry out, "Mom, Mom! You're home!"

She opened her arms and without another thought I took off like a rocket. "I missed you, Mom; I missed you!"

I leapt up onto her side of the bed, and although my father and Chip were probably yelling at me to be careful, I didn't tune into them. Only Mom being here mattered. I'd already flung myself onto her lap and was giving her the biggest hug in the whole wide world.

"Careful!" Dad shouted.

"Easy does it, honey; easy does it," Mom said wincing.

"I missed you so much, Mom."

"I missed you too, honey." She kissed me on my forehead and gave me a little hug, the best she could muster, I suppose, but until that moment, it had never really registered just how terribly weak she would be . . . or feel.

Then I realized what I had just done. I looked up at her, my lips quivering. "Oh, Mom, I'm sorry. I'm *sorry!* Did I break you? I didn't mean to."

She assured me she was fine, but as she spoke, her voice cracked, and I knew she was pretending. I started bawling, and that made everything worse.

By now both of my parents were rearranging the pillows to protect Mom's stomach. I wanted to run away and hide, but at the same time, I couldn't bear to leave my mother now that she was finally back home.

I heard Dad's voice. "Okay, Chip. Your turn."

I understood it was his turn, but while he and Mom shared their gentle hugs and kisses, I stayed on the bed, snuggled up to a pillow, and I kept looking at my mother's face.

Dark blue-black blotches circled her eyes. And those eyes, even though they were still beautiful, looked as if they'd been poked down into her face. It was confusing to see her that way. Her skin color seemed almost pure white . . . especially without lipstick or rouge. And her hair had lost its shine, and with it pulled back like that into a short ponytail, she looked as if she wasn't . . . well, my real mother.

I could feel my insides tighten up again. And then suddenly there was my father, stretching out on the bed right beside me, as though he had read my mind.

We stayed like that, the four of us, quietly and for quite a while. There was plenty of room for us all because my parents' big bed was actually two twin beds pushed together against a single headboard.

As my tears subsided, Mom glanced down and saw me watching her. She gave me a happy, dazzling smile just as she had done only minutes ago when I was running toward her open arms.

Maybe she really was okay.

If she was, then I was okay too.

❊ ❊ ❊

But Mom was not okay, at least not all the time. Her radical surgery left her with severe challenges, those side effects the doctor had warned of. The operation threw her at age thirty-three into heavy menopause, normally experienced by women in their later years. In the 1950s, hormone-balancing drugs for women were not yet available. So Mom had such intense hot flashes that she constantly felt miserably uncomfortable in her body. That's why my father made sure she had a hand-held, portable, battery-operated fan everywhere she went.

During this period, the worst part for me was that Mom would often get irrationally upset about the littlest things. When something didn't go the way she expected it to, she'd be unable to cope. She'd yell and slam things around and, many times, run out of the house, get into her car, and then speed away, tires screeching. It was as if my greatest fear had been realized, that she really had become someone other than my real mother.

Because I couldn't comprehend the root cause of her behavior, I too would become unreasonably upset. My father tried his best to explain that it wasn't really Mom who was "making mountains out of mole hills" but, rather, the illness inside her body.

Unfortunately, this explanation was of little consolation to me. I'd just cry and cry, run up to my room, slam my door closed, and throw myself onto my bed. I'd cry nonstop until no more tears were left for me to shed. Then I'd roll over toward my night table and reach for the chain on my Humpty Dumpty lamp. And once that light shone on me, I'd stare out the window across from my bed. "Please, God, please," I would plead, "bring Mom home safely."

Within a few minutes, Dad would always come upstairs and knock on my door. He truly was the most loving and patient husband to Mom and father to me. He was acutely strong but always in his quiet way with Mom and me. If not for his strength, I don't know how we'd have coped during this unfathomable period of time.

※ ※ ※

When I was four and a half, I was enjoying one of those gorgeous sky-blue summer days when people open all their windows to let in fresh air. I was outside in the backyard happily smelling flowers and tuning in to the whooshing sound of tree branches brushing against one another in the breeze when I heard my mother's voice. She was in the kitchen. Shouting! At my father!

"I can't take this, Bob," she screamed. "It's too much. Just too much!" The back door slammed sharply behind Mom as she stepped out onto the porch.

For a moment she just stood there, and then the next moment she was practically running around toward the front of the house.

"Mom!" I started to run as fast as I could, but when I heard the car rev up, I got this sickening feeling in my stomach, and then as the tires screeched speeding out of the driveway, I fell to my knees and beat the ground with my fists. "Mom, come back, come back!" I screamed. "Come back!"

Dad's arms were suddenly around me, scooping me up. On his shoulder, I cried my eyes out, asking him questions between my sobs. "Doesn't Mom love us anymore, Dad? Is she running away?"

He rubbed my back the way he always did, trying to soothe away my fear. He did his best to assure me she'd return. But he could not hide the fear in his own voice.

Chip wasn't at home during that particular incident, but he also witnessed this erratic behavior of Mom's because it continued periodically for many years. We never knew when Mom would go off.

That's why I made a vow to myself to make absolutely sure she never got upset again.

※ ※ ※

Shortly after that particular episode, I was with Mom in Burdett's Food Market in the village when I decided to go down aisle C in search of the animal crackers. It was a proud moment when I located the colorful little boxes. I helped myself to one of them, and holding it by its string, admired the cover art of circus animals in their cages. Then I twirled around to show my prized find to my mother.

She was missing.

I ran up and down the aisles, crying for her. *She wouldn't really leave me, would she? Did she?*

Finally, I spotted her at the dairy case, examining each egg in a carton to make sure there were no cracks. "Mom!" I called, running up to her in hysterics.

She set the carton down into her grocery basket. "What's wrong, Kimberly?"

"You lost me, Mom!" I said. "You left me!"

"No, Kimberly," she said, crossing her arms "You," she said, "wandered away from *me*."

"I'm sorrrrrry!" Had I upset her?

She rolled her eyes and then rummaged around her pocketbook until she found a tissue to wipe up the snot dripping from my nose. "What's that in your hand, Kimmy?"

"Animal crackers!"

"Hmm," she said.

"It's a good idea, right? The animals are so little they'll last a long, long time. Mom! I found them all by myself! Can we buy them, please?"

"That's some mighty fine salesmanship your daddy's been teaching you."

"Huh?"

Mom laughed. "Never mind. Okay. Hold onto that box. We'll take it home."

❊ ❊ ❊ CHAPTER 4 ❊ ❊ ❊

BETTY AND BOB

Elizabeth Wieghtorn Driggs, my father's beloved Betty, was born in 1922, one year after his own birth. Both births took place in Rochester. So, although they were raised in different neighborhoods, they were destined to meet in the same high school.

It was love at first sight for Robert Driggs. He was not alone. All the boys were smitten with Betty's beauty. Dazzling blue eyes. Light brown hair. Slender, with a tiny Elizabeth Taylor–sized waist.

Everyone, girls included, considered Betty Wieghtorn one of the most beautiful girls in high school, inside and out. She was extremely feminine, even in the way she moved with little lady-like steps. A shy girl, Betty was content to be an appreciator, rather than in the spotlight herself. This boded well for Bob, who was outgoing, popular, and handsome, as well as known for his great sense of humor. Betty appreciated everything about him.

Betty had been a baby when her father had died, and as the youngest of three girls she was raised by her mother, Ruth, and her strict German grandmother. Financially, the all-female family struggled to make ends meet. Even as children, the girls took on whatever odd jobs they could find in order to earn money to help pay the bills. At home, they all pitched in with household chores. Although Betty could do them all, and do them all well, her favorite responsibility was being in charge of meals. Even as a youngster, she had the knack. She'd find her favorite radio station and dance around the kitchen while pulling out pots and pans and this and that from the cabinets and the fridge. Next thing everyone knew, something deliciously creative would be waiting for dinner on the dining room table.

By the time Betty was in high school, her childhood wish to become a flying trapeze artist had become a thing of the past. Now, she still wanted to play the organ, but more than anything, she dreamed of falling in love, getting married, and raising children of her own.

⊠ ⊠ ⊠

While Bob and his brother Bud were still little boys, their father, Hamilton Irving Driggs, a Rochester attorney, was killed in a car crash. He had been in his early thirties. Hamilton's widow, Flossie, was left to care for their sons on her own. Fortunately, Flossie had the means to provide well for her boys. Bobby and Bud grew up enjoying the benefits of an upper middle class lifestyle.

When Flossie decided to remarry, others thought it scandalous for her even to consider marriage to someone so obviously beneath her class. But Flossie didn't give a hoot about what they thought. Joseph Wigton's kindness and compassion were what she valued. She saw Joe as a marvelous human being, who happened also to be a farmer. She could not imagine a more perfect mate for herself or a more exceptional stepfather and role model for her sons.

My father Bob grew up to be gentle and kind as well. I'm sure both Grandma Flossie's and Grandpa Joe's values influenced Dad and my uncle Bud, but I'd never believe it wasn't also my father's intrinsic nature that mostly made him the way he was.

⊠ ⊠ ⊠

Bob and Betty dated nearly exclusively in high school, and everyone regarded them as the perfect couple. After a while, though, Betty began to feel smothered by Bob's constant attention. She was flattered by his desire constantly to be with her, but at the same time, she had chores to do at home, homework to get to, as well as after-school jobs to fit into her overcrowded schedule. She desperately needed personal time—for polishing her nails, washing and setting her hair, soaking in a hot bath, and other girl stuff.

Bob couldn't understand this need, and she couldn't successfully explain it to him so that he didn't feel hurt. Consequently, at the end of their senior year, their relationship not only soured because of it. It also ended.

Shortly after Betty and Bob split up, World War II broke out, and my father immediately enlisted in the United States Armed Services. He joined the army air corp. I can just see him then, standing with his band of brothers, a man of average height but with fierce determination in his bright blue eyes, ready and able to do his part 100 percent.

I know very few details about his war experience because he didn't choose to talk about it. However, I do know that in 1943, as 2nd Lieutenant Robert P. Driggs, he was assigned to the 427th Bombardment Squadron as navigator for the *Memphis Tot*. On a combat mission over occupied Europe, Dad's plane was shot down. He took a bullet in the arm and parachuted, only to be captured in Germany and sent to a POW camp, Stalag Luft III.

For about three years, he was confined to POW camps, and during that time, he witnessed others he knew go mad from the experience of enduring the harsh and often unspeakable realities of war. According to a fellow prisoner of war, Dad was instrumental in easing the pain of his comrades. He'd come up with entertaining stories to distract them or persuade others to join him in presenting some sort of whacky skit. He once told me that to lift the spirits of his unit required nothing other than to do what came naturally. In Dad's case, that meant calling up his innate kindness and compassion but serving it up with creativity, his keen sense of humor and, for such a gentle man, his often larger-than-life personality.

Despite all his best intentions, however, the demoralizing conditions in camp were the undisputed reality.

At some point, Dad was sent to Stalag 13, and while there, he participated in the prison camp tunneling scheme that eventually became famous in the book, *The Great Escape*, and then the film of the same name, starring Steve McQueen. One way for the prisoners to get rid of the sandy dirt they' d secretly been digging to tunnel their way out of the camp was to hide the dirt in makeshift liners inside their pant legs. During daily exercises out in the yard, they'd run up to the exercise horse, jump over it, and upon landing, shake out the dirt from the lining. That's where Dad came in. He'd be standing adjacent to the horse in a position to shield the men from being seen by the guards. From one man's turn to the next, Dad nonchalantly spread out the dirt with his boots so the Nazi guards wouldn't catch on. Unfortunately, the prison guards did discover the tunnels, and many of my father's fellow POWs who attempted escape were killed.

Dad once talked about the moment he and his mates saw the lights of Patton's army coming over the hill to liberate them. "Every one of us wept like babies," he said.

That scene in my mind's eye rips at my heart.

At the time of the liberation of Stalag 13, my dad was on KP duty when General Patton came up to him. Dad told me Patton asked my father, "Lieutenant? What's for dinner tonight?"

I can't imagine Dad found his voice to respond.

※ ※ ※

While World War II was at its height, people everywhere lived each day with an unrelenting sense of uncertainty, and my mother was no exception. Longing to do her part to support the American war effort, she enlisted in the Women's Reserve branch of the US Coast Guard, and joined the SPARS, the nickname derived from the Coast Guard's fighting motto, "Semper Paratus, Always Ready."

The purpose of the SPARS was to release and replace male officers and enlisted men from shore duties so they could go off to fight for their country. After a month's training, the women reservists were assigned to various jobs, including administrative receptionist, messenger and driver, radio, telephone, and teletype operator, shopkeeper, and cook, and everything in-between.

Betty's SPAR assignment was in Washington, DC, where for the most part, she worked in administration, handling computer data cards. Unfortunately, dust from those cards ultimately caused her a serious case of psoriasis. Coincidentally, Bob's brother, Bud, was also stationed in DC after he joined the navy. He and Betty kept in touch and became close friends. So when Bud received word of Bob's capture, Betty learned the devastating news as well.

At the deepest level, she must have known she was and would always be in love with Bob. However, because their romance had ended so definitively, she'd moved on and was in a serious romantic relationship with another man, a Texan named Doyle.

Because of her relationship with Doyle, Betty did the best she could to push away her fears for my father's well-being as those concerns began to shift from back burner to front and foremost and always present, always pressing against her heart.

❋ ❋ ❋

After thirty-three months of confinement, my father came home a broken man.

I learned from my mother that, soon after her return from DC, she received a frantic call from Bob's mother. Never before had Flossie sounded so undone. "Please, Betty," Flossie begged, "can you come over? It's Bobby. . . . He's in terrible shape. I can't seem to help him. I need you!"

Betty was at first speechless but then said she'd try to get over there soon. The moment she hung up the phone, conflicting emotions surged. She wanted to go—Flossie clearly needed help, and she knew Bob needed her too. But if she went, how would Doyle feel about it? Back and forth, back and forth, she argued with herself until she decided there wasn't time to worry about Doyle now. There wasn't time to dawdle, even to bother with putting on makeup or changing out of her sweater and slacks. Flossie was desperate.

Halfway out the door, she ran back to her bedroom where she removed her engagement ring and tossed it into a bureau drawer.

By the time she arrived at Flossie's, the older woman was watching for Betty from the door. Betty stepped in.

As they embraced, Flossie said tearfully, "I don't know what to do. I can't seem to help him." She went on to explain that Bob had been drinking straight gin, nothing else, but that he'd contracted dysentery while "over there," and his stomach was in terrible shape because of it, not that he had talked to her about what he had gone through as a POW. "And he keeps asking for you." Flossie nodded in the direction of her living room. "In there."

Betty gave Flossie another hug, dropped her pocketbook onto the foyer chair, and took a moment to catch her breath before going in.

Bob lay stretched out on the sofa, his eyes vacantly staring at the window above. One hand limply held his drink with a burning cigarette hanging between his fingers.

She walked over, removed the cigarette from his fingers, and crushed it in Flossie's beautiful crystal ashtray, already overflowing with butts and ashes.

Bob didn't react.

Betty felt frightened to see him like this. She lifted the glass from his hand, set it on the coffee table, and then arranged his legs to make room for herself on the sofa. Still, he remained oblivious that she was near. Wordlessly, she took Bob's face into her hands. And she waited.

When her presence finally registered, his eyes instantly filled with relief. "Betty! You're here!" His head dropped forward, and he broke down and cried.

What had those bastards done to the Bob she had known and so adored? Tears fell from everywhere. From him. From her. From Flossie in the foyer.

My mother told me many times that, in that moment, she knew without a doubt she and my father were as hopelessly in love with each other as they'd ever been. She realized she needed him as he needed her. Whatever life threw at them, they'd get through it . . . together.

※ ※ ※

With very few exceptions, my father continued to avoid talking about the war years. As I think back on this, I know that despite Dad's remarkable ability to compartmentalize his daily life, those haunting memories from the war years still lived on within him. Furthermore, the scar on his arm served as a constant reminder of what he wished to forget.

Dad, standing, second from left, *with others from his air force battalion.*

Betty in US Coast Guard uniform.

CHAPTER 5

THE SENSITIVE ONE

Once, when I was about four years old, Mom watched me from the kitchen window while I stood in the backyard holding onto my favorite doll, Humpty Dumpty, the way I always did—tightly. (With me as his protector, Humpty Dumpty would never have a great fall or need to be put together again.)

Mom often told the story of how she saw on my face an expression so serene, so pensive that she had the impulse to capture it with Dad's camera. She snapped the picture moments before I turned and came barreling into the kitchen for a snack.

When I climbed up on the little stool at the kitchen sink to wash my hands, she asked what I had been thinking about out there.

"Well . . . I was wondering something."

"Do you remember what you were wondering?"

"What I'm doing here. I was wondering *that!*"

"In the backyard?"

"Um, no," I answered with uncertainty.

"Where then?"

I shrugged my shoulders. "Here."

"Hmm."

I got off the stool, wiped my hands, and skipped over to the table where she'd already set out a plate of chocolate chip cookies, still warm from the oven. She came over holding a cup of milk in one hand and a cup of coffee in the other.

I dunked the cookie into the milk before taking my first bite.

"Good?"

"Yummy, Mom."

We said nothing more until the cookie was completely in my tummy. Then I looked over at her with that same pensive facial expression. "I was wondering what I'm supposed to do. See, I don't know why I'm here again."

"Again?"

I nodded. "Uh-huh."

"Sorry, honey. I wish I knew what you meant."

My body began to tighten. With tears clouding my eyes, I added, "I can't say it." I just didn't know how to explain what I meant.

"Oh, Kimmy," she said. "I'm sorry. It doesn't matter, honey." She pushed back her chair, and when she opened her arms, I flew into them, pressing my nose against her apron, seeped with the scent of sugar and vanilla. Mom squeezed me and kissed my cheek. "There's nothing to worry about, Kimmy. Nothing at all."

With a little tickle under my arm, I soon was giggling.

"So," she said, "I'm okay; you're okay, right?"

"Right!" I agreed before running to the bathroom to pee before I went outside to play again.

School Days

When Mom registered me for nursery school at the Presbyterian church, I lasted only a few days. Mom couldn't even leave me at birthday parties without the birthday child's mother calling her to come pick me up as I hadn't stopped crying. It pains me to admit this, but I was a nursery school dropout.

Thank goodness, when I attended kindergarten, Miss Aladdin was my teacher. She stood a little taller than Mom and also had light-brown hair, but she wore hers in a very short haircut. Miss Aladdin was a new, young teacher, warm and outgoing. She had endless energy.

I loved her. That meant my mother could at long last leave me for a good part of the day without having to turn immediately around and pick me up. Because Miss Aladdin was so special to me, I never stopped to think about what it would be like when I'd have to be in a classroom without her.

On the morning of my first day of first grade, the thought occurred to me. I told Mom I didn't want to go to school, and she responded by saying quite simply, "Well, you have to go to school, Kimberly. So, c'mon. We're going."

Despite her assurances that there was nothing to worry about, I cried all the way there. "You'll be fine," she kept saying. (I later learned that she and Dad had already notified the school about my background and issues, and so for that reason, I believe, she actually felt secure about encouraging me to accept that all would be well.)

Lincoln Avenue Elementary School, situated on a nice residential street in town, looked nice enough, but as we approached the entrance to the old red-brick building, I felt myself becoming more and more apprehensive. Compared to where I'd gone to kindergarten, this place loomed enormous. Mom nudged me inside the school and then forward along several hallways.

"Smells like dirty socks," I said.

"Never mind," she said.

When we found my classroom and I first set eyes on Miss Daley, I saw a woman who appeared to be the complete opposite of my kindergarten teacher. Big and heavyset with dark grey hair, she showed no signs of warmth or enthusiasm. I pleaded with my mother to take me home. She didn't. So, at dinner that evening, I told my parents and Chip about my teacher.

"Miss Daley never smiled," I said. "Not once. All day!"

"That's surprising," my father said.

"And I don't like her voice, either," I added.

"Oh, she sang with you?"

"That's not what I mean, Mom."

"Well, what *do* you mean?"

I put my fork down and thrust my hands onto my hips. "I mean, there's no harmony in her voice!"

"Oh," she said. "I see."

⊠ ⊠ ⊠

If you were a first grader in Miss Daley's class and you needed to ask permission to go to the bathroom, her humiliating rule was that you had to hold up one finger to go pee and two fingers if you had to have a bowel movement.

Well, one day Sarah, whose desk was right next to mine at the back of the classroom, was wiggling around in her chair for a while before her hand went up with one finger raised.

Miss Daley didn't notice because her back was to us while she was busy writing letters on the blackboard. But the moment she turned around to address the class, Sarah kneeled on her seat and waved her hand higher to get Miss Daley's attention. Sarah was a shy, redheaded girl who always blushed when she had to say anything at all, but now, because Miss Daley seemed to be purposely not calling on her, Sarah's cheeks and ears were already the same shade as her hair.

That made me mad. It just wasn't fair. When our teacher continued to ignore Sarah, even though I could tell that she knew Sarah's hand was up, my body began shaking like a leaf. In my loud voice I yelled, "Miss Daley! Sarah has to go to the bathroom!"

She spun around and pointed her chalk at me. "Be quiet, Kim!" Then she turned back to the board.

Sarah started sniffing, and I thought I saw some tears trickling down her pale, freckled face. I leaned toward her and whispered, "Are you crying?"

She nodded and whimpered. "I couldn't hold it." Her yellow flowered dress was wet on the bottom, and underneath her seat, a little puddle of pee was forming.

By now children sitting nearby also noticed what was going on. Some had sympathetic expressions on their faces, and others were unable to control their giggling. That's why Miss Daley turned around and then marched down the aisle to Sarah's desk.

"Look what you've done now, little girl!" She took Sarah by the arm and shoved her little by little until she was out in the hall. "I'll be right back, children." Miss Daley turned to us and, pointing a finger, snarled, "Don't talk."

We didn't!

After she and Sarah returned from the girl's room, Miss Daley said, "Over to the tables, children. Take your homework with you and get ready. Be prepared to discuss pages one to three. Go ahead. No talking!"

I waited for Sarah, but Miss Daley told me to go ahead. Then she sent Sarah to the closet for a bucket and a rag and told her to clean up her mess. So I tried my best to save Sarah a seat next to me at the table, but I guess it was just not her lucky day.

I opened up my workbook, ready to read if Miss Daley called on me. I'd read ahead because I love reading.

Miss Aladdin, as well as my parents, said I read especially well for a child my age. This pleased my parents, of course. And I assumed the extra reading I'd done would please even Miss Daley. I hoped she'd call on me.

And then she did!

I articulated each word clearly as I read through the first three pages. When I turned the page and continued reading, Miss Daley stood behind me and, as her arm came around me, I thought she was going to give me a hug because she was so proud that I had read even more, but instead of that her hand slammed against my book, closing it.

"Ouch!" My pointer finger was in there!

"What do you think you're doing, young lady?"

"I . . . I . . . I was reading page four."

"Four?"

A furtive glance at the other children told me they were just as shocked. "Yes, Miss Daley. Aren't you proud of me?"

"Kim Driggs, were you instructed to read beyond page three, were you?"

"N-no . . . but . . . but . . ."

Pointing to the door, she said, "Out. Right now."

"But why?"

"Go!"

In disbelief, I rose and walked to the door, my head lowered in shame as she snapped, "You need to learn to do as you're told. Now think about that while you're out in the hall."

All eyes were on me. Did the other children know something I didn't?

I thought I heard Sarah, crying.

Don't you cry, Kimmy Driggs. Don't you cry! I told myself. A painful lump formed in my throat as I closed the door and then dashed to a corner so no one would see me or hear me as heaping gasps of humiliation erupted. How I wished I could call my mother and ask her to come and take me home or anywhere, just far away from my mean ol' teacher.

I'd been taught by my parents to be kind to others and to treat them the way I'd want to be treated. But no one apparently had taught Miss Daley the same thing. A bitter, raging emotion brewed inside me. Over and over, I thought, *I hate you, Miss Daley, I hate you, I hate you, I hate you.*

Another teacher walking down the hall saw me in the corner, crying. He stopped to ask why I was out there. I told him. He appeared sympathetic but didn't say anything or do anything. He just continued on down the hall and then down the stairs.

Somehow I got through the episode and, even through dinner, kept it to myself because I was afraid to upset my mother. However, when the phantom rash visited my buttocks that night, one thing led to another, and before I knew it, Mom had drawn the whole story out of me. The following day, she paid her own visit to the principal of my school.

He agreed Miss Daley had handled the situation abominably, particularly in light of the fact that the records about my issues were there at school. She should have read them. Rather than berate me in front of the children, she most certainly should have praised me, he told Mom.

Mom and he had quite a discussion, although I didn't learn about this until years later. It seems other parents had reported problems with this teacher as well. Consequently, she would be "asked" to retire. He said he suspected Miss Daley was experiencing an extreme case of menopause, not that that was an excuse.

So, good news for the next year's first graders! Miss Daley would not be back to harass them. Unfortunately, for my classmates and me, we were stuck with her for the rest of the school year.

Whatever the explanation might be for her damaging behavior, one result was a doozy. From first grade on, I developed another issue—fairly or not, I hated school. I began counting off the number of years left to go before I'd never have to go there again.

Discovering My Blue Star

When I was eight years old, Dad took Mom to Hawaii for a vacation, which she sorely needed. Our babysitter, Irene, had her work cut out for her that week not only because of how nervous I was with my parents gone but also because of a huge snowstorm that closed the school for a few days.

During one of those days, while I was out front constructing a snow fort with some friends, our mailman came trudging through the deep snow, waving a piece of mail in the air when he saw me. It was a postcard from my parents. Mom had written on it, "Aloha from Hawaii," and the cover picture showed a gorgeous blue sky and sea and a humpback whale breaching. I fell in love with that card, and it instantly became another of my most special possessions.

After my parents were back home again, I took that postcard and tacked it up on the wall of my play fort, which was a little log cabin that Dad had built out in the backyard. I loved that fort as much as or maybe even more than my super-secret room in my bedroom. On this day I was in the fort, relaxing with my eyes focused on the picture postcard. Then I closed my eyes and pretended to be inside the picture. I saw myself with a complexion even darker than my own, surrounded by gorgeous blue water, singing to the whale.

Then a shimmering six-pointed blue star that I hadn't deliberately envisioned appeared. It was right there inside my skull, directly behind where my eyebrows met in the middle. I wondered how it had gotten there. It was so vivid I thought maybe it was real and right next to me inside the fort, so I opened my eyes.

It was gone.

I closed my eyes, and it was vividly there.

Opened my eyes, gone.

Closed my eyes, kept them closed, and enjoyed the star and its magical quality. A wave of peacefulness came through me, all the way through, like a real ocean wave, reaching for shore, again and again, like the waves I'd been pretending about all those nights when I had trouble falling asleep.

As time went on, the star would periodically appear to me, although I didn't have the power to make it appear.

One time, however, as I concentrated on the beauty of the star, I heard musical notes, musical instruments way off in the distance, sweet sounds, like violins and flutes. They were so beautiful, filling my heart with something so big and good and warm, I thought it would burst out of me, but what burst forth were tears. Why would I cry when I felt filled to the brim with love and joy?

No matter, I decided. If crying was the price I'd have to pay to experience the star and music, so be it. That was an issue I could welcome.

Color Notes

One Saturday a few years later, mid-morning after another big rain, I went out to the front yard for a closer look at a blue jay that had landed on one of our maple trees. All seemed right with the world: sweet and clean air, tulips and daffodils all in bloom, birds singing in harmony, sun coming out; and . . . ah-ha, a rainbow forming over the tops of the elm trees lining our entire street.

I lay down on the damp grass, watching the rainbow's two beautiful shades of blue and yellow arch above the treetops. Then I closed my eyelids because it hurt to look directly at the sun, and when I did—holy cow!—I saw another rainbow, a rainbow inside me, magnificent colors layered one on top of the other, right there behind the middle of my forehead where the center of my eyebrows came together in a unibrow. Gorgeous colors, delicious colors, and except for the blue and yellow, all new colors!

With my eyelids closed, the beauty of color was so enchanting I looked deeply into each layer and felt my heart sing with ecstasy. As

I did, I realized I heard a different musical note with each separate color. It was as though each color belonged to the same musical scale. Astonishing. Wondrous. Effortless.

I opened my eyes, wondering if what had just happened was only in my imagination or if it . . . could be real. Had I imagined the rainbow up in the sky? Looking back to the sky, I saw the arc of the rainbow in shades of the same two colors, blue and yellow. And I heard no musical notes when I looked at them. Several times, I repeated the fascinating experiment, each with the same results: The moment my eyelids opened, the music stopped.

Jumping up, I ran to the house. I had to tell Mom about this, had to, had to had to! In the dining room, I found her setting a beautiful table for her dinner party that night. I begged her to hurry and come with me. She did, but extremely reluctantly, especially when I dragged her down to the ground to look up at the rainbow with me and tell me what she saw up there.

"What about the rainbow, Kim?"

"That's what I want to know. What colors do *you* see?"

She rattled off the red, orange, yellow, green, blue, and violet and then looked at me suspiciously. "What's this all about?"

So I told her.

The rainbow was already fading, so we had to work quickly, going from the bottom upward, naming the colors we each saw. We agreed the only colors I saw the way she did were yellow and blue.

"Mom," I said, "there's something else."

"Uh-oh," she said. "Do I want to hear this?"

"You do because this is the best part."

"Okay, hurry up. I have so much to do before tonight."

I tried my best to explain, and I could tell she was equally trying her best to understand.

She sighed. "I'm sorry. This is awfully confusing, and I need to get back inside be—"

"Mom! Wait! Think about the diatonic scale you taught me. When you play it on your organ or when we sing the scale, it's like that. If my eyes are closed, I see a different color for each of those notes." Then I sang it: "*Do, re, mi, fa, so, la, ti, do.*"

She got to her feet and then looked around. "Okay, Kimmy. Another experiment, okay?"

"All right."

Pointing to the car parked across the street in front of the Pitkins' house, she asked, "That car, what color is it to you?"

"Black? What's it look like to you?"

"Maroon."

This time, pointing to the house next to the Pitkins' house. "What color are those shutters?"

"A dark brown?"

"Dark green. Let's try this: What color is my apron?"

"I know that one, Mom, it's turquoise."

"Oh boy!" she said good-naturedly. "I don't know why I didn't realize this problem before now."

She encouraged me to enjoy the rainbows, no matter where I found them or how the colors appeared to me and that she and Dad would get me tested for colorblindness.

I jumped to my feet. "Is colorblindness a bad thing?"

She smiled at me sweetly. "No."

Over the years, I was indeed diagnosed as colorblind by more than one doctor, which in the scheme of things has caused me no serious problems. I've learned to ask for help in choosing color combinations before stepping out in public. But I never quite got over the fact of just how rare it is for a girl to be colorblind, and the fact that I was in that teeny tiny miniscule percentage of females with this "problem" in some ways pissed me off because, once again, I was different.

On the other hand, because I saw colors in a different way, we soon discovered that I had a rare ability to adjust our color TV so that the color would be perfect. Why? Who knows? All I know is that the word got out: "Having trouble adjusting your color TV? You don't need a TV repairman; just call Kimmy Driggs. She'll fix it for you."

Calls came in all the time. I loved that.

Kim holding her favorite Humpty Dumpty doll.

CHAPTER 6

PLAY TIME

During bad weather days, if playing outside wasn't an option, I was perfectly content to play upstairs in either my room or Chip's. Sometimes I'd set up my Johnny REB cannon from the doorway of my bedroom and angle it toward the bathroom. Chip would lift the toilet seat lid, and then we'd take turns shooting Styrofoam cannonballs aimed at the toilet.

If my brother invited me into his room, it usually meant he was bored. I loved going in there because he'd let me climb up to his top bunk, which was one of my favorite places to hang out. It wasn't an easy climb for me, but that was much of its appeal. I'd have to stand on the bottom bunk first, next get up onto Chip's desk—a shelf that Dad had built for him—and then jump from there and grab hold of whatever I could to hoist myself up and hurl myself over.

Usually Chip stayed on the lower bunk when I was up top. We'd tell each other knock-knock jokes, and then maybe he'd come up and play cards with me, like war or crazy eights. He taught me how to play baseball, and we practiced fake boxing together. Even with our age difference, we were very close back then.

⊞ ⊞ ⊞

In my room, I had a tall, white dresser that I liked to climb up on and pretend was a stagecoach. To authenticate the experience, I wore my cowboy hat and boots. At a moment's notice, I could grab my toy pistol from the holster buckled around my hips and fight off the bad guys to save the good guys. I saw it as my job, and I always took my job seriously.

One magical Christmas, I received an Indian brave doll from my dad's brother, Uncle Bud, and his partner Earl. I became infatuated with the doll's dark skin, black eyes, and long black hair, as well as the miniature authentic American Indian clothing. I loved this doll but didn't lug him around the way I did Humpty Dumpty or my Gerber baby doll. No. I kept my Indian brave somewhere else.

You see, my bedroom had two closets. One was used exclusively for my clothes and shoes and such. The other I used as a super-secret special place because it was a small walk-in closet with a window. This room within my room became a place to contemplate life or play with my special possessions, like the Indian brave.

When it came to this separate little room, I had my rules, just as Miss Daley had had hers. My rule was: DO NOT ENTER! (Entrance was by invitation only.)

Naturally, I invited Mom, that is, when she wasn't having hot flashes and being upset about everything. When I did invite her, she was almost always happy to come in for pretend tea, and often she'd step in with a real peanut-butter-and-jelly sandwich or a plate of real cookies. We'd talk about whatever was on my mind, and invariably, our conversations led to my questions about life and death and . . . just about everything.

The High Dive

One summer day when I was seven and a half and Dad was away on another business trip, Chip was playing a round of golf with Mom because he was such a good athlete and loved the game. Mom gave me permission to spend the afternoon at the Monroe Golf Club adult swimming pool on my own.

I had become a really good swimmer by then so she knew I'd be fine. Besides, Cap, the lifeguard who had taught me how to swim, was on duty. Still, this was a big deal for me. I loved the water so much; it was as though I were a fish.

For most of the afternoon, I stayed in the water at the edge of the pool, right near my stuff so I could harmonize with the songs on my transistor radio. I had it tuned to WBBF, my favorite station, and had the volume up just enough for me to hear without annoying other people.

Not a cloud in the sky that day. A real scorcher, though. So, I constantly ducked under water to cool off. Each time I popped up, the pool water dripped off my head into my mouth, open because I was always singing. I harmonized that day with singers like Neil Sedaka, Chubby Checker, The Beach Boys, and The Shirelles.

Later, at about the time I expected Mom and Chip's golf game to be over, I kept eyeing the gate. As soon as I saw them approaching, I hightailed it out of the pool, across the sunbaked concrete, and onto the ladder for the high diving board. After the twenty-fifth step up the ladder, I took a breath and then trotted out to the edge of the board.

"Hi, Mom! Hi, Chip! Look!" I waved my hands. "Up here! I'm up here."

Chip heard me first, and I think he started to laugh when he spotted where I was. Mom, on the other hand, looked horror-stricken.

"Jump straight, Kim. Straight!" she yelled and continued repeating it as she made her way around the pool to the deep end, across from the diving board. "You have to jump straight."

Only then did I realize why she was so upset. I had never done this before, and I hadn't thought about how the pool was oval-shaped. If I jumped even a little too much to the left, I'd land not in deep water but in deep doo-doo right onto the concrete.

A small crowd had gathered around Mom and Chip, which made me nervous but excited. Here I was, way up high, just as I wanted to be, with the hot summer sun beating down on my dark suntan and the trickling pool water from my bathing suit cooling it down at the same time.

Balance.

Deep breath.

The high board did not spring like other boards. It was just a flat plank of wood. I backed up and then walked forward. Wiggled my toes.

You are an Indian brave. You will aim straight as an arrow. You will not land on concrete.

Swimmers in the deep end moved out of my way. . . . Everyone was watching me, knees bending, arms swinging.

Ready.

Aim.

Deep breath.

Launch!

"Cannonball!"

Straight, straight, straight. Grab legs, tuck feet under butt . . .

Down, down . . . slambam alakazam!

Gigantic SPLASH.

Down, down, down . . . soles touching concrete on the bottom of the pool. Eyes open. Blue floor. Tiny lights. Wavy images of legs and feet. My head tilting up, arms spreading through water, water, water, feet kicking, body propelling up, up, up . . . and out!

Applause! Huge applause. For the little kid. For me.

I did it!

I swam right over to where I'd left my stuff, and by the time I had all of it in my arms, Mom and Chip were coming my way.

"Mom, you saw me, right?"

"Yes, Kim," she said, crossing her arms. "I saw you. I saw the whole thing."

"You saw me too, Chip, right?"

"Yup."

"See, I told you I'd do it!"

He laughed.

"Didn't think I would, did ya?"

"Nope," he said, "I didn't. But you fooled me good. Tell you what, I'm proud of you. I am."

"Really?"

He patted my shoulder. "Yup."

"Wow, thanks!"

Mom gave me a little hug. "Yes, honey. Very well done." She looped her arm through mine, and as we turned to leave, she elbowed my brother's rib, saying, "Now, pay the kid!"

I realized then that Mom must have gotten the truth out of Chip while I was up on the diving board.

As the gate latched behind us on our way out, I heard Cap call out, "Great job, little Kimmy Driggs, great job!"

"Wowee! Thaaaaaaaanks!"

What a day. A day of firsts.

First time at the pool on my own. First high jump. First time I felt really good about my courage, commitment, effort, performance . . . about myself.

When Chip sauntered into my room later that day to pay off his bet, he seemed anything but pleased about now having to part with his own money. Still, here he was wiggling a flimsy, old five-dollar bill in front of my face. "Go on," he said. "Take it."

"Oh . . . I don't know."

"What don't you know? You don't want it?"

"That's not what I said."

"So then take it."

"It's just that . . ." *Maybe I shouldn't take it. Wasn't high praise from my brother reward enough?*

"Gonna take it or not?" Chip said. "I don't have all day."

"I'm thinking about it! Give me a minute."

"Look, Kim, just take it or leave it. Okay?"

"All right!" I snapped. I took it. I took the money.

❈ ❈ ❈ CHAPTER 7 ❈ ❈ ❈

THE DARK SIDE

Night Wanderings

One night in October 1961, around nine o'clock, while Chip was away and my parents were in their bedroom reading, chain-smoking their Pall Malls, and watching TV, they had no idea I was coming down the stairs, opening the front door, and walking out into the chilly night.

Still in my Dr. Denton pajamas, I crossed Rand Place and continued on down the block. My parents, still unaware of what was going on, were not the only ones. This wasn't my first time sleepwalking, but it was my first time sleepwalking outside.

Once, while I was at my friend's house for a sleepover, Suzie's mother found me wandering down the hall in the middle of the night. She simply guided me back to bed without making a big fuss about it. In the morning when we talked about the incident, I remembered parts of the experience but more as though it had occurred in a dream.

This October night was a totally different story.

Out on Rand Place, I could have just as easily turned right or left. I thank my lucky star that I turned in one direction and not the other; otherwise I might not be writing this story today.

Halfway down Rand Place, Mr. Way, who owned the local pharmacy, was sitting by his living room window, smoking his pipe, and reading a book when he miraculously happened to glance up just as I was passing by. When he threw open his window to get my attention, it squealed like fingernails being dragged across a blackboard.

"Kimmy Driggs!" I heard and turned in the direction of the man's voice. I was now somewhat awake, stunned by hearing my name being called and then to see Mr. Way staring at me.

"What're you doing out there in your pajamas?"

The cold night air slapped my face, fully awakening me.

"Are you alone so late at night?"

I stood there, speechless and shivering.

"Kimmy," he said, "are you okay?"

Embarrassed, ashamed, scared, and horrified, I shouted out, "I don't know!" I turned and ran all the way home. When I got there, I couldn't open the door and panicked. It had locked behind me. I slammed my hand against the wood crying and shouting for someone to come and let me in. Finally the door opened.

Dad took me in his arms. Behind him, I saw Mom running to find out what all the commotion was about. Between sobs, I told them what had happened.

"It's not your fault," my father said, and he promised to change the locks in the morning, put them up higher so it couldn't happen again.

Mom took my hand and led me into their smoke-filled bedroom. She wanted me to stay with them for that night, so I wouldn't worry. I'd know I'd be safe.

I climbed in between Mom and Dad, knowing that as calm as they tried to act, they were the ones worried; I'd seen the concern on their faces.

You know what, Mr. Way? I'm not okay! But I don't know why. What's wrong with me?

When I was younger, thunder and lightning storms would send me fleeing down to my parents' room, and I'd spend the night with them. I'd just gone an entire year without doing that and had even learned to enjoy being in my own room during those storms. But now, here I was again, on the crack between Mom's bed and Dad's, feeling frightened, not of thunder and lightning this time, but of myself.

Dealing with Death

At the end of each school day, I could hardly wait to get back home to Rand Place. During the winter season, after a big snowfall, everyone in the neighborhood was outside shoveling or playing. Snow forts. Snowball fights. Snow angels. And, best of all, the magical snow tunnel created by a glistening, white canopy of snow-laden tree branches that stretched across Rand Place from both sides of the road. We would pretend all sorts of wonderful things going on under there.

During summer vacation from school, Chip and I practically lived in the pool at Monroe Gulf Club where I took swimming lessons, starting out in the kiddy pool. I loved being in the water and playing at the pool. If Mom and Dad were on the golf course, Chip was old enough to babysit me; plus there was always a lifeguard on duty.

During spring and autumn, I spent ages hanging out in one of my forts, indoors or outside. Outside, I usually pretended to be an Indian brave or a cowboy, always on the search to help an animal or else stop something bad from happening.

One day in early June, I nearly stepped on a baby bird. It was under one of our cherry trees at the side of our house. I didn't want to scare him, so I stood absolutely still, waiting to see whether he'd fly up to the tree again or fly away altogether. I kept waiting, but he didn't move; he only chirped. I waited so long it finally dawned on me that not only couldn't he fly, but also he couldn't even walk.

His teensy chirp made my heart ache. When I bent down to be closer to him, his eyes darted around, and he smelled like moist dirt.

I was hoping we could sing together, but when that didn't work, I took my toy gun out of the holster and nudged him until he was in the palm of my hand. Then, I galloped to the house and into the kitchen to show Mom.

We placed the poor little guy in a shoebox and kept him out on the back porch. While we added leaves and bits of food to the box, my mother prepared me for the worst. Of course, she tailored her comments appropriately for my age, but the message was that the bird would most likely die.

Not for a single moment did I believe it. Weren't we taking care of that little birdie? Wasn't I wishing with my whole heart he'd get all better? I just knew he'd recover, and he'd fly back to his tree branch or wherever else he wanted to go.

But the very next morning when I hurried out to the porch to check on him, I discovered my mom had been right. The injured birdie was lying flat on his back in the shoebox with his tiny legs sticking straight up in the air as stiff as a couple of twigs.

Lifeless.

※ ※ ※

After I'd experienced one too many failed healing attempts, I became obsessed with death. I'd ask Mom, "Where do they go when they die? Is there really a heaven? Why can't we fix them?"

Again and again, Mom would say, "Kim, you can't help all the sick birds in the world, honey. Nobody can." At the time I thought she meant what she was saying literally.

I had been seeking answers to many questions about life since I was three or four years old. Are we alone in the universe? What is death? What happens and where do you go when you die? I had heard the occasional story on the TV, and when I was older, I'd read an article or two in magazines of people who claimed to have seen a light and tunnel upon their near-death experience. Finally when I was fifteen years old, Mom shared with me her experience of dying on the operating table that day when I was just a child.

She told me she had seen a bright light and a tunnel. She had felt peace and love and wanted to move down the tunnel to the light. I asked her if she had seen any people at the end as I had read others claim to see. She said, as she had been traveling down the tunnel to the bright light, suddenly a voice had spoken to her saying, "No, Elizabeth, you cannot go now. It is not your time. Kim needs you. You must go back." She continued, "It is then, Kim, that I woke up."

※ ※ ※

In August of 1962, I was in my log cabin fort having a terrible time shaking my distress about Marilyn Monroe's death, which was all anyone seemed to be talking about. I'd failed to understand why someone would deliberately take pills to go to sleep and stay asleep forever. Pictures of Marilyn Monroe being beautiful and alive decorated newspapers and magazines everywhere, and moving pictures of her that way dominated television news programs.

Each time I thought about just how unhappy she must have been, I found myself visualizing my mother, that year after her hysterectomy. At the time I was contemplating all this, I was in my cowboy outfit, loading plastic bullets into the toy rifle when a loud screeching noise from out on the street made me jump, and a moment later, another noise like a thud made my heart race.

I dropped the bullets and rifle and ran around the side of the house to the front. Over on Jefferson Road, I saw a car stopped in the middle of the street with the driver's door still open. Other cars and trucks were pulling over to the side. People were getting out of the vehicles. I walked to the curb and saw a man who must have been the driver leaning over a teenage girl. I couldn't hear what he was saying, but I just knew his car had hit her because the poor man was sobbing.

Off to the side, some people were with a boy, who was crying hysterically. I looked back at the girl, who just lay there like one of my injured birds, unmoving, lifeless. Even though I knew I wasn't supposed to go out into the street, all the traffic was stopped, so I stepped off the curb. I had to get closer to hear what the man was saying, so I stepped into the circle of bystanders that had formed around the man and the girl.

"I didn't see them; I didn't see them," the driver shouted out to the crowd. "They came out between those parked cars. I didn't know they were coming. When I saw them, I couldn't stop in time. I tried, but it was too late! Too late. I was too late."

Sirens were screaming by now. Commotion whirled around. And suddenly, my mother appeared beside me.

"Come, Kimmy. Come away from this."

"No, Mom. Look!"

The police and an ambulance pulled up just as nuns from the Catholic church up the street came running over. I recognized some of our neighbors as well.

"Kimberly," Mom said, "you don't need to see this."

"But I do, Mom. Please, I have to stay! I want to do something. I want to help."

"I know you do. But unfortunately, you can't. Come with me."

"I can do something!" I took a step away from her and readjusted the string on my cowboy hat. Mom must have understood my need to experience whatever was unfolding in front of me in my own particular way.

"Oh, please," I said softly, "help her. Don't let her die! Please, don't let her die." I closed my eyes as tightly as I could and tried to find the star, but it didn't work. I so wanted that special feeling and somehow to make it go into the girl.

By then the paramedics were trying to resuscitate her, and I think that was why my mother forced the issue. "Come," she said. "We're going home. Right now."

At that point, I didn't argue. But as we walked toward our house, I glanced over my shoulder several times. I caught a glimpse of the paramedics lifting the girl on a stretcher into their ambulance, and although I didn't see the vehicle as it sped away, I saw the lights flashing over the treetops, and I heard the sirens.

That night in bed, I couldn't bring myself to pretend the noise from Jefferson Road was ocean waves crashing. And later, when raindrops pelted against my windowpane, creating music that under normal circumstances would have lulled me to sleep, I lay awake thinking about the girl. The boy. And the man.

And all I could hear were sirens. Just sirens.

Because it had rained so hard during the night, I spent most of the following morning down at the creek, just loving the music of the rushing water's babble and letting it sing to me, rather than the other way around.

When I heard my mother call me in for lunch, I looked at the little frog in my hand. "Gotta go," I told him before setting him down. "Have fun!"

With one last whiff of the sweet wet grass, he went his way, and I went mine. On my way up the slope, I spotted something on the ground over by the cherry trees that hadn't been there the day before. I ran over to see what it was and, when I got there, saw that it was a shoe, a penny loafer. As soon as I picked it up, some muddy liquid spilled out of it. The copper penny in the slits had mud on it too, so I tried shining it up with my finger, and as I did . . . I smelled blood. All I could imagine was the girls shoe flying off her foot when she was hit and the impact so great that it had sailed over the cherry trees into our backyard. That was the only explanation I could come up with.

Next thing I knew I was running home with the shoe.

Mom was in the kitchen spreading egg salad on slices of Wonder Bread.

"Mom," I said, "look!"

"Just a minute," she said, still concentrating on making our lunch.

"But Mom, look at this. Look what I found."

"Wait, Kim! Let me finish."

She topped the egg salad with lettuce and tomato, then sliced the sandwiches, and placed them on our plates. After she opened the can of Charles Chips and began placing handfuls on our plates, she finally glanced over at what was in my hand.

"What've you got there, a shoe?"

"Yes! Mom! It's that girl's from yesterday, isn't it?"

"Oh God, is it?" She wiped her hands on her apron and then took it from my hand.

I told her where I had found it.

"Oh my. It must have been . . ."

"Is that blood in there, Mom?" *Say no! Please, say NO!*

"Aw, honey. I'm so sorry. I think it is." She set the shoe aside and turned back to me. "I know you're upset, Kimmy, and I'm sorry you had to be the one to find this. But I'll take care of it. It's okay. There's nothing we can do to change what happened. You go wash your hands and face now."

Silence.

"Go ahead, Kimmy. After you get washed, take your plate to the table. I'll join you in a minute."

During that lunch, my mother carefully paced the information she already knew from the morning news. The girl had actually died in the ambulance. She'd been fifteen. The boy with her was her brother, and they'd been on their way home. They lived on the other side of Jefferson Road, three blocks up. Just as the driver had said, they'd run out from between two parked cars, instead of using the crosswalk.

And Mom agreed with me—the girl must have been hit hard for her shoe to have landed in our backyard. It was a terrible tragedy, and it looked as if the driver would not be charged. "He wasn't at fault," she said, giving me a love tap on my hand. "I know it's hard, but . . . life goes on."

But how? If I can't forget what happened, how will he? How will the girl's brother? Why? Why, why did this have to happen to her? Why do my hurt birdies have to die? Where do they go after they leave their bodies?

Why am I back here again?

"Kimmy," Mom said, "just take comfort in knowing she's in a better place now."

"What better place!" I roared, surprising even myself. I shoved back my chair and slammed my hand on the table. "I'm going to my hideout, and you're not invited! I want to be alone!"

My mother seemed to ignore me as I stomped out of the room suddenly complaining, "I wish I had my own dog."

Hidden Anger

One year after that episode, my mother agreed that I could have my own puppy, so that's when a precious, grey miniature poodle came into my life. I named her Gigi, and on the first day she came home with me, I promised her and my parents that I'd be the best, most perfect, most responsible dog owner any puppy could possibly wish for.

I fed her and potty-trained her and brushed her and walked her and taught her tricks and cleaned her off when she got dirty and everything else a dog owner is expected to do. I could never do enough for my baby girl puppy because I simply loved her to pieces.

If Gigi or I ever felt down in the dumps, we'd instinctively seek out the other to offer comfort by sharing the sadness. If she were the one who was sad or hurt, I would sing to her. If I were the one, she'd snuggle against me so I could pet her while she licked me. No words. Just comfort and peace for a while. But then, I'd sense her intense dark eyes staring at me, waiting for me to connect, and the moment I'd do that, a playful energy would transfer from her body to mine.

Her nose would nudge me until I'd giggle. It was always as if she were announcing, "Time's up! No more sorrow. C'mon, let's play." I think it would be fair to say that Gigi was my best friend.

By the time Gigi had grown from teeny new puppy to full-grown size, she still was so small I continued to see her as my little baby girl puppy.

One early summer evening when she was about seven months old, we were upstairs playing together on the bathroom floor. I was still dressed in shorts and a sleeveless blouse but probably was supposed to be getting ready for a bath. While we were playing, I suddenly became upset and angry. What triggered it, I can't recall, but the next thing I remember was hearing my mother's voice from the doorway.

"Kimberly, stop that!"

Her shrill tone shocked me nearly as much as the fact that she was even there. I hadn't heard her come up the stairs or known she'd been watching us. The expression on her face was one of horror.

What had I done?

"Let go of her legs, Kim! You're hurting Gigi!"

My mind raced to make sense of what she was saying. I must have appeared as dumbfounded as I felt.

"Look where your hands are, Kim. Shame on you."

Sure enough, Gigi's front legs were caught in my fists. *Had I actually been pulling them? Why would I do that to my beloved puppy?* Alarmed, confused, and ashamed, I withdrew my hands and backed away. "I'm sorry!"

"You're too rough with her, Kim. Too rough."

"I didn't know I was hurting her, Mom!" *Why didn't she whimper or cry to let me know?*

Seeing my mother's face so obviously disappointed in me accentuated the degree to which I'd so miserably failed at being Gigi's perfect owner. I began to sob and, through gasping breaths, cried out apologizes to them both.

Gigi stood and seemed to tiptoe to me and circled around my legs until she was on my lap.

Mom said nothing as I squeezed my puppy and kissed her all over—face, back, paws, legs—all the while begging for her forgiveness. As if in answer, Gigi responded with the same unconditional love as always, licking me everywhere like crazy. Our eyes locked, each of us communicating love for the other. Gigi had to know I hadn't hurt her. *It couldn't have been me.*

"Kimberly," Mom said, "I'm sorry to have to say this, but if you can't be gentle with Gigi from now on . . . well, we're going to have to give her away. That's all."

"No! I love her more than anything!"

My mother gave me one last disappointing shake of her head before turning and walking out the door. When the door slammed behind her, I felt my insides quiver. How my heart ached. For us all.

Gigi and I stayed put while I tried to make sense of what had just happened. Something I'd been thinking about had made me feel . . . like when Miss Daley had sent me out to the hall to punish me. For the life of me, though, I could not recall what had triggered that anger.

Gigi snuggled even closer and whimpered.

We sat motionless for several more minutes until I felt the intensity of her love. I lowered my head and met her stare. I was not alone in my sorrow.

Nor was she.

※ ※ ※

It still irks me that I can't recall what had caused such rage that day, but I do acknowledge back then, at any given time, I encountered situations, incidents, hurtful words that might have triggered such uncontrollable anger. Fortunately, by about the fifth grade, my stuttering and *s*'s were under control, and my sleepwalking was an occasional problem and no longer a serious one. My parents made sure of that.

But as they say, when one door closes, another door opens, and for me, that meant new issues.

Kim holding and kissing Gigi in backyard of Rand Place, Pittsford.

⊠ ⊠ ⊠ CHAPTER 8 ⊠ ⊠ ⊠

DEFINING MYSELF

Guitar Girl

After seeing the Beatles debut on the *Ed Sullivan Show* February 9, 1964, I had an epiphany. At ten years old, I knew it was imperative for me to learn how to play the guitar. It made sense. I'd been banging out rhythms on every table in the house for years by then. Not everyone appreciated it, either. Even Mom had ceased hiding her distaste for this habit of mine.

Grandma Ruth, who came over for Sunday dinner quite often, never had a problem letting me know how she felt about it. She and I would play cards when she visited, but each time she took a long time deciding whether or not to pick up a card or which card to put down, I'd start beating out rhythms while I hummed. She hated when I did it and said as much, which of course hurt my feelings until Mom told me that Grandma Ruth's mother, Mom's grandmother, was an even stricter and more forceful German mother.

So when I approached my parents about getting a guitar, the timing was impeccable. It had become abundantly clear to them both how much I detested having to go to school, and learning to play the guitar would give me something of value to focus on without beating the furniture to death.

A couple of days later, Mom drove me to Pittsford Plaza on Monroe Avenue so we could go into The Music Lover's Shoppe and at least look at some guitars. I shoved that heavy glass door open and dashed over to the counter. Behind it, a variety of guitars hung on the wall, each with a price tag and an identifying label: acoustic, nylon string, electric, and so forth.

As I was viewing guitar accessories, like picks, tuners, strings, and straps, in the showcase beneath the counter, I heard a man's voice greeting us. Mom and I both turned as he approached us from a rack of sheet music.

"How can I help you today?"

To my shock and delight, Mom said, "We're here to buy my daughter her first guitar."

He smiled and gave me an "okay" hand signal. Then we were off and running. He answered all Mom's questions, recommending a Kent guitar to start out with and lessons right there in the back room with Mike DeFrancisco, Tuesdays and Thursdays, beginning in one week.

Then, heaven: He handed me a Kent acoustic steel string guitar.

As I took a whiff of the dark wood's aroma, I heard my mother say, "She always does that. Smells everything."

"Look, Mom," I said, "see the sunburst on the front? Isn't it pretty?"

Her gorgeous smile gave me her answer.

I strummed the strings, and the sound was sweet. Not knowing what else I should do to test it out, I closed my eyes and visualized my new idol, George Harrison. I moved my body to mimic his stance while playing rhythm guitar and singing with the Beatles. I heard them both chuckling but didn't care. I just started belting out, "She loves you, yeah, yeah, yeah," and then segued right into "We'll take it, okay, Mom?"

"That guitar? You don't want to try some others?"

"Nope. This is the one."

While mom paid the $49.99 for my Kent, plus whatever it cost for the accessories I needed, she sent me over to look through the songbooks at the other side of the store and told me to choose a few.

I had the best time selecting three to take home with me. Meanwhile, Mom had arranged for me to take guitar lessons with Mike on Tuesdays, starting the following week.

On the way out with all my treasures, I chirped like a bird, "Thank you, sir," and then on our way out to the car, "See ya next week when I come for my lesson!"

I saw him smile and roll his eyes.

On the way home, I sat in back so I could study the chord chart in one of the books and attempted playing G and C chords. Then I flipped through some of the songs to find one I could sing right there and accompany myself. "You Are My Sunshine," "Down in the Valley," "The Man on the Flying Trapeze," "Oh My Darling Clementine," . . . and then finally, "Row, Row, Row Your Boat." Ah! I tried that one. Strumming the rhythm felt natural, easy. But wow! Pressing down on the strings sure was not! I wondered if I should have asked the man why the strings were so high up off the neck of the guitar. How would I ever make chords without hurting my fingertips?

No matter. I would master those chords and those strings and prove to my parents and to myself just how serious I was about this, my new dream: to become an entertainer. Nothing was ever going to get in the way of that!

Self-conscious Preteen

Before I was even eleven, I had to wear a bra. My girlfriends didn't have to. I needed all new clothes because of weight gain and because I hated that I now had body hair to deal with. It grew fast and as dark as the hair on my head. Humiliating!

And speaking of the hair on my head—naturally thick and wavy—I had to accept the fact that as much as I wished it could grow long and silky, it wasn't going to.

I became more and more self-conscious of how different I was from everyone else. Mom complimented my striking Mediterranean skin tone, dark eyes, and dark hair, saying I looked exotic. How desperately I wanted to believe her, but how could I when the boys at school mocked me about my body hair and thick unibrow? No matter what my mother said, I still felt in my bones that I was ugly.

One day, she came home from shopping with something she hoped would help me feel better about myself: Elizabeth Arden's cosmetic depilatory wax kit. The cute pink plastic box contained a small aluminum pan, the wax, and a Popsicle stick. Mom heated the wax in the pan and then used the wooden stick to apply it one section at a time wherever we wanted to remove or thin out my hair.

With each application, when she pulled off the wax, I couldn't help but scream, "Ouch." Was it worth it, though? Oh yes.

What a glorious moment to peer into a mirror and see myself as not ugly anymore, and well, maybe even a little bit pretty without all that unwanted hair. With my self-image boosted, I felt much better about going out in the world, and frankly there was no reason why this positive step in my life couldn't have continued merrily along.

Except for the fact that it didn't.

One day after deciding that I was perfectly capable of waxing without my mother's help, my left eyebrow took the major brunt of my recklessness. A sizeable glob of wax accidentally dripped onto the thickest part of that eyebrow. With no other choice, I had to grit my teeth, rip it off, and scream bloody murder. I had no one but myself to blame for botching it up.

For nearly a month, I walked around school with my head lowered, as though doing so would save me from ridicule. Ha! Now, *that* was the laugh! For the boys in my class, my one and a half eyebrows provided them an uproarious, month-long laugh and a half.

Was it any wonder I hated going to school?

❋ ❋ ❋

In my preteen years, girls and women began wearing a new kind of wig known as a "fall." Falls were all the rage, and I had no difficulty understanding why. To me, it seemed the answer to my prayer.

Some falls were made using real human hair, but most women I knew of wore synthetic falls in a shade that blended with their own hair. The long hairpiece, gathered together to be clipped into hair at the crown, fell down past the shoulders onto the back. The fall looked so natural others thought it was your own hair.

When I learned about it, I made my appeal to Mom. "I'd feel a lot better about myself if I had one, don't you think?"

She worried about it for some reason but eventually agreed to shop for one with me. After a few visits to different beauty salons, we came home with what I thought was a perfect match.

The second we were home, I started practicing how to put it in securely and then how to take it off without hurting my scalp. *Practice makes perfect.* Just to be sure it wouldn't fall off, I secured it with extra bobby pins, slipping them in fast enough to assure that when I did it in the morning there'd still be time to get everything else done before going to school.

So, the next morning I arrived in school with my new, silky, long hair. I felt far more attractive than ever before. Not as attractive as Cher, of course, but certainly more attractive than . . . well, me.

While I sat in Mr. Carol's fifth grade class that morning, I hoped my being more attractive would make school life more bearable. It seemed to be going well so far. My friends liked how it looked on me and supported my decision to wear it.

When the bell rang for our lunch break, I hurried over to my locker to put away my books. A boy named Larry called my name, and when I turned, he was walking over to me, smiling. He stopped and leaned back against the locker next to mine, still smiling. This was going even better than I expected. Here was Larry, flirting with me.

His hand reached up to the back of my head, and he began to stroke the hair of the fall. "Hey, Driggs?" he said.

"Yeah?"

"What's this up here?" he said, and he grabbed hold of where the fall was clipped in.

"Stop that!" I shouted.

But he didn't. He just ripped the fall right off my head with one nasty yank.

"Ouch, Larry! Darn you, that hurt! Give that to me!"

He threw his head back and laughed.

"Give that back!"

Of course, if he did that, it would ruin all his fun. No. He had to launch it down the hallway.

"Imbecile!" I shrieked as he backed away.

I could hear him and his gaggle of stupid laughing hyena friends behind me, as I stood there, mortified that this was happening.

Again.

Why, why, why were these people so nasty to me?

The hell with them.

Riding on a wave of rage, I made it over to my hairpiece and then back to my locker. I threw the thing in and slammed that door closed.

That night, when the phantom rash flared up, I ended up telling Mom about what had happened, but changing a few details, that I had walked away from those knuckleheads holding my head up high and marched into the cafeteria to sit with my friends.

Mom saw through me, I'm afraid, and once again talked about how my looks were striking and unique. She said I was handsome, in a female way, which made no sense to me whatsoever. Still, I did appreciate her effort to make me feel better.

Oh, it was hard to fall asleep that night. I finally gave up trying and walked out of my bedroom to sit on the top step and stare into space.

Unfortunately, I overheard Mom and Dad talking about me down in the living room. My mother said, "It breaks my heart to see our girl so unhappy." My father tried his best to console her when she began to weep. The one person in the world I wanted with all my heart to make happy was down there miserable. Because of me.

I ran into the bathroom, thinking I had to throw up. I was wrong. It came out the other end.

Ugh.

Religious Freedom

On one of my bedroom walls, I had a framed picture of Jesus Christ with a little light over it. Where it came from, I don't remember, but once in a while, I'd sit on the floor in the dark and stare at his lit-up face.

The night I heard my mother crying over my sorrow was one of those times. Under normal circumstances when I'd attempt to communicate with Jesus, I'd ask my typical questions. Who is really

God? Who made God? Where do we go when we die? Is there really a heaven and hell? We're not the only people in the universe, are we? When will I see a UFO?

This night, I asked him what I could do to make my mother happy.

As was his custom up there on my wall, the Son of God said nothing and just stared back at me from within his golden hue.

I fully trusted that Jesus had been an extraordinary man, a master teacher with a beautiful gift of helping others through loving words and deeds. In my mind and heart, it was unnecessary for him to be remembered only as a God or Son of God. I admired who he was based on how he was. My mother's belief pretty much followed that of the bible from a Protestant point of view. I, however, could never relate to any of what was in the bible. It just didn't answer my questions. But I did my best not to upset my mother, so although I didn't relate well to going to church and being told what to believe, I kept most of my feelings about religion to myself.

During my childhood, therefore, I went along with Mom's wishes. She was somewhat religious. Even though she'd been brought up as a Lutheran, she made sure Chip and I attended the First Presbyterian Church of Pittsford.

Ironically, Dad, who had been raised as a Presbyterian, preferred not to go to church at all. If Mom pushed the matter, however, he'd accompany the rest of us. Easy enough to do. The church was conveniently located at the end of our street.

By the time I was thirteen, not surprisingly, Mom requested I continue my religious education by attending confirmation class with Reverend Kesel. Because I still hadn't shared my disbelief in many of the stories of the bible and much of church dogma, I agreed to go. But, she agreed to something as well: Once I was confirmed, I'd be free to follow whatever religion I chose.

In his classes, unfortunately for the reverend, I bombarded him with my endless questions. One evening I asked if we could please discuss reincarnation, explaining that I believed in it and had had strong feelings throughout my life that I'd been here before. Reverend Kesel, in his kind, soft-spoken way, peered at me over his eyeglasses and asked me to speak with him privately after class.

When we were alone, he said, "Kim, you're interrupting my classes too often. I expect you to pay close attention to the class at hand, not your questions about other topics. Now, if you don't like this class or how I'm teaching it, then you may leave it. However, if you stay, this must not continue. If it does, I shall have to ask that you not return."

"You would expel me?"

"I'm sorry, yes. That's how it would be."

I could never knowingly disappoint my mother, and if I dropped out of Reverend Kesel's class or if he expelled me, I surely would, wouldn't I? Consequently, for the next several weeks while he droned on and on about all that dogma, I sat absolutely still and kept my big mouth closed tight.

At the graduation ceremony, I received a gift for having gotten through the class. We each were presented with our own, brand-new blue bible. I loved the feel of it in my hand and its thin and silky pages, each of which had a fresh, clean scent.

Afterwards, when I skipped down the steps at the back door where Mom had been waiting for me, a bubbly, perky Kim smiled at her and showed her the bible. Mom seemed so pleased to see me happy.

I could have left it at that, but as we turned to leave, I thought about what Dad had taught me always to tell the truth. Now I would, not about Reverend Kesel's confrontation but the truth about my feelings about religion. During that four-block walk home, I confessed that I had decided it was not for me. I said how sorry I was to disappoint her.

"You're not disappointing me," Mom insisted. "I'd have loved for you to feel comfortable with my faith, but I'm proud of you for sticking with what feels right for you. I understand you need to find your own way."

Whew.

That night, with such a huge weight lifted from my shoulders, I trotted up the stairs to my bedroom with the bible, thinking, *That's that!*

But before retiring myself to bed and the bible to my bookcase, I flipped through the pages one more time, taking in the clean scent and looking at the text as though the answers to all my questions might magically pop right off the pages then and there.

I glanced up at Jesus's picture. "Sorry," I said. "But I love you, anyway." After that, I called it a night.

Earliest Record

I often asked my mother to repeat the stories about when they first saw me and took me in. So one day when I was in my teens, I asked her to tell me again about my birth story.

She let out a huge sigh and then, changing the subject, said, "How about we go to Carrols Drive-In today for lunch?"

"Cool!" I said because as far as we were concerned they made the best hamburgers and milkshakes in the world!

"Okay then, we'll do that, but first we need to go to the Rochester Pubic Library."

"We do? How come?"

"To find a newspaper article," she said with a sparkle in her eyes.

"What about?"

"About you, honey. About when you were born."

"Really? You mean they have it?"

"We'll find out."

So there I was, jumping up and down as though I were still a little kid and not the fifteen-year-old teenager I'd become.

An hour later, Mom and I were there in the library following a man in a dark suit and tie. He may or may not have been the reference librarian, but either way, he was happy to help us find what we were looking for.

"Should be on microfilm," he said. "Come, ladies, and I'll get you set up." He led us through many rooms of floor-to-ceiling books and finally into a small room in back. One window. One desk. One large, metal gizmo.

"Have a seat, ladies," he said, gesturing to the stools in front of the monitor. "I'll only be a minute." He slid out a deep file drawer and thumbed through the microfilm inside. "*Democrat and Chronicle*," he muttered to himself. "January 1954."

Nervously, Mom and I reached for each other's hand, both of us eager to see a baby picture of myself pre Mom and Dad. Finally!

"Here we go!" the librarian said.

Music to my ears.

He walked over to us with the treasured microfilm, and we waited while he installed it into the back of the machine. Then he came around, powered up the machine, and showed us how easily the turn handle scrolled through the pages so we could watch them on the monitor. He explained what button to press for a printout, told us to take our time, and wished us luck.

We were on our own, shoulder to shoulder, looking at the screen. He'd set us up starting at the newspaper's January 15, 1954, edition.

We scrolled. And we scrolled. And then, Mom said, "Here it is, Kim! January 26. And look. There you are!"

The photo of myself as a newborn nearly took my breath away.

"Oh, Mom!" I said. "Thanks so much for doing this! I can't believe that's me!"

She wrapped her arm around my shoulder and gave me a little squeeze. "I should have thought of this a long time ago."

"Oh, she's so cute."

Mom laughed. "*You*, honey. She's you."

I read the headline of the article, aloud: "Police Seek Identity of Foundling's Mother." Immediately, I felt nauseous. *Mother!* I hadn't thought about how painful this could be for Mom. I glanced at her as she began reading the article aloud and then followed along by reading the screen.

"So," she said after we had finished reading. "now all we have to do is print it out. Want to press that button, honey?"

I nodded.

"And this is how it should be," she continued. "You'll have this to keep with you forever."

"Mom?"

"What is it, honey?"

"I just hope . . . you know . . . you're my . . . only mother. I hope you're okay that I asked about this."

"Aw, honey, I am. I'm perfectly okay with this."

Her beautiful blue eyes gleamed with love, not apprehension, and so I knew she was more than okay with it.

"Now, go ahead," she said. "Print it out, and then let's blow our minds with burgers and shakes!"

Born to Be Wild

The same year Apollo 11 landed on the moon, I landed my first date. A really cute boy named Dave invited me to go to a dance at McQuaid Catholic High School, although he wouldn't actually be taking me to the dance. We'd have to meet up there, but then we'd be at the dance together.

That was the date. Mom happily obliged, and when Friday rolled around, she drove me to the school, as well as a friend of mine, Lorrie, who had asked for a ride.

I hoped we'd see Dave waiting by the entrance when Mom dropped us off, but we didn't, so Lorrie and I followed the sound of the blaring music. Gotta say how great I felt not to be walking into the gym by myself. Not only that, but I was with a pretty girl who at any given moment would be approached by one boy or another, but I was the one who already had the date!

The Typical Blimp band's earsplitting music and the strobe lights accosted our senses as we wove through the crowd to get closer to the dance floor. There was no way to have an actual conversation, but Lorrie already knew I was looking for a really cute boy with light brown hair.

Even though I didn't spot Dave right away and should have been looking for him, I couldn't take my eyes off the drummer, Eddie, who was by far the best drummer I'd ever seen. While absorbed in watching him beat out rhythms on not one but two bass drums, I heard Dave's voice yelling my name. When I turned, there he stood, right beside me, his lean but muscular wrestler's body neatly hidden beneath chino pants and a blue button-down shirt. After I greeted him, I introduced him to Lorrie.

And from that moment on, what had begun as a night of high expectations turned sharply into heartbreak.

Lorrie sashayed right up to him, flipping her long blond hair to swish behind her where it trailed beyond her ass. I couldn't believe she would flirt so shamelessly with the boy who was there to be with me. She knew damn well how much I liked him, how excited I was to have this date.

As they talked in each other's ears, I rationalized that perhaps Lorrie's flirtatious behavior was simply her way of bringing attention to herself, to get other boys to approach her. That rationale lost its luster, though, as we three stuck together like glue while going for Coca Colas at the refreshment table, while circling the dance floor, and while getting closer and listening to the band.

But then when the band began Steppenwolf's "Born to Be Wild," Dave turned to me and—*thank God!*—asked *me* to dance. All bets were off again. I felt incredibly relieved. "Sure!" I shouted. "I love this song."

Being out there on the dance floor with Dave made me feel . . . wonderful, as if I fit in, was one of the crowd. I lifted my chin to glance up at his face. His dark brown eyes gleamed. He seemed as happy as I felt.

When the song ended, I hoped we would stay for the next, but I felt his hand on my back, nudging me to turn and return to Lorrie.

In no time at all, Lorrie literally stood between us. She shouted above the music, "So, Dave, tell me about yourself, won't you?"

He laughed, took her hand, and asked her to dance. On the dance floor, he pulled her close, and they took turns talking into each other's ears.

I could not believe my eyes. Why would she monopolize his attention this way? How could she deliberately hurt me like this?

After a few songs, they returned to me.

I soon excused myself to go to the bathroom. And once I was in the girls' room, I seriously considered staying there until it would be time for Mom to pick us up. Then I thought, no, I had to return to the battlefield.

I should have known better. There they were in the middle of the dance floor, slow dancing to the Young Rascals and their hit song,

"How Can I Be Sure?" I noticed that by now Lorrie had intimately discovered Dave's arm muscles as she rubbed her fingers over them.

For the next several dances, I moseyed around with a Coke close enough for them to see me should they wish to. The lump in my throat grew larger. Was I a glutton for punishment? Did I require further proof that boys didn't go for me, further proof that I didn't fit in, never had, and never would?

My *friend* betrayed me!

I elbowed my way through dancing couples to speak with the one pair standing out, the one in the center, in the pelvis-to-pelvis, slow-dancing embrace. "Lorrie," I roared, "I'm leaving. You'll have to get another ride home. Can you?"

"Oh," she said, feigning disappointment. "Well, I think I can."

"Don't worry," Dave assured me. "I'll see she gets home."

Then he and the girl in his arms, who should have been me, returned to getting lost in each other's adoring gaze.

Anxiety said, "Run! Get out of here." But I walked as nonchalantly as I could out into the hall where panic set in. *A pay phone!* "Where is a pay phone?" I asked, and someone pointed to it by the water fountain. As the Led Zeppelin tune, "Stairway to Heaven," began from the gym, I dialed home.

Several couplings of students out in the hall glanced my way, and the last thing I longed for was their rapt attention. As I waited for Mom or Dad to answer the phone, I forced myself to will away the pending explosion of tears.

"Hello?"

"Mom!"

"What is it, honey? What's wrong?"

"Please can you come and get me?"

"What happened?"

"Lorrie's with Dave. I want to go home."

After a brief pause, she replied, "I'll be right there. Wait for me outside."

"Thank you!" *What would I ever do without you, Mom? Again.*

Going Solo

School continued to be something merely to be endured. Being away from school, on the other hand, was something to be celebrated, which I did by devoting my attention to my family, and that absolutely included my beloved Gigi and the one of her litter we kept, Tiger (a tough little dog that became Dad's constant companion; he'd even take her to work on Saturdays when he'd go in to catch up on his work), my few true friends, my guitar lessons with Mike, and singing. Always, singing.

The one and only exception to total disdain for being in school was that, as a member of the chorus, I'd developed a special relationship with our music director, Dr. Tappen. Early on, he had recognized my talent and spent time with me apart from the other students. In fact, he became my mentor.

For the past five years, I'd been working with Mike DeFrancisco weekly at the back room of The Music Lover's Shoppe. I had decided to focus on rhythm, rather than lead, guitar and had even saved up to buy my new Martin 12-string guitar. Often, I sang and played for Dr. Tappen, and he decided to feature me with my Martin in the end-of-school concert that year in solo performances. We agreed on the two songs I'd perform, and he surprised me by composing backup harmonies for the chorus to sing behind me.

Until that decision, I'd been nothing more than just another voice in the school chorus. However, outside of school, I'd been performing professionally in coffee houses, as well as a couple of small bars, getting paid under the table but with my parents' approval. Without that experience, I don't know how I would have reacted to this opportunity to showcase my talents at school. Dr. Tappen's enthusiasm for it, for me, well . . . it was contagious. I focused on the work, not on the spotlight.

And when blips of that spotlight on me began asserting themselves into my consciousness, 1 closed my eyes tightly and thought about the friendly faces I knew would be in the audience. My closest friends— Ann, Joan, and Jan—would be out there cheering for me. They were the only other students who knew about the professional aspect of my life. And of course, my parents would be there.

On the night of the big concert, though, the jitters, the butterflies, the shaking knees, the tummy aches all came along for the big night too. Bastards! From behind the stage curtain, I snuck a peek at the audience, hoping to quickly spot those friendly faces. I needed something to calm me down. It didn't help. I was going to have to make a run for it. . . . Oh, shit! . . . I made it to the girls' room in time. But still . . . ugh. Diarrhea.

Why? I had prepared. This would be a piece of cake for me. Dr. Tappen had requested I sing "What the World Needs Now," not by mimicking Dionne Warwick but by singing like Kimmy Driggs. He always told me I was a natural talent—I had my own style, and I should never try to sing like anyone else. So, that's what I would do. That's what I always did! And for the second number, I'd be doing, "It's Not Unusual," which had been Tom Jones's huge hit. I would do that my way too.

I loved both those songs. I could do this! I could do Dr. Tappen proud.

At the sink, I washed up well, took deep breaths, and visualized the faces of my parents, Gigi and Tiger, Dr. Tappen, Mike DeFrancisco, my friends, and anyone and anything that had a positive influence in my life, even Humpty Dumpty and my frog friends. I looked in the mirror admiring the way I looked in the red pantsuit Mom had bought me for this special occasion and loving my new guitar.

Back behind the curtain, I took another peek. House lights were flashing. Thank my lucky stars, right there, tenth row center, sat Mom and Dad, facing the stage with heads held high, confidence in their demeanor.

Lights out.

Only blackness.

As the school orchestra filled the auditorium, thoughts filled my brain. Performing in local coffee houses and bars was one thing. Performing in front of hundreds of my peers and their parents—oh my God! This would be something else! As we were getting closer to when I was to perform, I waited in the wings with my guitar, trying to will away my topsy-turvy stomach, remembering words from those I loved. Mom's voice in my head said, "Sing like a bird, honey. Sing like a bird." In my mind, I heard Dad's "Come over here and sit with me, little Kimmy Driggs, girl singer."

Back to the present, Dr. Tappen's voice, over the mic, said, "And now, Pittsford's own Karen Carpenter, Kim Driggs."

Too late to run and hide.

Dr. Tappen's coaching ticked off in my mind. "Just be yourself, Kim. Close your eyes and be in your music. Nothing to think about. Just sing. You're perfect just the way you are. Don't change a thing."

"Ta da!"

The spotlight followed me as I walked to center stage. *Ugh! Damn! This seemed so unfair. Don't think! Sing. Just sing. Play. Just play. Your guitar's your couch.* Shaking like a leaf, I had no choice but to begin. I sighed, gave a reluctant smile to the bright light, and prepared to strike the first chord.

Here goes nothing but everything.

I closed my eyes. "What the world needs now is love, sweet love . . ."

My Martin 12-string guitar resonated as magnificently as if it were a concert grand piano, but my voice was quivering. *Don't think! Sing!*

And then I got there, into the music, taken over by the beautiful spirit of my collaboration with Dr. Tappen. From the corner of my eye, I caught sight of him conducting and felt fueled by our special connection.

As my hand strummed the final chord, I think I stopped breathing for several seconds. I'd gotten through it without having to make a humiliating run to the bathroom. I took a bow.

The auditorium rang out with applause and whistles.

Immediately I launched into my own upbeat rendition of "It's Not Unusual." While I strummed away on my Martin, my body swayed with the music, and I caught another glimpse of Dr. Tappen. He beamed with pride from offstage. The joy he emitted was immense and, like a giant lick of fire, reached out for me and engulfed me in its flames. The warmth in my heart surged.

How could I not take pleasure from providing such happiness to others, simply by singing?

My eyes remained closed at the completion of the number. Applause grew louder and louder. I opened my eyes and stared out into the blackness and then was able to make out that in the first few rows people were on their feet. Yes, I received a standing ovation.

Not only did the members of the chorus and audience see me in this new light during the night of that concert, but so also did the entire student body. From that point onward, I was no longer Kim, the oddball who didn't fit in. I was still me, being me to myself. Yet to them, I'd become someone else: Kim, the singer and guitarist.

"When will you be performing again?" they now asked, stopping me in hallways or leaning across their desks. "Where?" "What time?" Now, even boys interacted with me as someone to admire and respect when only the day before they wouldn't have given me the time of day.

ACT II

On the Road with Mom

We're switching drivers again after a timely stop at Joplin, Missouri, to pee and grab a bite to eat. Mom takes the wheel, and we're back to singing together, one song after another, almost as though there were no tomorrow.

Then she asks me to sing alone without her. "Sing like a bird, honey. Sing like a bird."

So, I do because I'd do just about anything in the world if it makes her happy, just as she did for me.

CHAPTER 9

A Date, a Friend, and Inklings of Love

A Real Date

A few months after the concert at school, while I was singing in a local coffee house, a guy who turned out to be a senior from the next town, Penfield, was watching me and later, during my break, came over to introduce himself.

Tim was a good half-foot taller than I and yet another guy with light-brown hair—nothing like the dreamboat whose photo I kept in my wallet in those days. The guy in that magazine picture was an incredibly handsome Italian-looking male model with dark brown hair and eyes. I always imagined I would one day meet a man who looked like him. We'd get married. I'd have a fairy-tale romance just as my parents had had. We'd raise a family together and live happily ever after.

Tim, I noticed, was a little chubby in the middle and not at all the athletic type, but he still received high marks simply for showing interest in me. And at the end of the set, because we seemed to instantly hit it off, I wrote down my phone number on a napkin when he asked for it.

Here's the thing: Tim actually called and asked me out on a date. A real date! As in a Friday-night date. As in come-to-my-house, pick-me-up, take-me-out-for-dinner date.

When I told my parents about Tim, they seemed as euphoric as I was.

That Friday at five thirty when I sauntered down the stairs, I felt quite grown up and pleased with myself—and with the new outfit I had on and that Tim would be picking me up in our newly built house. We'd been living in it for about a year, but only recently had Mom completed all her fabulous home decorating. I thought I'd take Tim on a tour of the house first, just to show it off, and then we'd go out for the evening.

My parents greeted me from their chairs in the living room as I crossed the Italian-marble foyer. Dad had gotten home only minutes before. Already he had a martini and cigarette going, as well as the *New York Times* crossword puzzle, all of which were part and parcel of his decompression routine after arriving home from the office.

Tim wasn't due to arrive until six, so Mom and I sat together on the loveseat and chatted mostly about the big date, placing bets on where he might take me. There were only so many restaurants worth naming, however.

When the grandfather clock struck six fifteen, Mom and I both stood up and headed for the foyer where we paced, only to make repeated visits to the front windows in search of headlights approaching from the driveway. Mom plunked her tush down on the bottom step of the stairway and, in an effort to distract me, engaged me in discussions about decorating skills. But after a while, neither of us could bear the pretense.

By 7:00 p.m. with still a no-show and no-call, the deed was done.

"See, Mom, this is what I mean. No boys like me! I don't know why I even try!"

Thundering past her, I stomped up the stairs, and when I was in my room, I slammed the poor door as hard as I could.

When Mom and Dad came in several minutes later to console me, they discovered I was inconsolable. What could they possibly do or say to ease the pain? That only deepened the pain—I knew perfectly well that for every tear I shed, they shed a tear themselves.

For Life!

On the last day of my junior year at Pittsford Sutherland High School, while other students tore out of that building to get on their buses and head home for the summer, I took my sweet ol' time. With only one year left on my countdown, I chose instead to soak up that joyous reality along with the hot summer sun.

Wafting from the side of the building came the unmistakable aroma of cigarette smoke . . . and marijuana. The hippies had boldly gathered for their final hurrah together before departing.

Only one other student seemed to linger, and the way her shoulders slumped, I thought she seemed a bit lonely. She sat down on the front steps of the school. I skipped down the steps to see if she was someone I knew. She wasn't, but I said hello, and she looked up, blocking the sun with her hand while I introduced myself and squinting at me with a cute freckled face and a great big smile. Within less than five minutes, we learned so much about each other that it was as though we were old friends.

Sue had just moved to Pittsford from New Jersey because of her father's new job and worried about how her summer would go since she hadn't yet made friends. As she was telling me about how hard it was to leave behind her boyfriend, I heard someone shouting for us to get on the buses, that they were starting to move. Sue walked to school, but I had to hop on that bus. I scribbled down my phone number just before I ran toward my bus and she began her walk home. I stopped before I boarded the bus and looked back to wave good-bye again. I noticed Sue standing there as if she was waiting for me to do just that. Waving good-bye, I felt my heart expand as if I had found a long-lost love.

I didn't hope she would call the way I had hoped Tim would call after giving my phone number to him. I *knew* she would call. It was a knowing, an unwavering certainty that I never thought to question. She and I had in those few minutes already made plans to speak by phone that evening, get together in person in a couple of days, and arrange for our parents to meet each of us and us to meet each other.

I'd even invited Sue to go to Bermuda with me later that summer for my promised vacation before my senior year.

It all went according to plan.

Sue and I were indeed fast friends and more—we were friends for life.

Inklings of Love

During that senior year in high school, I always sat in the front row for my French class. I admired and respected our French teacher so much that I kept looking at her, feeling suddenly love for her. Not like the love I had for, say, my parents or my friends, or even Gigi or Tiger, all of whom I loved wholeheartedly and unconditionally. No, this love caused a strange tingling inside me, as though it emanated from my core. Heat radiated from somewhere around my heart area, or was it all the way down to well past my stomach? I remember shifting around uncomfortably, especially if she turned her head toward my side of the classroom.

One day, as I was leaving her class, she called me over to her desk. "Kim," she said, "I want to talk to you about your homework."

"Okay, sure." I had hoped mine would stand apart from the others. I so wanted to please her.

"Kim, when you do your homework, all you have to write are the answers. You're creating more work for yourself by writing out the questions first."

I looked at her and thought, *Wow, she's so beautiful and sweet.*

"There's no point in overdoing it. Know what I mean?"

"Oh," I said, realizing I hadn't answered her yet. "Well, I just wanted it to look nice on the pages. But if you don't want me to do that anymore, I won't."

She said, "I don't want you to bother. Okay?"

"Sure."

I thanked her and then slowly and no doubt awkwardly backed out of the room, still thinking more about what she looked like and how lovely a person she was and far less about what she'd just said to me, so totally smitten was I.

For the next several weeks, I loved watching her when she walked down the hall or came into the classroom, each time concluding she looked more gorgeous than the time before.

Then one day it dawned on me: These thoughts and feelings about my French teacher—a woman!—were so odd that I ought not to share them with another living soul. I'd feel embarrassed if anyone knew, although I was uncertain exactly why.

Another thought dawned. I knew my parents accepted Uncle Bud and Uncle Earl's unusual relationship, their homosexuality, yet Mom and Dad would surely not accept mine, should I be the same way. *No. Don't think about that. Don't think that!*

That is why, for the rest of the year, I continued to be diligent about my homework but even more diligent about keeping my eyes on my French books and off my French teacher. The last thing I'd ever want to do was knowingly hurt my parents.

I never even told Sue my secret. I kept my real feelings to myself, stuffed them down, deep inside me. With Sue and my other close friends, Jan, Ann, and Joan, I often whipped out the photo of the handsome male model that I kept in my wallet.

"See this guy?" I'd always say. "Someday I'm going to meet someone like him." And that was, in truth, what I really wanted. "We're going to fall in love, have a fairy-tale romance just as my parents did, get married, and live happily ever after."

Trying to Love

Finally, in my senior year, I had my first real boyfriend, Chuck. I don't even remember where or how I met him, but he was five years older than I was. Chip approved of him, though, and that was good.

Chuck was by no means a "looker." He was starting to go bald, had very fair skin, and was somewhat overweight in his midsection. His taste didn't match mine, either—he wore polyester pants, which I hated, and his idea of fine wine was Lambrusco, although in fairness, I guess that was the wine of the times. He was, however, a lovely person and adored me for who I was. He treated me well, which made me, in turn, care for him deeply.

Sue's boyfriend would come to visit when he was on leave from the navy, and we would double date. Chuck did everything right that a wonderful boyfriend should do; yet I found myself struggling somehow inside.

All my close girlfriends had had sex by now at eighteen. Not me. I wanted to wait for Mr. Right and have it on my wedding night. Yes, old fashioned I know, but it sounded so romantic.

Yet I felt uncomfortable being the only virgin in my group. As my senior year drifted on and it came closer to graduation, I felt this need to see if I could go all the way with Chuck. He was getting really serious about me, and I knew he was thinking of marriage. But I wasn't ready for that so soon . . . or was I? I did feel all the normal sexual feelings I was supposed to and got turned on at times with him. I knew he would be gentle and kind with me if I were willing. He never pressured me, though. So, I decided to take the plunge anyway. I made sure I had the proper rubbers on hand for him.

One weekend Chuck was hosting a BBQ at his new home he had bought. I could tell he was hoping I'd move in with him after I graduated and bag going to college.

I played the dutiful hostess role for him, learned from my mother, of course, and tried to find common interests with his friends. It all felt so trite to me, but he seemed thrilled that his friends liked me.

After everyone left, and we cleaned up the dishes of dip, chips, buns, burgers, beer, and such, he motioned me up to his bedroom. He put on candles and some nice seventies music. (That was my favorite decade of harmonies.) He started to undress me. I knew this was the night if I was to do anything. He stripped me down naked ever so slowly and with kindness. I unbuttoned his shirt, belt, and then pulled down his jeans. I had made him throw out all his polyester pants and switch to jeans or corduroy pants. Then a bit frightened but very excited I pulled down his underwear to expose a most definite hard-on. At the sight of him, I should have been more excited myself, yet I could feel nothing in the sexual department.

After preparing his manhood with the rubber, he lifted me onto the bed and starting kissing my face, lips, neck, and breasts. Nothing. I felt nothing. I begged God to please let me get excited, but nothing happened. I went through the motions and tried desperately to imagine everything I had thought about in my dreams and had seen in movies that this moment would hold for me. Why was I so excited in the past when we'd kiss? Why did I feel ready before but, now that the moment was here, was I shut down?

Mom once told me, when I was seventeen and she and I were having a serious talk about sex, that I was ripe and ready at twelve due to my passionate personality and nature. Then where was it? Why didn't I feel it now?

Chuck tried to have intercourse with me.

Come on, Kim, you can do it, I said to myself. Attempt after attempt failed. I begged my body to open up to him, but the harder he pushed the more I shut down.

After about five minutes, he gave up. "Honey, what's wrong?" he said sadly.

"Chuck I'm so sorry. I don't know what is wrong with me." I didn't want to hurt his feelings, and yet, maybe, I wasn't ready. I just didn't know. Was it men I wasn't ready for? Was something wrong with me? Was he not the right guy? "Chuck, I think I need to go home now. I'm really sorry. It was a great party."

We both dressed, and he drove me back. I kissed him goodnight and tiptoed up to my bedroom where I lay down on the bed staring up at the ceiling.

And then a tiny bit of awareness crept into my consciousness. I started to have awareness that I was equally attracted to both men and women. I also realized that I had impending guilt about having sex prior to marriage. My parents probably would not approve, and not wanting to disappoint my mother in particular was looming over my head during the time I was trying to have sex with Chuck.

I remembered all the boys I'd been attracted too in high school and whom I so desperately wanted to like me yet didn't. I also remembered my attraction for my French teacher, which I had totally pushed into a black hole. Hmm. Interesting. But I went no further. I was tired and couldn't deal with all that then. I fell asleep dreaming of rainbows.

Chuck came to my high school graduation, which unfortunately had to be held in the stinky gymnasium, due to weather. Afterwards, Chuck and I got together to talk, and I told him I would never be able to be who he needed me to be. Basically I broke up with him. I could see I broke his heart.

✠ ✠ ✠ CHAPTER 10 ✠ ✠ ✠

MOVING UP . . . AND OUT

Tradeoffs

In my later years of high school, my brother was off on his own, Dad's business trips took him to countries around the world, which meant longer stretches of time without him, and I was more independent after my junior year. All made for a rather empty house, especially for Mom, and contributed to her issues with moodiness. Mom kept busy but doing what others expected—involved in the community and the club and fulfilling the role of exceptional corporate wife, helping her husband climb way up high on that corporate ladder—even while he traveled.

One evening in my senior year while Dad was in California on business, I was up in my room holding a rhythm stick as though it were a microphone and singing into it songs by the Carpenters and Carole King. The yellow hue of the closet light served as a spotlight in the darkened room. Imagining myself up on a stage, I was content for hours.

After numerous songs and imaginary standing ovations, I decided to call it quits for the night. Mom had been in the kitchen, cooking and baking all day for the big bridge party at the club. The aromas had been tantalizing and finally teased me into trotting downstairs for a closer look and perhaps a taste.

The kitchen light was off. Covered platters of baked goods lined up on the counter. Pots and pans, back in their places. Everything, spic and span.

Gigi and Tiger moseyed over to me from their bowls, and then we three walked around the house looking for my mother. Back in the foyer, I breathed a sigh of relief. Mom's Pall Mall smoke led me out the front door. There in the dark sat Mom on the stoop, cigarette in one hand, gin on the rocks in the other.

"What're you doing out here, Mom?"

She said nothing. Took a puff. Then a sip.

"Mom? What's the matter?"

"Leave me alone."

Her tone pierced me to the quick and worried me even more. I'd seen this mood before, one that could send her fleeing angrily away. It brought me back to overhearing her say, *I can't take this anymore, Bob. I'm fed up!*

"Mom, how about coming inside with me now, okay?"

"Damn it, Kim," she fired back, "I said leave me alone! I'm fed up. Go. Please!"

"No, *you*, please! Come inside."

"Stop it!" With her glass she tried to bat me away.

"Fine!" I spun around and ran into the house, left the door open, started up the stairs, and then changed my mind and sat on the bottom step. Both dogs cowed and went into the living room to get away from the negative energy.

What, I wondered, had I possibly said or done earlier that might have upset her? How I wished my father were home. He'd know how to handle this situation.

My sniffer kept me informed of another cigarette being lit, and I casually walked back to the kitchen where Mom's pocketbook sat on the table. Inside, I found her car keys and slipped them into my pocket. Then I called Chip. I told him it wasn't an emergency but explained about Mom's condition. He offered to come over and hang out, help me keep an eye on her. Then I heard the front door slam. Mom had come inside. I heard her plodding up the staircase and told

Chip I'd call him back. When I ran out to the hall, I saw her holding onto the bannister. No cigarette. No glass.

After I heard her bedroom door slam, I retrieved her belongings from outside, locked up the house, and went up to bed. It broke my heart to see what had become of my sweet, loving mother.

Years later, I understood more fully the crisis she was undergoing at the time. But at this time, I had only an inkling of the tradeoff she'd made. Immersing herself into the country club lifestyle with all its socials, bridge parties, cocktail parties, and dinner parties had taken its toll on her. She'd had to invent an outgoing personality to excel at everything that had been asked of her. That Betty Driggs was not who my mother truly was—only who she had become. She was still that shy, quiet girl inside. And with her husband away more often and for longer stretches of time now that he was on a dizzyingly high rung of that corporate ladder, my mother was lost, exhausted, and miserably unhappy.

But I also remember why she did all that. And if she had to do it all over again, she'd probably do it the same way.

Rochester Club

Christmas time in our family had always been synonymous with jolly good times. We went all out—decorated the house to the hilt, inside and out, had delicious meals, exchanged beautifully wrapped gifts, attended parties galore. But a new tradition had been initiated by my father the Christmas before I became a teenager: our private father-daughter luncheon, always at the Rochester Club in the heart of Rochester's cultural East End district.

In December of my senior year, as Dad and I set out for our annual private lunch at the beautiful private club, I wondered if during our talk he would bring up Mom's recent depression and, if not, if I should.

Upon entering the building, I forgot about all that as I noticed—as though for the first time—the beautiful Waterford crystal chandeliers, the classic architectural details, and felt myself wrapped in sophisticated elegance. Had I developed a new appreciation for artistic details and décor simply because I was maturing? I wondered. Or, did my cultural awakening have more to do with my mother's refined taste and my acquiring it through osmosis?

The man who greeted us looked like a prince in his tux, as always. This year, though, I noticed how his handsome face reminded me of the photo of the male model in my wallet.

"Hello, Mr. Driggs," he said. "Nice to see you and your lovely daughter again."

Dad shook Carl's hand.

Just outside the main dining room, a second "prince" waited for us with menus and greeted us as we approached.

"Please follow me," he said. "Your table is ready." His manner made me feel like royalty but also family, and I enjoyed both in that moment.

With my father's hand pressing my back, I moved forward still glancing around, realizing that I didn't need to read the menu to start salivating. Lusciousness was everywhere: the Victorian décor, bounteous fresh flowers, crystal wall sconces and chandeliers, tables draped with starched white linen.

At our table, I allowed the waiter to help me into my chair and then hand me a menu. Rather than immediately examine every word of every offering on the menu as I had in the past, I continued to devour the fine touches spread out before me: silver cutlery, fine stemware, and the bright-white linen napkins folded to resemble flowers.

Something had clearly changed in me since the year before. I hadn't yet taken a bite but already sensed that this particular father-daughter luncheon would live on in my memory forever.

I was only a month away from being eighteen, the legal age for drinking in New York State. That's not to say I didn't go drinking with my friend Ann, who looked older than her age. During those occasions, my drinks of choice were based on whatever other kids drank: Sloe Gin Fizz, Whiskey Sour, Tom Collins. Looking back, it's a wonder bartenders didn't know we were underage just by the silly drinks we ordered.

Now, when the waiter came over for our drink orders, I knew what my father would order for himself but was uncertain if he would order me a Shirley Temple, as he always had in the past. Sure enough, he ordered himself a gin on the rocks.

"And for my daughter?" He turned to me. "What would you like to order today, Kim?"

"What would I *like* to order?" I said, noticing how his eyebrows had risen and he had a twinkle in his eyes.

"Whatever you want," he said, grinning.

"Hmm," I said. I glanced up at the waiter. "I'd like a Tom Collins, please."

"Very well," the waiter said.

Dad smiled at me but said nothing more as we both picked up our menus again to consider the divine choices: lamb, steak, prime rib, and veal.

When the waiter returned with our drinks, my father told him to wait for a while before coming back for our meal orders.

This surprised me. Under normal circumstances, he'd have been joking with the waiter about some past antics that would have had something to do with fine dining. On this day, however, that life-of-the-party father had suddenly left the table. Even as we raised our drinks and clinked our glasses for our annual father-daughter toast, the sparkle was gone from his eyes. Something was up. He probably did need to talk about Mom's condition.

Dad lit another cigarette. "Kimberly, I'd like to talk to you about something."

"Okay."

"Nothing bad, don't worry," he said quickly. "It's an opportunity that's come up for your mother and me."

"Good." I took a big swig of my drink and then leaned forward.

"I've been offered a new position. It's temporary. I'd be working for French's parent company—Reckitt & Colman."

"That's good, I suppose. What is the job?"

"Well, my title is worldwide director of food and wine development. How's that sound?"

"Impressive, Dad. Important. Congratulations. Mom happy about this?"

"Well, actually she is."

"That's great."

"If I accept the position," he said, "your mother and I would need to move to England, and—"

"Wait a minute, wait a minute. *Move?* To England?"

"London, Kimmy. We'd live in London."

"You're not kidding?"

"No."

"Dad, that's not what I expected you to say."

"What *were* you expecting?"

"Not this, that's for sure. I thought you wanted to talk about Mom's depression."

"Well, in a manner of speaking, I am." He leaned back in his seat and held up his hand. "Now, just listen, and I'll explain."

I did exactly that. I sat there numbly listening as little by little he revealed more of the plan. Each additional detail seemed a layer of bricks to wall me off from Mom and Dad.

He and Mom would have the opportunity to either accept or not the assignment, depending upon how they felt about living in London after a trial period—another trial period—that would be six months long and that would begin in March.

"That's only three months from now!" I finally said. "What about the fact that this is my senior year? I'm almost through it. I don't want to have to start over somewhere else. Not now."

"Of course not." He leaned forward now. "We agree. You need to stay here and finish up. Study and do well on your finals. You can handle being on your own without us. You've grown up into a responsible young woman. And you know what? I believe you're going to love this chance to be responsible for yourself, not just with schoolwork but also with your gigs."

He went on to explain that I'd stay with their close friends, the Connellys, from March through June. After I graduated, I'd be able to spend all my summer vacation with them in London before having to fly home to get ready for college. It would be a great opportunity for me, he said. The experience would be, in fact, wonderful for us all. "Your mother has come alive just at the prospect of this change."

I gave Dad a smile. Not easy. But it felt like the right thing to do. Looking back, I remember feeling scared and hurt that they'd so readily leave me for four whole months and live so far away from me—*three thousand miles* away. But . . . I didn't want to think about that. I didn't want to feel that way. If they were happy about this, I should be too.

"Kim? Are you listening?" Dad said.

I nodded and tried another smile. "Go on."

"Your mother will fly back with you to help you get ready for college and then drive you up to Boston."

I glared at him. "Aren't you going with us?"

"I'm sorry, Kim, but I'm scheduled for an important business trip then around the world. I'll be gone for a few weeks."

I forced a smile and nodded—words wouldn't come.

"While we're in London, Kim, if we decide to take the job, you'd be in college for two of the four years anyway. So, in that way, it all works out." He held up his empty glass for the waiter to see.

As Dad spilled more of the details involved with his promotion, they left a bitter taste in my mouth. He kept saying "if," but I could tell he'd already decided that this move was right for them. He explained that if—that word again—the trial period went well, they'd put the house on the market after they returned and would move in January the following year.

The waiter arrived just then with Dad's drink. He also casually replaced the ashtray with a sparkling clean one. Dad lit up another cigarette and, sure enough, requested we be given more time before ordering our meals. He waited for me to say something, I suppose, but I couldn't find my voice. He picked up his menu and appeared to read it but kept eyeing me, waiting for a response.

I just sat there, numb.

He reached across the table and patted my hand.

I thought about Dad's ascension up that corporate ladder, how valued he'd always been, how he deserved everything he'd earned, how rewarding that had to be for him. Vice-president and director of marketing. Next step would be the presidency. His dream. But poor Mom. What about her dream?

"Another drink?" the waiter asked me. I hadn't even noticed him coming over.

I shook my head no.

Dad slid his menu to the side and lifted his glass. "Well, I've decided what I 'm going to have. You?"

"Still deciding . . . "

"Take your time."

"Dammit, Dad, this is hard."

"No rush."

I closed the menu. "Mom's been more miserable than ever, lately. You've seen the weight she's put on. She's not happy at all. You know that, right?"

He nodded.

"So . . . the change . . . well, maybe it would be good for her. And . . . I probably could like being here on my own for a while. As you said, not really alone. I'll have the dogs, at least."

"Well, actually, the dogs can't stay at the Connellys. But, hell, you can go over and see them any time you want. They'll be at the house with a sitter. Someone needs to stay there."

Someone. Tears spilled from my eyes. "Me, Dad. It should be me."

"No, honey. The only way we could do it is the way I just said." Suddenly he seemed so weary. "But look, nothing's written in stone yet. Not yet. We're still just talking here."

"No, Dad. Do it!"

"You sure?"

I nodded.

"I understand how you feel, honey. But I promise you, you *will* like living in London next summer. You'll see. It will all be worth it."

❊ ❊ ❊

The second half of my senior year in 1972 was spent unhappily living with my parent's bridge-and-drinking buddies, the Connellys. Their kids were all grown up, married, and with kids of their own. Oh, don't get me wrong here; it isn't that I didn't like them. Actually, when they were sober, I liked them very much. It's just that Mrs. Connelly started sipping the sauce around noon and, by dinnertime, was pretty sloshed and unreasonable.

I did everything I could to stay busy. Most of the time, I was hanging out with Sue, Jan, and Joan. I spent as much time at Sue's house as possible. Chip would check in on me from time to time. He was off having his own life by now.

The house-sitter my parents got to stay at our house and care for Gigi and Tiger was nice enough, but every time I drove over to the house to see my pups, I was offended by her being there. I could tell Gigi and Tiger missed us and didn't understand the new living arrangements. I'd stay a few hours at a time before grabbing them both up in my arms, singing a little song, usually "Over the Rainbow," and then driving back to the Connellys miserable.

Mom and Dad would call me from London every few days. Mom could tell I was miserable, and I felt bad to have unveiled those emotions to her, but I just couldn't help myself. So again, I felt guilty for making Mom worried or unsettled about my issues when all I really wanted was for her to heal and be happy. Yet, in spite of my miserable situation and however she felt about it, I could tell from the tone of her voice she was doing just what I'd hoped—healing and feeling happy. She wanted the same for me and kept saying, "Hang in there, Kimmy. Soon you'll be over here in London with us. Just hang in there. I'm okay; you're okay, right?"

"Right, Mom."

London Trial

During the six months my parents were in England before I joined them, they had experienced a great deal about the UK. All who knew Bob and Betty Driggs loved them. Mom had fallen head over heels in love with England in every way. After graduating, I arrived to a woman who had lost twenty-five pounds and had a smile and twinkle in her eyes I hadn't seen in years. She walked everywhere. Dad too seemed different, happier, more challenged by the possibility of a new role with the parent company.

I arrived a week after graduation, and just as Dad had said, I too fell in love with England and all she offered. The three of us dined out at all the great restaurants Mom and Dad had found—Il Portico, Maggie Jones, Oscar Pub, Wheeler's Alcove, Snooty Fox, and Hungry

Horse. We frequented the theatre weekly down in Piccadilly Circle in the West End. I was honored enough to see some of the greats live on stage, including Jimmy Stewart, Henry Fonda, Jean Simmons, Debra Kerr, Michael Crawford, and even Haley Mills.

Mom and I would take day trips on the Tube outside of London to visit all the charming little villages giving special attention to her favorites, the churches and cathedrals. The history of the royal family enchanted her. She could tell you every duke, duchess, prince, princess, king, and queen of Britain, who they married, and where they were in history. Mom was alive and vibrant. Her transformation was extraordinary.

I too resonated with the lifestyle, the people, and the endless possibilities my musical career could have in a cosmopolitan city like London. By now I was the proud owner of two Martin guitars. The six- and twelve-stringers were my pride and joy.

By the time September came along, I could pretty much tell my parents had made up their minds to move in January 1973 for the four-year project. As much as I wanted to join them, I couldn't—college was calling.

⌘ ⌘ ⌘ CHAPTER 11 ⌘ ⌘ ⌘

COLLEGE QUITTER

College . . . or Not

Back in the States, Mom was with me getting me ready to attend Dean Junior College in Franklin, Massachusetts, for two years. After that, I'd join them in England.

She had plenty to do prior to dad arriving home with putting the house up for sale and finding movers, plus driving me to Dean.

Too soon, it seemed, Mom and Sue dropped me off at the dorm after making the long drive from Rochester to Franklin. They got me settled, met my roommate, Shelly, and then left. I watched them drive away, the two closest women in my life, with Sue waving out the window, tears in her eyes.

After they were out of sight, I cried in the dorm bathroom stall silently as I didn't want anyone to see me and think I was a big baby missing Mommy already. I felt sick. What was wrong with me? Why did I have such trepidation so quickly? Why weren't any of the other kids feeling or acting this way?

Obvious differences in other ways quickly appeared and told me so strongly this just wasn't the place for me. Within twenty-four hours of arrival, the entire dorm set up dope smoking, beer, and pizza parties.

That wasn't who I was. Not that I didn't like beer or liquor. But I was most definitely not into dope and hadn't come to college to party.

I had just spent a summer in London enjoying all that living in a cosmopolitan city offers—great food, wine, theatre, music, history—and experiencing it in another country just made it all the more exciting. I loved England and the people. I realized upon my return I didn't really want to go to college after all, but I had to. I was committed.

My first night at Dean, Shelly and some other gals asked me to sing and play. I sat on the floor in our little dorm room and performed. I felt happy when I sang and played.

They all said, "WOW, Kim, what are you doing here? You should be out making records and singing in clubs."

"Yes, I know. That's my dream."

I tried to fit in, but I couldn't relate to any of the student body, the curriculum, or anything the college had to offer. There was not one thing that resonated with me on any level. Even Mom's words of wisdom telling me to "give it a chance" over the first three days of phone calls to her in tears didn't work.

Since I loved music so much, I thought entering college with music as my major was a no brainer, right? Who knew I wouldn't understand one word of the music theory class on the first day. I couldn't keep up with anything the professor said. Damn. I should have known better. I could barely pass theory in high school. Yet here I was in college and couldn't understand the theory class from the first day.

I always loved the art of psychology, so I thought I'd at least like that class. Nope. I couldn't stand the professor. He was the most boring, mundane, monotone, zero-personality person I'd ever met.

Every class I was in, I hated. I felt out of place and totally alone. I had hated school my entire life. Why would this be any different? What was I thinking?

After four days, I realized my decision to attend Dean Junior College was a catastrophic mistake in judgment, and I told the dean I was quitting. He tried talking me out of it as I sat opposite him in a short leather chair, he behind his huge desk.

There was a large window behind him, and the sun was beaming colored rays of light onto his desk. Something possessed me to ask him what this was costing my parents having me here every day.

Rather than answer my question, he zeroed in on the real damage my dropping out would do and said, "If you quit now, they'll be out two thousand dollars."

He failed in his attempts to get me to stay, as I was determined this was a huge mistake for so many reasons. *Let's cut our losses*, I thought, as it was inevitable I wouldn't stay, no matter what anyone said to me.

I signed some piece of paper saying I was quitting. I remember walking out of his office feeling both elated and terrified. My college roommate and gals I had met in the dorm drove me to the train station, suitcase and guitar in hand. I traveled to Boston's Logan International Airport where I bought a ticket home to Rochester, New York.

Having to wait a few hours for the flight and knowing I had to make the dreaded phone call to Mom that I had quit college after four shitty days, I took my time finding a phone booth near the gate. I located one as far away from people as I could find. Pushing on the door, it swung inward. I tried to navigate my Martin D-18 guitar case and me inside the phone booth. Unfortunately, the case stuck out of the booth door allowing the door to shut only halfway.

I had sold my Martin 12-string guitar to a local recording artist who played lead prior to going to England. She would make love to it better than I could since I played only rhythm.

The phone booth smelled musty inside. A filthy film of grime covered the windows with wads of gum stuck to the glass. The dirty phone book was encased in a plastic black cover with a hook through the top as it hung from a black dusty shelf.

I was an emotional mess. My body was trembling with uncertainty, and my colon was already reacting to the stress and worry with several bouts of diarrhea that had sent me to the restroom prior. The phantom rash had reappeared all over my ass and on my scalp. I tried twice to dial zero for the operator to make the collect call and hung up the receiver. Leaning back against the glass with tears filling my eyes, I reflected on the whole experience. What had I done?

Mom and Dad hadn't made me to go to college. Hell, they had even said, "Kim, we are not forcing you to attend college. We do feel it would be a good experience and help you in life down the road, though." Even so, I had thought if I didn't go they'd be disappointed on some level. This was clearly something I had put on myself.

"Charleston, North Carolina, Flight 459 Alleghany Airlines, last call, Gate 23 for Charleston."

The loud speaker shook me back to reality. Taking a deep breath, I dialed zero for the operator.

"Operator, may I help you?"

"Yes, I'd like to make a collect call to area code 716-555-5674."

"Whom shall I say is calling?"

My voice was cracking, and my hands were sweating. I bowed my head staring at the dirty floor with candy wrappers and dust. "Say it's Kim, please."

"One moment while I connect you."

I prayed she'd be home. What if she wasn't? Then I heard the phone answer and Mom's voice.

"Hello."

"Yes, this is the long-distance operator with a collect call from Kim. Do you accept the charges?"

There was a pause. My stomach sank, and I could barely keep the tears in. I was about to disappoint the most wonderful person in the world. I felt so guilty and worthless. "Yes, I will accept." Mom's voice sounded slightly frustrated, as if she thought, *Oh no, not this again.*

"Go ahead, please," the operator said, and I heard her click off.

"Mom?"

"Kim, what is wrong?"

"Mom, I'm so sorry. I can't stay here. I made a big mistake. This isn't right for me. I'm at the Boston airport. I bought a ticket, and my flight arrives in Rochester at four forty-five. Will you pick me up?" Before she could answer, I blurted out again with tears streaming down my cheeks sobbing. I kept bowing my head further down into the booth and turning my back so people walking by wouldn't see this pathetic young woman holding her guitar and balling her eyes out in the phone booth. I must have looked like a runaway. "Mom, I know you told me to give it a chance, and it's only been four days, but I know this is not for me. I can't explain it; I just know this is a huge mistake. I shouldn't have come here. I have nothing in common with any of these people. I want to move to England with you and Dad next year. I can't stay here. I'm so sorry."

She jumped in, "Kim, Kim, stop. Take a breath. Where is your trunk full of clothes?"

"I left it at the school with Shelly. I have my suitcase and guitar with me."

"Okay, look, I will be at the airport to pick you up. Calm down. We will work this out."

Still sobbing, I replied, "Mom, when does Dad get home from his business trip? What will he think? He will be mad and disappointed too."

I heard her take a big breath and say, "Kim, your father comes home in a few days. Don't worry about him. He loves you, and together we'll figure this out. Just come home. I will be there at 4:45 p.m. I love you."

My sobbing started to subside, and for a moment a wave of peace moved through my solar plexus, and for that instant, I thought all would be okay. "Okay, Mom. I love you too. See you in a few hours."

"Bye, honey."

"Bye, Mom," I replied. I hung up and stood in the booth thinking how lucky I was to have a mother so understanding and kind. She knew me so well, and even though I didn't know what the ultimate outcome would be, I knew I was going home.

I gathered myself up, opened the door to the phone booth, picked up my guitar, and strolled over to a café and ordered a tuna sandwich and cup of black coffee.

Seated at my gate looking out the window eating and drinking, I watched the planes take off and land imagining and hoping my parents would let me move to England with them for their four-year journey. I wanted to experience life first-hand, to *taste, touch, and feel* it. And I wanted to be a professional entertainer in London, England.

⌗ ⌗ ⌗

Dad arrived home from an exhausting three-week trip around the world in his new position. He came down the jet way wearing his suit, wingtip shoes, and hat and carrying his briefcase, always a professional, my father.

"Hi, honey," my mother said as she kissed him.

Before Mom had a chance to say anything else, he asked, "So how's Kim doing at school?"

Mom took a deep breath and said, "Well, Bob, she's home. She quit. She's miserable and has been beating herself up for days worrying what you will think. She was not happy there and wants to move to England with us and do her music."

"What?" he exclaimed. "What happened? I thought she wanted to go," he said, as they continued walking to the baggage claim area.

Mom held his arm as they walked briskly, which Dad always did, several steps ahead of everyone else. She continued, "Bob, I don't think Kim wanted to go to college at all. I think she did it for us, thinking we would be disappointed in her if she didn't attend."

Dad didn't say a word, and for several minutes, they walked in silence while he processed the situation. Arriving at baggage claim, he asked, "How did she get home?" "Well, she took a train from Dean to Boston, bought a ticket with the cash she had saved, called me very upset, and flew home. I picked her up a few days ago. She's home now wearing out the carpets pacing, worried about what you will think and do. Bob, she doesn't want to go back to school. She wants to move with us to England and pursue her dream in music."

The bags came down the conveyer belt, and Dad grabbed his as Mom took the briefcase from him. They walked to the parking garage.

"Betty, you know Kim will not be legal in England. I will be legal as an employee of the company that is sponsoring me, and you will be as my wife. Kim being over eighteen will not be covered as a child of mine. She would have to leave the country every six months and talk her way back in to get stamped for an additional six months.

She'd have no friends and have no job, other than singing gigs she might obtain under the table. She can't get a legal job either due to the laws. You know companies in England have to prove why they'd hire an American over one of their own."

"Bob, I know all that, but she is dead serious," Mom replied as she opened up the back door to the car and tossed the briefcase on the seat.

Dad opened the trunk and put in the bags and his hat. Then he got behind the wheel, shut the door, and sighed. For a moment, he sat staring out the windshield in silence before turning on the engine. I could imagine the wrinkles on his brow turning downward.

Mom said she sat quietly too. She told me later when we talked about this that as she was sitting in the car silently waiting for Dad to turn the ignition on, she thought to herself, *I'm okay; you're okay, right, Kim?* Anytime something challenging in our life came about as a family, this was the phrase my mother always said to me to help us get through it and to calm me down.

Dad turned the ignition on, and as he turned his head to look over his shoulder to back out, he said to Mom, "I'll talk to her more about this tomorrow, and we'll figure it out."

"So, honey, how was the trip?" Mom finally asked him.

⊠ ⊠ ⊠

I heard the garage door open, the car pull in, and then the back door open. I had been pacing from the living room through the kitchen to the back door and back again for hours biting my nails until Mom and Dad returned from the airport. She walked in first and threw me a subtle loving look while putting his hat and briefcase on the counter. My stomach was in knots in anticipation of him at the very least being extremely disappointed in me, if not angry.

Dad looked exhausted. Walking slowly into the kitchen, he saw me standing there with what I can only guess was a terrified look on my face. He came up to me, looked into my eyes, and with no emotion, simply said, "Kimberly, we will talk about this tomorrow evening." He kissed my head, grabbed the suitcase, and went upstairs.

I looked at Mom in shock and was about to ask her a million questions when she said, "Kim, not now. He will talk to you tomorrow. I have to help your father get settled; he needs to nap."

"Okay," I replied grabbing Gigi and Tiger, one in each arm, and went out to the backyard to contemplate what had just happened.

Pros and Cons

The next evening after dinner, Dad sat me down, and we began the process to determine whether I would go back to college or go to England with them in January 1973.

"Kim, come here and bring some paper and pencils," he said as he positioned himself on the sofa in the living room. Sitting in his favorite corner on the couch, shoes off, legs curled up around him, and cigarette smoldering in the ashtray on the coffee table, he sat comfortably. Nervously, I grabbed a tablet of paper and two pencils joining him on the couch.

Mom was busying herself in the kitchen cleaning up from a fabulous beef stew she had made. She truly was an amazing cook.

Dad drew a straight line down the middle of the yellow pad and labeled one side "College" and the other "England." Then he drew another line straight down the middle of each of those two sections, writing "Pro" and "Con" over each pair.

"Okay, you and I are going to make the lists together so we can all see at a glance what the pros and cons will be if you go back to school or come with your mother and me." Taking a toke from his Pall Mall cigarette and rubbing his almost bald head with his right hand, he exhaled. I turned my head away from the smoke. Mom peeked around the corner of the kitchen and then went back to cleaning up the dishes.

"Kim, you go ahead and list all the pros for going back to school." Rested from a good night's sleep, he leaned back into the couch and waited as I sat there staring at the blank page. He kept observing me.

Shit. I didn't want to disappoint him, but I couldn't think of one reason that would be a pro for going back to that hellhole. "Well, I guess the only pro, Dad, would be to get an education. But, honestly, it just doesn't work for me in any way, shape, or form, so I don't feel good about putting it down on the list. But if I had to write something, if I could have stuck it out, I guess an education," I said stubbornly and jotted the word education on the page.

"Is that it from you?" he asked.

"Yep, that's all I can come up with," I replied.

Dad tried to list some pros for school, aside from education, such as meeting new people my age, but I countered that should be listed as a pro for going to England too. He was losing the battle on the college front, I thought.

"Okay, now the cons," he said.

I had several reasons for not going back to school. It was limiting, I didn't like the teachers, I had chosen the wrong major as it was way over my head, and I couldn't pursue my dream of singing professionally. The kids were immature, into partying, and weren't serious. I was serious and knew what I wanted out of life. I couldn't relate to any of them. I felt I could actually obtain a better education living in England than attending college. I wanted to go back to England, pursue my dream, and experience more of living in a foreign country in a cosmopolitan city; college couldn't do that for me. The whole college atmosphere turned me off. I acknowledged that college is a great thing for many people but not for all. It was definitely not for me.

"Okay," Dad said, "let's do the list for going to England."

I wrote down many pro reasons, such as my need to *taste, touch, and feel life* in real time, meet international people, get an agent, sing in clubs, go for my dream, experience more of living abroad.

Dad wrote down all the cons. I wouldn't be legal, I'd have to leave the country every six months and talk my way back in, I wouldn't know anyone, I couldn't get a legal job, and I might regret not having a college education and some level of degree.

Mom finished the dishes and came into the living room sitting in an easy chair by the fireplace. She had a cup of tea and was listening but not saying anything. I noticed Dad gaze over to her with apprehensive eyes. She looked back with love and encouragement to him. I could see they both only wanted what was best for me, and this was a truly difficult decision that would determine my fate for years to come.

After making our lists, Dad said, "Kimberly, I want you to take this list and go to bed and think about all of this. In the morning, I want you to come down and tell your mother and me what you have decided. Whatever you decide, your mother and I will stand behind you 100 percent. However, you must live with your decision for the rest of your life." The wrinkles on his brow were pointing downward again.

I said, "Okay, Dad, fair enough." I grabbed the paper, leaned over, and said, "I love you, Dad."

He said emotionlessly, "Me too. Now go to bed."

I walked over to Mom, hugged her, and said, "Love you, Mom."

She smiled sweetly and replied, "Love you too, honey," and then whispered in my ear, "I'm okay; you're okay, right?"

I beamed a big smile and knew I had her support while I bobbed my head up and down in an acknowledgement of yes.

※ ※ ※

Needless to say I didn't sleep much that night. I lay in bed gazing out at the stars. It was dead quiet that night. With the sheet of pros and cons clutched tightly in my hand, I wondered if this list really was the turning point in my life. Could a single piece of paper change one's life so much? I read the list over and over again trying to find any reason to stay in school that resonated with me. I couldn't find one. I needed to go back to England. I needed to *taste, touch, and feel life*.

The summer I had spent with my parents was the most incredible I could ever recall. Mom was happy, she was losing weight, she wasn't drinking as much, she laughed, she was totally submerged in the history of England and the royal family heritage. She was a different person. Mom loved the lifestyle, the people, and all that England had to offer. She was alive again.

Dad seemed excited and interested in this new work. If he took the job, he would be in charge of helping bring to market a prenatal formula that would help pregnant women in Third World countries ensure that their babies would be born with at least normal intellect and brain function. It was an exciting venture, and I hadn't seen him so enthusiastic in a very long time. For my parents, the move to England was the right thing to do.

For me, I felt the same. In those two and half months I had spent in London, I had been finally finding myself. Mom and I traveled around to various villages and took in the sights and sounds. I adored the people, the butcher, the baker, and the fishmonger. It didn't matter how bad the weather was, the workingman always thought it was a glorious day to be alive. It could be brutally cold and rainy, and the fishmonger would say, "Top of the morning to you, mum and lass. Beautiful day, eh?"

The butcher, the produce man, the baker, they all viewed life with a smile on their face and a song in their heart, no matter what was going on. They taught us a great deal about appreciating the little things, the important things. I found myself starting to come out of my self-loathing shell while in London. I started to view life differently and knew I had much more to learn by being there. For me, that was the best education I could have received. I wanted—needed—more of that.

As I lay in bed, I asked for help and guidance from God, whoever that was. "Please, God, help me make the right decision for the good of everyone," I prayed. I shut my eyes, and there it was, that six-pointed, bright-blue star inside my head between my eyebrows. WOW! I hadn't seen that in a while. As I lay there focused on that blue light, I could hear the faint sound of violins in my head. Suddenly I was fast asleep clutching my paper full of pros and cons.

Early the next morning, I woke to the sound of birds singing and a lawnmower starting up. I twisted my head around to look at the clock radio sitting next to my pink Princess phone—seven thirty— and thought, *It's a bit early to be cutting your grass, don't ya think?* I found the pros and cons list scrunched up under the covers. Sitting up in bed and looking out at the backyard, I realized I felt happy. I felt at peace for the first time since we had come back from England and I had quit college. It was as if something had come over me and turned my whole life around. The sun was shining, and so was I. Pulling the covers off, I sprang out of bed and headed for my bedroom door, list in hand. As I opened the door, I could hear my father's voice echoing in my head, *Whatever you decide, your mother and I will stand behind you 100 percent. However, you must live with your decision for the rest of your life.*

Down the stairs I flew dashing into the kitchen where I found Mom and Dad finishing their breakfast. Mom was reading the *Democrat and Chronicle* drinking her coffee, and Dad was engrossed as usual in the *Wall Street Journal*. Both had cigarettes burning in ashtrays.

"Morning, Mom and Dad," I burst out enthusiastically.

Mom looked up from the paper with an inquisitive look on her face. "Morning, Kim," she said.

Pouring myself a cup of black coffee, I sat down at the breakfast table with them.

Dad put down the paper, took the cigarette in his hand, looked over at me with a pensive expression, and said, "Well, Kimberly, have you made up your mind? Do you have an answer for your mother and me?" Both parents stared at me and then looked at each other and back to me again. Mom picked up her cigarette too and took a puff. I pulled my chair back slightly to get away from the smoke.

Replying confidently, I said, "Yes, I do. I have decided to move to England with you guys and not go back to college."

Dad replied, "Are you sure, Kimberly? You will need to live with that decision—"

"Yes," I said interrupting, "I know, Dad, for the rest of my life. I want to *taste, touch, and feel life*. I want to go with you, and I will not be a burden; I promise."

Mom had a cute expression on her face and said, "Kim, you are never a burden."

Dad replied, "Okay, then, the decision has been made."

Mom and I smiled at each other.

"Ya know what?" I said. "This will be our last Christmas in our new house. Kind of sad, but think about all the Christmases we can have in England. But I wish that Gigi and Tiger didn't have to go into quarantine for six months. That's the worst part of all of this."

Mom replied, "I know it is, but your dad found a safe, clean quarantine facility for the girls two hours outside of London, and we'll visit them every couple of weeks."

"Then off to London we go," I said as I got up from the table.

Dad gave me a whimsical smile over the top of the financial section. Mom added, "Yep, off we go."

The only thing my father asked of me if I was to accompany them to England was that I go to school to learn some backup skills, especially how to type. He said if you can type you can always find a job. He wanted me always to have a backup to my musical career. I promised him I would.

I went into the backyard and sat thinking about what had just happened. The sound of the lawnmower was fading away as my brain started to play back some of my most favorite times here in Pittsford living with Mom and Dad.

Scenes of my life on Rand Place flooded my brain like an MGM movie. At Christmas, Mom and I would gather pinecones in the winter from Monroe Golf Club on the fairways and make Christmas ornaments together. I'd go door to door selling them for spending money. The sounds of our favorite Christmas albums would resonate throughout the house with vocals by Johnny Mathis, Perry Como, the Ray Conniff Singers, Nat King Cole, and Andy Williams. I grew up on those artists, and all of them played a role in my musical development. We'd always get a big tree. Mom was particular to Douglas firs.

We had real winters always with a white Christmas and huge snowstorms. I remembered making angels in the snow, having to hang my snow-crusted mittens on the radiator, and smelling the wet wool drying. Monroe Golf Club made an ice rink in the tennis court and had a trailer set up for us kids to change our clothes and put our skates on and off. We'd put the protective guards over the blades and clumsily walk into the clubhouse grillroom where we'd have hot chocolate with tiny marshmallows on top. I'd say the famous words, "Charge it."

I also remembered one summer when the club's bill came in and Mom and Dad had sat Chip and me down and had the conversation about "money doesn't grow on trees." I guess we had rung up too many hamburgers, hot dogs, fries, and Creamsicles that year.

The memories of growing up on Rand Place and all my childhood friends playing kick the can and capture the flag warmed my heart. My times gathering pollywogs and frogs and trying to help the sick birds will stay in me forever.

CHAPTER 12

London for Longer

We moved right after New Year's Day and three weeks before my nineteenth birthday. I'll never forget kissing Gigi and Tiger good-bye at the airport. Mom, Dad, and I watched as their little kennels moved down the conveyor belt into the wall. We'd pick them up at Kennedy Airport and then see them off in the international terminal, not to set eyes on them for two weeks. That was the law in England. We were all very sad and worried about their voyage to the UK and about spending six months in quarantine.

Saying good-bye to Sue was the hardest for me, although she promised to visit in the summer. As I sat on the plane gazing out the window, I saw Sue and her mom and dad waving good-bye. In those days, you could see your loved ones off at the gate. As the plane was pulling away from the gate, Sue was getting smaller and smaller in the window. I was crying, and I knew she was too. I had been her source of strength in a strange new town, and she had been my rock. Dad was engrossed in the *Wall Street Journal*. Mom was reading a book about England and how to communicate to the butcher on the cut of meat you want since they butchered the cows differently over there. She looked at me with sincere eyes and knew I was having a hard time.

My mind ran over and over my decision to move with my parents and give up my life in the States and school. Suddenly as the plane taxied down the runway, I noticed a rainbow sitting over the airport terminal. At that moment, I knew I had made the right decision.

Living in London

After arriving in England, we lived in a hotel until we found a flat in Nottinghill Gate off Holland Road across from Kensington Gardens for a couple of months while waiting for our mews house to be ready and furniture to arrive from the United States. The flat was decorated in Victorian décor throughout. Dad set up a small barbeque in the tiny patio out back. Up the flight of stairs was the master bedroom where Mom and Dad slept. Their bedroom had red-and-black curtains hanging from the windows and a huge king-sized bed.

The bathroom I remember the most. It had a freestanding, huge soaking bathtub, large enough when filled with water for a grown man to spread out and float. There was a toilet with a pull cord to flush and a bidet. I asked Mom how it worked, and she showed me with her clothes on how to use it. I thought it was cool, so I tried it after she left. Honestly, it didn't really work that great. There was a tiny shower that wasn't anything like what we had in America. It was a small, freestanding unit. My dad could just fit in it, and he was only five feet seven inches.

On the third floor was my bedroom. It had a window that looked out onto Holland Road. The room wasn't as grandiose as Mom and Dad's, but it was private . . . somewhat. The first night we slept there, I could hear the police sirens going most of the night. They sounded like the sirens in those World War II movies during the Nazi invasion. It was un-nerving. Suddenly, the reality of my moving to a foreign country hit me. As I lay in bed, worrisome emotions enveloped me. I felt the loss of my friends and felt a little insecure wondering what I was going to do with the rest of my life. I had to find a way to stay here and not get kicked out of the country but also make a living and pursue my singing career. Instead of being a burden on my parents, I wanted to give them reasons to be proud of me.

I also felt exhilarated with anticipation of the journey ahead. Mom was thrilled to be living in England, and Dad was excited about his new role with the company. Yet, I could feel he was holding some heaviness inside. He didn't think I noticed, but I did, and so did Mom.

Setting aside my concerns, as well as excitement, I finally drifted off to sleep for the first night in our rented flat only to awaken to those nasty sirens again.

※ ※ ※

Dad finally got word from the owner that our mews house was ready. The all-white house had three levels. Originally, it had held horse carriages in the lower level, falcons on the next, and caretakers' quarters on the top level. Now converted to housing people, the bedrooms were located on the second level while the third floor housed the living room with vaulted ceilings, a small kitchen, and a small water closet (bathroom). French doors opened up to a tiny four-foot-wide by twelve-foot-long balcony.

We found our mews a delightful place to spend the next several years while exploring England. It was located at 3 Fulton Mews, just off Porchester Terrace, off Bayswater Road in London's West End and directly across from Kensington Gardens. It was a five-minute walk across Bayswater Road to Round Pond where the famous Peter Pan statue stands. Canada geese and swans would flock at the pond, and Mom and I would go daily to feed them. I was always feeding birds; it didn't matter if they were pigeons, swans, or geese. Mom called me the Pied Piper of London.

The driveway into the mews was typical English cobblestone. Walking on it felt like a gentle massage through your shoes, and vehicles driving on it made the most delightful sound and alerted us to their passing—or arrival.

It was sixty-eight degrees out and partly sunny just a day after we had moved in when I heard a truck pull into the mews and a loud knock on the front door located thirty-five steps down from the third-level living room. The container had arrived with our furniture and Mom's organ from the States. What a feat it was watching and listening to the burley English men with Cockney accents hoisting the organ and couches up to the third level over the patio bannister and carefully into the living room. The rest of our worldly possessions were placed in the bedrooms below.

Mom loved playing her organ, especially "Get Me to the Church on Time" and "I've Grown Accustomed to Her face" from *My Fair Lady*, and I loved singing with her. Her feet would dance on the pedals while her fingers struck the keys with delight.

All the mews were the same, so you could look into your neighbor's living room from your living room windows on the third floor. We noticed immediately our neighbor John, who loved to walk around naked every day and who looked like the actor Dudley Moore. He had a different gorgeous blonde with him overnight every few days. He also seemed to deal in very expensive cars. It was common to see Bentleys, Rolls Royces, and Ferraris being bought and sold right out of the mews. We wondered if it was legal.

We had other adjustments to make to British ways. The plumbing was archaic and stubborn, and we no longer took for granted the simple things we had in the United States, like the desired mix of cold and hot water coming out of a single faucet. In this kitchen, we had two faucets, one for cold water and one for hot. We hired a plumber to combine the water into a single faucet. But much to our surprise, when we positioned our hands under the newly created faucet, expecting a beautiful blend of hot and cold water running over our skin, instead we felt hot water on the left side of the flow and cold on the right side. The two flows were touching each other but were definitely not blending into one perfect temperature. Mom asked the plumber why this was. He just shrugged his shoulders, said in his Cockney accent, "That's how it is, mum," and packed up his tools and bid us good day. Mom and I shrugged our shoulders and laughed hysterically.

The small quarters also meant small-size appliances by American standards. Our three-foot-tall by two-foot-wide refrigerator required filling up every couple of days. Pulling our wheeled cart, Mom and I would walk to Queensway and hit the butcher, the baker, the produce man, and the fishmonger.

About every other day, Mom would ask, "Hey, Kim, do you want to go blow your mind today?" I'd always say yes, and then we'd go to the French bakery and have espresso and some wonderful pastry.

In our explorations of London, we quickly caught on to the Brits' attachment to order, especially in waiting—or queuing up—for the bus. Each person had a place in line, unless some pushy, loud-mouth American came by and attempted to jump queue. The Brits would give him a dirty look, and we'd speak up and say, "Excuse me, sir, you need to queue up."

Mom and I used to laugh about other aspects of the bus system. The bus signs read, "The London bus system does not undertake that its busses will run in accordance with the schedule if at all or at all." We'd reread it over and over and just giggle.

The city had other signs that made us roar as well. "Any dog found fouling the footpath will be liable to £20 fine." Right under the signs would be piles of dog crap.

Working

I kept my promise to my father and enrolled in the London School of Business for a while. I picked up all sorts of skills to help me in the business world should I need a backup for my singing career, and yes, one of them was how to type forty words a minute without making a mistake.

Meanwhile, I looked for non-secretarial work. Passing myself off as a Canadian, I found work under the table, as several employers wanted to hire me. I worked at a camera shop for a while and then found a great job as a phone operator running the old manual switchboards at the Prestigious Royal Oversees League in the West End off Knightsbridge Road.

My musical career was progressing well. I teamed up with an Australian, Richard Bennet, who was a fine guitarist and vocalist. We played dinner clubs in the West End of London. When Rick had to move on to other opportunities, I was a solo act again.

I found an agent who arranged gigs in nightclubs throughout London. Dad let me drive to my gigs, even though I didn't have a license, although he didn't either. He was on a temporary license, and every time his test would come up, he'd be out of the country on business. In the entire four years we lived there, he never got his permanent license.

Paris

From time to time, Dad had business in Paris, and Mom had been several times with him. She thought it would be a good experience for me to go. Unfortunately, Dad and I were there during their holiday, Armistice Day, and everything was closed. I still had a ball though. I'd walk up and down the streets window shopping, stopping at cafés, and drinking espressos while eating croissants. I tried out my high school French and barely got by. I loved Paris and said I'd return someday.

Dad took me to the Crazy Horse, a nightclub, but first treated me to dinner at a fabulous restaurant on the Champs-Élysées. I wore my red velvet dress Mom had made for me to perform in. At the table next to us in this chic dining establishment, a poodle and her owner were having dinner. I thought, *Now that is the way it should be; your pets are your family.*

After our meal, to kill time, Dad took me to a local bar for after-dinner drinks while waiting for the 11:45 p.m. show at the Crazy Horse. He played some local card game with a Frenchman at the bar counter. Not speaking any French, Dad likely got taken by the Frenchman for the equivalent of a hundred dollars.

At the Crazy Horse, which has been around since 1951, we had seats in the front row by the stage. The classically trained dancers perfectly integrated a sensuous choreography. Each dancer was bathed in richly colored and textured lighting designs. The colors and images from the stunning lighting effects were so overwhelming that it was hard to determine where skin ended and the color reflections began. It was the most sensual thing I'd ever seen. While the show has changed over the years, the one we saw had many lesbian overtones. I'm sure Dad was embarrassed and hadn't realized what the show entailed when he had suggested we go. Men were looking at him with approving eyes that he had this young woman on his arm. I heard him say to the guy next to him who made some remark, "No, she is my daughter." The guy shook his head as if to say, "Oh yeah, sure she is." After all, I didn't look anything like Dad.

I remember the girls undulating on top of each other with colored lights streaming over their beautiful bodies. The women were naked in some of the scenes. We were so close to the stage that two of the woman who had their bodies entwined were only a foot from my face. Both of them gave me a big smile. I felt my inner feelings stirring about my attraction toward woman again. *Quick,* I told myself, *put that away!*

Dad leaned over to me and said nervously, "Are you okay with this show?"

I replied, "I love it." Then I knew what Mom meant prior to us leaving for Paris when Dad told her he was planning on taking me to The Crazy Horse. I overheard her from the other room say, "You're planning on taking Kim to the Crazy Horse? Well, I suppose that is okay. She is years ahead of her time, and she'll totally appreciate the theatrical and musical side of the show."

On our last night in Paris, Dad and I had dinner at our glorious hotel on La Rive Gauche, the southern bank of the Seine River in Paris. There was a beautiful nightclub in the hotel with live entertainment. Of course, as Dad always did, he had to tell the bandleader that his daughter was a singer. I hated that. I was so embarrassed and always shy to get up and sing at another performer's gig. It felt invasive to me.

The bandleader encouraged me to come up, and to please Dad, I did. I sang a couple of songs and received a very positive response from the audience. Dad sat in his booth with a huge smile on his face, a cigarette in one hand, and a cocktail in the other. He was so proud.

Isle of Jersey

Back in London, the agent I found arranged for me to audition to be one of two lead singers for a stint on the Isle of Jersey with Ivy Benson's swing band. She'd risen to fame in the 1940s, and her band was still popular in the 1970s. I aced the audition in one hour.

Excited about my new gig and thinking this was a big break for me, Mom and I shopped for new performing outfits. She bought me a stunning embroidered, dark-blue pantsuit that looked like a woman's tuxedo, along with a yellow halter dress that showed off my natural dark skin tone.

While I was nervous about spending a couple of months in a strange place with people I didn't know, I was more nervous about Ivy herself. She was rough around the edges and could be very curt. I tried to ignore her less-than-friendly approach, as this was a big opportunity. I wanted everyone to be proud of me, and I wanted to be proud of myself.

We were to reside in flats in a city by the water on the Isle of Jersey in the English Channel. Half the girls were to share each flat. While on the boat ride to the island, I noticed the other lead singer, Shirley, was overly friendly to me in an odd way.

"Kim, you will stay with me," she kept insisting.

I didn't know what to say, other than, "Okay."

"Let's play golf one day, Kim. Do you play?" she said.

I replied, "Yeah, I do actually. My parents were big golfers."

The bass player, Pam, took an interest in me and could see how green I was. She took a protective role and kept interrupting the conversation between Shirley and me, "Shirley, no; Kim is staying with us, so hands off" or "Shirley, Kim is not playing golf with you."

I wouldn't understand till several days later while Pam and I were strolling through the lush green countryside looking at Jersey cows that Shirley was a lesbian and she was coming on to me. In fact, Pam said Shirley's entire flat of musicians were gay, and they wanted me with them. The only gay people I knew were my Uncle Bud and Uncle Earl. However, Pam said, "You will not be safe with them. You are staying with us girls."

Before opening, the other female musicians who shared my flat told me the new pantsuit Mom had bought me looked grand. My performance warranted a standing ovation, and I didn't make any mistakes. Thank God. Yet, the show was a disaster. Right after the final curtain call, back stage, feeling overwhelmed with pride and joy, I saw Ivy storming toward me. She screamed at the top of her lungs, "Kim, don't you ever wear that outfit again. You look like a dyke."

I had never been screamed at like that. I was stunned, crushed, and confused. Turning to Pam I said, "What did she mean, I look like a dyke? What's that?"

Pam glanced over at the trumpet player, who looked upset for me, and took me aside. Kindly she said in her thick Lancashire accent, "Kim, dyke means lesbian, hard core."

"What? I do not look like that. What is she talking about? She never told me what to wear and not to wear, anyway." Tears were rolling down my cheeks by now. I felt humiliated.

Pam could see I was in no shape to stay and party with the other entertainers, which was the norm after the show. She took me back to the flat and tried to calm me down. For the next week, Ivy found some reason to scream and mock me after every performance. Even with huge applause for my performance, she abused me verbally. What the hell was happening here? I thought.

All the girls in my flat felt bad for me, but they all said the same thing, "That is Ivy lately. You just have to go with it."

Well, I couldn't. This wasn't for me. This wasn't what entertaining was supposed to be like. This was supposed to feel good and harmonious. Ivy had hired me for my talent, so why was she treating me like shit?

After a week, I'd had enough. So there I was in the phone booth in the tiny city on Jersey in the middle of the English Channel calling Mom again and weeping.

"Hello," Mom answered the phone.

"Mom it's me. I can't stay here. Ivy is treating me horribly. She hated the pantsuit you bought me; she told me I look like a dyke. She screams all the time at me. I can't do anything right. I'll never make the eight weeks."

Mom replied, "Kim, listen, you have to get tougher if you want to be in show business. Just ignore her. Do your best. You said you made a new friend when you called before, Pam, isn't it?"

"Yeah, but if I can't do anything right, why did she hire me? Everyone else likes me and my singing, so why is she treating me like shit?"

"Kim, I don't know why, but try to give this a chance. Call me back in a few days. Okay? Just be strong, honey. You can do this," she said trying to comfort me. As I hung up, I had a flashback to me standing in the phone booth at the Boston airport dealing with this same emotional crap. What the hell was wrong with me? As Mom had said, if I couldn't be tough, I'd never make it in show business. I felt like an idiot and failure.

I made it another five days and called my mother. "Mom, I tried, I really did, but the abuse is just too much for me. I hate it here. I can't find any happiness being here if all I do is get yelled at and ridiculed every night. Even Pam said it is wrong, and she's not sure why Ivy is treating me this way. It could have something to do with the other lead singer, Shirley, trying to get me to quit. Maybe she's jealous because I'm getting too much attention and the other singer isn't. I don't know. I need to come home now. There is a ferry that leaves tomorrow; I'll be on it."

Mom sighed. "Okay, Kim, we'll be there to pick you up."

Failure, failure, failure. That's all I could think of myself.

As I hung up the phone, I noticed one of the show's comedians was sitting at a table in the café near where the phone booth was. He had been watching me intently talk on the phone. As I exited the phone booth, I raised my hand as if I was saying hello and good-bye. He waved back and didn't appear to be very happy himself.

I strolled aimlessly back to the flat to pack, feeling worthless again. What was wrong with me? I just didn't understand what the problem was—me, Ivy, or something else. Despite what Mom had said, I asked myself over and over, *Why should I have to have tough skin to take that kind of shit from anyone? No one should, show business or not! I can't help it if I'm sensitive. I'd understand if I was doing a lousy job or doing something terribly wrong, but I'm not. Singing always made me happy, but not now.*

If this singing wasn't fun and didn't give me the happiness and love inside that it always did, then why do it? I sat on the bed, looked around at the flat, and realized this big break was nothing more than a big bust. I knew my agent wouldn't be happy to hear the news either and would probably dump me. I had to go back to London and try to find work in clubs on my own.

Vocal Cord Surgery

After the Ivy Benson disaster, I set out on my own. My agent did dump me in disgust, but I persevered with the support of Mom and Dad. I auditioned at clubs all over the West End and had several gigs playing my guitar and singing for three to four hours in the evenings several times a week, mainly at lounges and supper clubs. Everything was going fabulously with my career, and I was on top of the world. Hell, I didn't need any idiot agent; I was doing it on my own.

At the top of my singing career in London, I had a setback for over eighteen months, which put my career on hold and basically ended it in England. Singing in too many smoky bars and clubs damaged my vocal cords. Plus, in a few establishments, I'd had to push my vocal cords harder to be heard above the noise, even with my microphone and amplifier turned all the way up. The strain was too much, and I lost my voice due to severe nodules on my pharynx and larynx. I had the best doctors from my father's health insurance plan with the company. A Harley Street ear, nose, and throat physician told Mom and me that I had to be silent for two weeks. Not one word. If after that time, the nodules were still there, I would need a severe vocal cord strip.

I went through six legal pads of paper. Mom and Dad kind of liked the quiet for a change, but after two weeks, the verdict was surgery. I stayed at The London Clinic on Harley Street. It was like a first-class hotel. A porter walked Mom and me up to my room carrying my overnight bag. I was given a menu to choose my dinner, which consisted of choices of several healthy gourmet items.

The drawer in the nightstand by the bed held paper with The London Clinic letterhead and beautiful pens. I could even order a half-bottle of wine if I wanted from the menu. Of course, I said yes. The porter would fetch it from the liquor store just outside the front door of the hospital. Now that was class. I had the best care. How appropriate, I thought, that in England they call the "operating room" the "operating theatre."

A speech therapist, Dr. Juliette Glover, came to the hospital the night before my surgery and talked to Mom, Dad, and me about what to expect. She clearly stated that when I woke up from the surgery I would not be able to make any sounds, so shouldn't try. She said she would have to teach me how to speak and form sounds again. Even though my brain would know how to form the words, my vocal cords wouldn't. The last thing I remember saying to the nurses as they wheeled me into the operating theatre was "thank you for taking such good care of me."

When I woke up in my room after the surgery, the first thing I did was reach for the phone to call downstairs to the front desk just to see if anything came out. Nothing did. Mom and Dad came into the room shortly thereafter. I attempted to say, "Hello, Mom and Dad." But my lips only formed the words, and no sounds came out.

Mom looked sad. "Kim, stop trying," she said. "Dr. Glover said don't try, remember?"

When they saw I truly couldn't make any sounds, they both had tears in their eyes. Silence is golden . . . until it's not.

Dr. Glover came to our flat at Fulton Mews every week for several months to work with me. My parents were getting worried that my relearning to speak was taking longer than expected. So was I. Dr. Glover said that sometimes this happens, and we just have to push on.

Then three months after surgery, it happened. Mom was just entering the mews house pulling her little cart filled with groceries from the fishmonger, French bakery, butcher, and produce man just two blocks away on Queensway. As she was attempting to pull the cart up the stairs, I ran down to greet her enthusiastically at the front door while Dr. Glover watched grinning from the top of the steps. We had been working on the *m*'s, and I squeezed out the words "mother" and "money."

The expression on Mom's face was nothing short of elated joy. She took my face in her two hands, squeezed my cheeks together so my lips puckered up, and planted a big kiss on them. I could see tears welling up in her beautiful blue eyes. That's all she did. No words needed to be said. Then I helped her pull the cart up the two flights of stairs to the kitchen.

The vocal tones were scattered and uncontrolled, and I couldn't carry a tune for more than a year after the surgery. After eighteen months, I was able to start singing again but limited in terms of how long at any one time.

Dr. Glover told me I have sensitive vocal cords and whatever line of work I end up doing shouldn't be where I use my voice all day.

Phased Out

While Dad was thrilled with the job he did while in England and loved the lifestyle, nearing the end, Mom and I noticed him getting unhappy and drinking a bit more. His temper was short, and he snapped at Mom and me, which he hadn't done before. I wasn't sure about all the details, but I knew it had to do with his job that was or wasn't waiting for him back in Rochester.

One day I heard Mom and Dad arguing and went upstairs into the living room where I heard Dad do something he'd never done as long as I'd known him. He stood up and screamed at Mom with anger in his heart. It frightened Mom and me. This patient loving man, where was this coming from? I don't know what came over me, but instinctively I screamed at him, "Stop it! Stop it, Dad," then bolted from the living room, ran down to my bedroom, and slammed the door.

Minutes later, there was a knock on the door. Mom and Dad entered my room. They both had been crying. Mom sat close to me on my bed, and Dad on my other side. Taking my hand, she said, "Bob, look what we are doing to our little girl."

I had never seen my father look so sad. He spoke softly with tears in his eyes, "Kimmy, I'm sorry I blew up like that. I've been under a lot of stress. I apologize to you and your mother. It will be okay." They both hugged me and walked out.

While I accepted that explanation, I knew there was more going on with my father, and I was worried about him. So was Mom.

Later on I learned that Dad was being phased out so the company could hire young, less experienced men for less money. Yet the company wanted my father to teach his replacements his job and stay on as a consultant for a little while after he returned to the United States. Dad had made it to second in command and wanted the presidency but recognized that was clearly not going to happen. He was crushed and, I'm sure in some way, felt betrayed. He had given more than thirty years to that company.

Remembering

In August 1976, our time in England came to a close. While we were looking forward on some level to returning to Rochester to our friends and family, we were overcome with sadness as well. We had been infused with the English style of life and had grown to adore London in every way, even the weather. For someone like me who craves the warm temperature and sun year round, I found myself enchanted by the need for London to show the many facets of her charm.

While packing the mews house up for the movers to tote our worldly possessions back into a container to travel the thirty-five hundred miles back to Rochester, I leaned back against the wall in the living room and time-traveled my last four years in this sensational country.

Smiling, I remembered the day we freed our dogs from quarantine and their daily five-minute walks with me to Round Pond where I fed the birds. The movie in my mind played back all the churches, cathedrals, and villages Mom and I visited throughout England. We walked around the wall at York while she read, as she usually did, to me from her English history books. How happy Mom was telling me what had happened historically on this day in this city. We'd sing appropriate songs, such as "Winchester Cathedral" as we toured the grounds of that famous building.

The fabulous live theatre in Piccadilly Circus had kept us entertained throughout our stay. We saw *Jesus Christ Superstar, Joseph and the Amazing Technicolor Dreamcoat, Hair, The King and I, Harvey,* and so many others.

I recalled connections that soured and others that were cemented. Twice I had attempted relationships with men that failed almost as soon as they started. Yes, again, all they really wanted was my body, not me. And then there was my experience with the Ivy Benson Band. But my meeting Pam the bass player who watched over me was worth the agony as, over forty-two years later, we are still friends and stay connected.

Our daily trips I treasured to the butcher, baker; produce man, and fishmonger dragging our little pull cart to fill our tiny refrigerator with fresh, healthy food. I loved all the pubs and restaurants we discovered and the routine Mom started. Every time we came out of a restaurant, we'd gaze up at the moon, and she'd start singing a made-up tune, "I see the moon, and the moon sees me."

It was the best decision for me to choose England over college. I did get to *taste, touch, and feel life* in every way, shape, and form.

Kim feeding the swans, Canada geese, and other birds at Round Pond, Kensington Gardens, in London.

CHAPTER 13

BEGINNINGS OF TRUE INDEPENDENCE

Before we arrived back in the United States, my parents had decided not to return to the suburbs. Instead, we moved into the city of Rochester off East Avenue and rented a classic refurbished carriage house that had been featured in *Better Homes and Gardens* and resembled a mews house in London. After living in Britain, they realized they were really more city folks and didn't want to return to the energy or lifestyle of the suburbs. I was happy to hear that.

And so were Uncle Bud and Uncle Earl, who lived in a gorgeous old brownstone only fifteen minutes from East Avenue where the carriage house was located. The carriage house was situated behind one of the larger mansions on East Avenue. Made of red brick, it had three lofts, one where Dad had an art studio set up in hopes he'd start painting again, although he never did. The other loft was a sitting room with TV. Those two lofts were accessible by a winding wrought iron staircase from the main part of the house. The third loft was accessible from a ladder in the living room up against the wall in the front of the living room, where you could climb up and sit gazing out into the front yard. We had books and pillows placed in that loft and called it the library.

The kitchen was small but magnificent with state-of-the-art appliances for Mom to cook her fabulous gourmet meals.

The living room was large with a sensational chandelier hanging in the middle, which came from the old Rochester Savings Bank Building. It had a dimmer switch,. which could give the room a romantic glow at night.

Moving Out

After living in the carriage house almost a year, I approached a sensitive subject with my mother. "Mom, I really feel I should get my own place. I'm twenty-three years old. Sue and Jan are married and starting families. I still live with my parents and don't even have a boyfriend. Hell, I'm still a virgin."

Sitting in the living room, Mom replied, "Look, Kim, I don't want you to feel pressure about any of this. You are and always have been a pleasure to be with. You have always helped out enormously when living with your father and me. Your day will come, and you will meet someone, so don't put pressure on yourself about that. You can stay with us as long as you need, but if you really want a place of your own, I will help you find something, and we will decorate it together, okay?"

❋ ❋ ❋

My first apartment was in the attic of an old mansion off Vick Park B, off East Avenue and Park Avenue, about five blocks from my parents. Small but cute, it had a little kitchen, tiny eating area, a bathroom, and small open room. The main room had a bed, table, and lamp. We had a lion doorknocker made with a small sign for the door. Although no one ever called me by my first name, Mom liked the sound of "Ann's Attic," so she had a sign made for my door with that name. Since dogs and cats weren't allowed, I had a yellow parakeet named Tweedy.

Picking up the last of my clothes from the carriage house, I kissed Mom, Dad, Gigi, and Tiger good-bye. While I would be only a few blocks away, we all knew this was a turning point for them and me.

"Bye, Mom and Dad. I'll call you tomorrow, and let's plan that I'll have you guys over for dinner next week, okay? I'll make Cornish hens. Oh, and bring the girls. We can sneak them in for just a few hours."

Smiling and kind of sad, they both replied in unison, "Okay, honey, that sounds good."

As I waved good-bye walking to my brown Camaro I had bought from Mom, I could see the look in their eyes mixed with hope, love, and concern. The first night I slept in my new flat was emotional and exciting at the same time.

That First Kiss

I had been teaching guitar for a year out of my parents' place and now transferred it to Ann's Attic. Doing that on Sundays for eight hours, plus working at Executive Placement, Employment Agency full time and singing Thursday, Friday, and Saturday nights at local clubs as a solo act, I made out just fine financially.

One of my guitar students, Sally, was sixteen years old going on twenty-five. Her parents were casual friends of my parents. Her mom didn't care for the boyfriend Sal was involved with at school, and feeling I was a good role model, her mother encouraged me to have Sal over for weekends. We'd play and sing for hours.

One night I took her out to dinner to The Park Avenue Pub around the corner from my flat. Sal looked at me and said, "I love you."

I replied, "I love you too, kid."

She fired back, "No, you don't understand; I am in love with you. I want to make love with you."

To say I was shocked would be a lie; I wasn't. I could feel the sexual tension between us. There was something remarkable stirring inside me, that familiar feeling I'd had before yet tried to ignore. But how could I have these feelings for a woman almost seven years younger than I? Was I nuts? I had never been with a woman, nor had she.

Although I had long ago torn up the photo I used to carry around of the tall, dark, handsome Italian model, thinking that was the kind of guy I'd end up with, I still tried to make relationships with men work. After my family moved into the carriage house, my Uncle Bud and Uncle Earl introduced me to a Frenchman named Andre. I was really attracted to him, dark and handsome with a thick French accent. Unfortunately all he wanted was to screw me and had no real feelings for me. I didn't screw him; instead, I sent him packing like all the others. My luck with men always ended in disaster. Why? Why couldn't I find Mr. Right? Was I not attractive enough?

But then I noticed, even when I was with a man I thought I liked, I kept looking over my shoulder at women. Why was that? How could I be with a man for life if I kept doing that? I was totally confused. Was I bisexual? Oh great. That's all I needed.

So I tried to shy away from what I was feeling for Sal but knew it was hopeless. She was dead serious on this issue, and I knew I wanted to give in to these feelings. I had grown quite fond of her.

We went back to my apartment and sat on my couch staring at each other. The longing in Sally's eyes tore at my heart and emotions. She was assertive and moved in on me before I could evaluate the situation any further. I'll never forget the first kiss with a woman. Never before had I ever experienced anything so sensual and exciting both sexually and emotionally. My skin tingled; my solar plexus became hot and tightened in my gut. The kiss had a profound sensitivity, intimacy, and sensuality nothing like what I had felt with any man before.

We fell deeply in love and had an affair that lasted almost two years. We constantly had to hide our affair from her school friends, my friends, and our parents. Exciting as it was, we both were terrified of being discovered.

One day, however, our luck ran out when her mother caught us in a compromising position in her bedroom during an afternoon we thought her mother would be out. After that, I was banished from her life and their home. I was so worried her mother would say something to my mother, but she didn't.

I was living a life of secrecy. Who was I? What was I? I was still attracted to men. I was attracted to woman. I guess I was bisexual. I didn't want my parents to know anything. The last thing I ever wanted to do was disappoint them, yet if they found out, it would have crushed them, or so I thought.

Sal and I had our challenges since I was banished from her life. While we tried to see each other from time to time, I knew I had to move on. She would be leaving for college, and I knew she would have many other lovers. I was heartbroken, and so was she, but I had to let her go.

Mark

I had a new job by now working at the law firm Middleton, Wilson, Boylan, and Gianninni in downtown Rochester, midtown plaza. I was the receptionist. That typing came in handy.

One of the firm's client's was Manufacturers Hanover Bank. Their contact was a guy named Mark, a divorcee with two children. He stood five foot ten inches, was thin with light-brown hair, and drove a beige VW Beetle. He wasn't what you'd call gorgeous and certainly didn't look like the Italian model I use to keep in my wallet, but he had a beautiful, huge smile that showed off his perfect pearly whites, along with a funny sense of humor. At least twice a week he'd come to the firm, and he'd flirt with me at the front desk all the time.

He even told Rob, one of the lawyers, that he wanted to take me out. Mark thought my voice was sexy on the phone. I was twenty-four years old and hadn't had sex with a man yet. So I decided to go for it. I was still trying to find Mr. Right and get rid of the feelings for women that kept rearing their head. We began dating.

While Mark wanted to get down to serious business within the first thirty days, I told him I wanted to be properly courted for several months before I gave myself to him. I really was kind of old-fashioned. He agreed.

I started to fall for this guy, although there were hurdles—or maybe warnings—along the way. He decided it was time to introduce me to his two children, who were between five and eight years old, but when I met them, it felt strange. Plus, because his ex-wife was receiving alimony and child support, Mark didn't have much spending money. When we'd go out to dinner, sometimes I had to pay, and that felt oddly uneasy. The kids liked me, but none of this felt totally comfortable or natural. I was confused by these emotions.

In addition, Mom and Dad were not thrilled with Mark. Mom especially didn't like the idea of my hanging out with a divorced man with no money, no future, and two kids. She kept telling me I was in love with the idea of being in love but not really in love with the man. Mom and I knew that Mark was getting ready to ask me to marry him, but she wanted me to take it slow and cautious and wait for the right one.

One weekend, Mom, Dad, and I were at Canandaigua Lake where she ran a short-term rental business Dad had set up for her. They had a powerboat there, named *Bristol Holidays*, which I wanted to take out for a spin.

Before they gave me the okay, Mom sat me down and said, "Kim, listen. I know you've been ripe and ready since a very young age. It's just who you are, passionate and sensual. I know you want to find love, but I'm asking you to take the boat out, sit in the middle of the lake, and ask yourself about Mark. Is he really the one for you? Are you in love with him or the idea of being in love? What can he really give you?"

I did as Mom had instructed and realized floating on the lake that maybe I wasn't sure about Mark. I thought I loved him, but did I really? And how would I know unless I gave myself to him? He adored me and thought I was beautiful, or so he said. The bigger issue for me, which I couldn't share with Mom, was could I find sexual happiness with a man. Would I shut down again as I had with Chuck?

Secretly, I went to the gynecologist and got a prescription for birth control pills. I didn't want my parents to know, as I didn't want to disappoint them, but I had to find out about my sexuality once and for all. Was I going to be with a man or woman? For me it wasn't about the gender but the person inside. I knew I could love either one. Let the best man or woman win! But until I really had a meaningful relationship both emotionally and sexually with a man, how would I know whether men were even in the running?

※ ※ ※

One snowy winter evening, Mark was making me dinner at his apartment. When I opened the front door, I saw he had placed candles from the front door leading up the stairs all the way into the living room and bedroom. His patio off the bedroom had snowdrifts on it. He had placed champagne in the snowdrift. How romantic. We started off with cocktails. Mark had vodka; I had Johnnie Walker Black. He made steak, baked potatoes, and salad—couldn't go wrong with that.

After dinner, we went into the living room and started drinking champagne. I was tipsy and ready. Being the entertainer that I am, I started to remove his and my clothes in perfect syncopation to the verses in the song "Tonight's the Night" by Rod Stewart, which was playing on the stereo. For a moment, I flashed back to my disaster with Chuck in my senior year, but it passed. Mark and I spent the next three hours making love on the living room floor in front of the stereo and then moved into his bedroom. I'll never forget him saying, "So are you sure you've never done this before?" Unfortunately or fortunately, depending on how you look at it, it unleashed a passion and desire in me that had been bottled up for years. Sex was so easy for me, so natural. Why had I waited so long? I thought he had to be the one, as it was a total success.

The next morning, I had to rush back to my apartment, shower, and go to work. I was so sore, I was almost walking bow-legged. That started a yearlong passionate affair with Mark.

Mom and Dad were not thrilled.

I started to think that maybe I wasn't bisexual and certainly not gay like my Uncle Bud and Uncle Earl. However, I still had some sexual feelings for the office manager, Mary, at the law firm. Focusing on Mark, I pushed those feelings aside. Still hiding from my parents that I was having sex, I played the relationship down, but I think my mother knew. My dad never said a thing. Although I was certainly old enough to have sex if I wanted and was living on my own, wondering what my parents thought of what I was doing did bother me. In truth, I wanted their approval and knew I wasn't getting it. There was a definite tension between Mom and me when it came to Mark.

Betrayed

Nearing the end of 1978, my musical career was making huge strides with my performing in better clubs and gaining more plaudits, including articles written about me in the local newspapers. Instead of supporting my success, Mark was becoming jealous of my singing. When I'd perform at the Top of the Plaza, Mark would show up, sit at the bar drinking and looking pissed off while I'd perform.

Once after the show, I asked him, "Honey, what's wrong with you? You seem distant and unhappy."

He pouted and replied, "I don't like your getting all this attention now. I feel your music is pulling you away from me."

"That's not true," I said. "All I've ever wanted was my music and a relationship. Why can't I have both? I love you," I said as I held his hand. Mark had asked me to marry him a few months back, and something inside had told me not to accept. I had put him off by saying, "I'm not ready yet, Mark. Please, give me some time."

❈ ❈ ❈

By now I had moved from Ann's Attic to my new larger flat, a one-bedroom, three streets down from my parents in the other direction. One day at work, I developed excruciating pain in my abdomen. I was doubled over and couldn't stand straight. Somehow I drove myself home. I was running a high fever, perspiring profusely, and becoming delirious. I called Mom for help.

When she arrived, she found me passed out on the floor and rushed me to the hospital. Mom had quit smoking for a month, only to start up again while waiting for me in the waiting room at the hospital. I felt guilty that I had caused her to start again.

After the doctors put a twelve-inch probe into my vagina, I heard one of them say, "Oh my God, the infection has spread."

What infection? What the hell are they talking about? I thought as I winced in agony biting down on a thick cloth while they did the procedure.

They took tests for which the results wouldn't come back till tomorrow. Then they launched a six-inch needle filled with penicillin into my upper thigh. One of the emergency nurses was the mother of my ex-boyfriend Chuck. She was talking to Mom in the waiting room. I felt so embarrassed but didn't know why . . . yet.

Mom took me home to the carriage house. When Dad got home, she told him I had a bad case of the flu. She put me on the couch with lots of pillows and blankets, instead of in my old room, so I would be closer to their bedroom and she could hear me if I needed help. She fed me a baked potato and watched over me all night constantly putting cold washcloths on my forehead. I could see they both were very worried. So was I.

I hadn't felt such pain before and wondered what kind of flu bug could this be that it would send me to emergency and infect my vagina?

The next morning the penicillin had kicked in, and I could start to upright myself.

The phone rang around ten. I grabbed it in the kitchen leaning on the counter and said, "Hello."

"Hello, this is the Emergency Room at Genesee Hospital calling for Ann Driggs."

"This is Ann."

"Ms. Driggs, your test results are back, and the findings are you have gonorrhea. I believe we treated it in time, so you will still be able to have children if you desire. We ask that you notify all your partners to seek medical attention."

I was knocked over and in total disbelief. I didn't have multiple partners. I had only one. "What! Are you sure?" I fired back.

"Yes, we are sure. Please notify all partners. Let us know if you have any other complications. Good bye."

For a moment, a strange feeling flooded through me, that this was the same hospital that had cared for me in 1954 when I had been abandoned as a newborn. Wouldn't they be disappointed to know that same little girl was now being treated for gonorrhea? What a disappointment I turned out to be.

But how could this have happened to me? I had waited all these years to give myself to a man and now this?

I had to tell Mom what the hospital had said. *Shit.* Now she would know I was having sex with the very man she and Dad didn't approve of. Oh my God. How was I going to do this? I would be the disappointment of a lifetime. *This just can't be happening*, I thought to myself. I felt trapped with no way out.

Always tell the truth, Dad had taught us. *Your mother and I will stand behind you 100 percent if you always tell the truth, no matter how bad it is.* I had to tell them the truth.

Dad was at work. Mom was in her bedroom making up the beds. I walked in the bedroom shaking with humiliation. "Mom, that was the hospital that called, and they said I . . . I . . . have . . . gonorrhea." I burst into tears and fell into her arms. "I'm so sorry Mom. I know I've disappointed you and Dad. I'm so sorry. It is only Mark I've been with. I had to know if I loved him. I did love him. How could he do this to me, Mom? I thought he loved me."

Mom was gentle, kind, and understanding. I think she had known all along. She hugged me for what seemed like a long time. Then trying to wipe the tears away, she looked me straight in the eyes and said firmly, "Kim, it's okay. It's okay. You will be okay. I love you. Listen, Kim. We can't tell your father or brother. They'll kill Mark. We need to keep this to ourselves, okay?"

"Okay," I sobbed." I knew Mom was livid at Mark, but her main concern was tending to my emotions.

Dad never knew.

I did tell Chip some twenty years later, and he was pissed even then to hear Mark had done this to his little sister.

When reality hit, anger and disgust followed. I called Mark and confronted him. That pig! How could he do this to me? He loved me, didn't he? Hell, he'd asked me to marry him. Then it came to me. Ah ha! Several months back, he had flown to New York City on bank business and looked up an old girlfriend. I didn't worry as he was in love with me. He must have had sex with her, and she had passed the nasty bug onto him.

When I told him what I had, he denied it. I told him he knew damn well I was with no one else but him and asked if he had had sex with her. He finally admitted it over the phone. I told him he was an insecure pig and he should tell her if she didn't know already what she's carrying. Saying never to call me again, I slammed the phone down.

Then standing there in the kitchen staring at the phone, I thought how odd that in one hour you could go from being so in love with someone to totally abhorring the person. I was through with men. I was through with love.

❈ ❈ ❈ CHAPTER 14 ❈ ❈ ❈

FOLLOWING MY MUSIC MUSE

Stu, who was married to my grade school friend Ann, was a professional arranger and in 1978 was working for Berkeley College of Music in Boston, Massachusetts. He arranged my original songs and had the musicians and recording studio time booked. Stu believed in me.

A group of investors comprised of lawyers from the law firm I worked in and some of their real estate clients had heard me sing many times in clubs and decided to invest in me. They formed the AKD Corporation and promised to stand by my side through thick or thin.

Mom and Dad, while incredibly supportive as always and enthusiastic, did have some reservations about the AKD Corp. but didn't stand in my way. Their biggest concern was that these men didn't know the first thing about the music industry and might not be willing, despite the "thick or thin" promise, to stay with me for the years it could take to build my career.

Regardless, onward I went. The first step in making a career of my singing was getting a professional demo tape, which we scheduled in a recording studio in Boston. I drove my Camaro there from Rochester flying high all the way with eager anticipation. Finally, I was living my dream—performing my music in a studio recording with live musicians. We recorded two of my original pieces at the time, "Jas Vas

Lu Blue" ("I Love You" in Russian) and "Spotlight Routine," a song I had written in London about the city.

I was in heaven and could have stayed in the studio for days on end. This was home to me. The sound booth was dimly lit, and I first played the guitar track without vocals along with the other musicians. Then Stu would play it back into my headphones, and I'd sing to the tracks. My entire being tingled with delight as I felt a rush of warm energy flood my body and spirit. To hear what you've created with only your guitar and voice manifest and transcend into a complete work of multiple instruments, layers, and colors is the most gratifying experience for any musical artist. It was like being a part of a rainbow.

It took over twelve hours to get the tunes how we wanted them. I did all my own harmonies. The layers of melody were like layers of colors on top of one another. It reminded me of how The Carpenters created all their musical harmonies. I'd close my eyes and see all the colors of the rainbow as I imagined them in my head with each color having its own note. I had never been so happy.

Hearing the playback in the engineering booth of each layer of my voice being mixed to perfection with the next layer and assisting with the mix was better than sex. This is what I had been waiting for all my life for my music. I didn't care if I ever performed in public again. I could have just made records in the studio and been totally happy.

By this time, I had found a manager, as the investors insisted I needed one. I agreed. His name was Clark. He sent the demo tape to multiple record producers he said he knew.

Then we waited.

Guidance from the Other Side

My blue star, my ability to connect with animals, even my singing that often helped people through rough times showed me there is more on this Earth than meets the eyes. And I have had several close calls that hammered in that point.

One happened on a bright sunny afternoon, as I was driving through a canyon, angry and too fast and carelessly, swerving around the turns as if I had a death wish. All of a sudden, I lost control of the car, and it started to swerve and spin. It kicked up so much dirt that the entire windshield became opaque. I knew the car was only a few feet away from going over the embankment into the gulch. My heart was racing, and I could feel a pit of fire in my chest with fear.

Suddenly, I had a sense of someone or something telling me to let go of the steering wheel. *Just let go, Kim.* Incredibly, I did; I gave into it. Then the car stopped abruptly. I didn't know what direction I was heading at that point. I turned the windshield wipers on and could see I was facing the oncoming traffic. All other drivers had stopped when they'd seen my car out of control. I was alive and safe, and so was everyone else.

Taking a deep breath and waving to the oncoming cars, I put the car in gear, moved it to the right side of the road, and continued slowly down the canyon on my way. I realized what had happened— that the angels had intervened and saved my life. I thanked them, apologized for my childish behavior, and said I would never do that again. I have kept my word.

I had another extraordinary experience with the angels years later. I was on my 750 bright-yellow Honda motorcycle going only three minutes away to get the bike inspected at the 76 Station. I had the green light, right of way, and was going straight ahead. Suddenly, a huge, bright-yellow, long-bed truck in the oncoming traffic turned left in front of me to beat me through the intersection. He wasn't going to make it, and I knew we were going to collide. I was wearing shorts, T-shirt, tennis shoes, socks, and my helmet.

Swerving quickly to avoid the collision, I could hear voices from the other cars in the intersection gasping in horror. I could feel the bike falling and the pavement getting closer to my face. It was then that these words raced through my brain while the panic and fear ran through my veins. *Oh my God, after all I've been through, now I'm going to die on this bike.*

Just then, as before, a voice yelled into my ears, *Let go of the handlebars. Let go.* I let go and let God. Suddenly, the bike was upright and off to the side of the road, out of the intersection. I was alive with only a bad burn from the engine on my leg. The truck was long gone, and everyone was yelling, "Are you okay?" I waved back knowing my angels had again saved me.

I told them how much I loved them and appreciated them. Right then, I promised I'd sell the bike, and the very next day, I put it up for sale.

※ ※ ※

With those experiences in my background, my talking with a psychic did not seem so odd. Maybe, I thought, I could get some clue about whether I was on the right track in my life.

The woman led me along one of the first-floor hallways toward the back of her rambling Victorian home. At the end of the hall, we turned left. She mentioned that her elderly mother resided in the opposite wing. One more turn, a few more steps, and . . . *voilà*, our destination, a cozy, windowless sitting room. Ornate frames decorated oils and sepia-toned photographs, tasteful portraits, mostly. She gestured for me to sit on the cushioned loveseat while she sat across from it on a matching upholstered chair.

Now settled, she raised her eyes to meet my gaze. Her smile was warm. "You have something?"

"Yes." I dug into the pocket of my tight jeans. "She said to bring something along. My friend's mother, the one who recommended you. So here. I brought this."

I notice her eyes closed as she held out an open hand.

I dropped the item onto her palm and watched her fingers curl around it and then lift her cupped hand to rest against her heart.

Her eyes opened. In friendly but muted tones, she prepared me for what was to come. She might go into a trance and say things that made little or no sense. But I mustn't worry or be frightened.

"Please," I said, "whatever you need to do." *I'm not spooked. Optimistic, that's what I am.*

"Very well." Eyes again closed.

I waited.

Waited.

Waited.

"I see a priest . . . and two nuns. There, by your shoulders."

Really? I had no sense of their presence, none at all. "That's odd," I said aloud.

Her other hand shot up as though to quiet me.

"Sorry," I said.

She frowned. "Slow down; you're going too fast!"

"I am?"

Still frowning she shook her head, and then I got it: She was annoyed with them, not me. *Them! The priest and nuns? Why a priest and nuns? What sense could that possibly make . . . and what made me think this would work? . . . Aw, shoot!* Distracted with my thoughts, I missed what she was telling me. "I'm sorry," I said. "Would you mind repeating that, please?"

"A stage," she repeated. "Lights. On you."

Ah ha! Now we're getting somewhere!

"You're on the stage, doing . . . something . . . I'm unclear what exactly but . . ."

Performing! I'm performing!

"Above you, a blue light." Eyes still closed, she added, "It shines like a star in the sky. Watches over you. Protects you."

Oh, this woman's good; she's really, really GOOD! She DOES have the gift. Nancy's mother was right!

"Your friend. She has problems with her foot."

There's nothing wrong with Nancy's foot. Or . . . is there? How would I know?

"The friend here with you today."

"Oh, you mean Wendy?"

"That one. In the living room."

What a laugh! Wendy has no foot problems! . . . Don't say anything! Don't embarrass her! Remember no one can be 100 percent right all the time. Psychics are only human.

Silence.

"In a few days," the psychic continued, "you'll be leaving for New York City."

Close, but no cigar. I managed to hold back my grin.

As though she'd read my mind, she laughed, but pleasantly. "You're not going where you expect, and she won't be going with you."

"She?"

"Your Wendy."

Oh yes, she is too. She wants . . . to go with me . . . to help . . . to be my personal assistant. Her idea, not mine.

The psychic was speaking again but . . . wait . . . in a different tone. A deeper register. "And it's winter," she was saying. "It's snowing. Very heavy. Heavy snow. Oh dear. A young woman . . . exhausted . . . lying down . . . near a curb in an alley. She's shivering. Poor dear."

My hand covers my mouth.

"Such a lovely young woman. Blonde. Pale skin. But she's in terrible pain . . . another with her . . . younger woman . . . a girl? . . . she's to go . . . to fetch . . . there's a restaurant. "

Blonde? Pale?

"Oh, I see. The girl returns with a paper sack and . . . scissors, blanket. . . . The blond woman, I see. Of course. She's been in labor . . . and now giving birth."

Oh my God!

"Screaming pain . . . she's not doing well . . . not at all well."

I wanted to speak, but I couldn't. Barely could I breathe.

"Scissors, now."

"Scissors?" I ask.

"To cut, yes. The umbilical cord."

I waited for more, wanted more. Leaned forward. Bit my bottom lip.

Silence. Stillness. Her eyes remained closed, face straining . . . but nothing. Nothing more? Was the session over? Silence.

The psychic sighed. "She was . . ."

Oh good! Here comes more!

"Liked to sing . . . a happy soul . . . no longer here . . . not on this physical plane. . . . That man . . . the Sicilian . . . not someone you would care for . . . not a nice person. . . . He did *not* want the baby. . . . They were in Florida, I think that's so. . . . And yes . . . she fled from him . . . from there to . . . here . . . some family.

Here? Family? But I thought . . .

The psychic cleared her throat.

More, please!

Silence. A big sigh. Then she said with deep sadness, "Painful. It was so very painful to let her baby go."

"It was," I said aloud. "It was." Not a statement. Not a question. What, then?

A long silence.

The psychic's cupped hand lowered to her lap. Her chest expanded and then relaxed. Her eyes opened now, wide open, smiling. "So?" she asked with raised eyebrows. "I hope I didn't frighten you."

"Not at all." *Surprised, yes. Frightened, no.*

"May I ask, dear? Was any of what came through of help to you?"

"Oh yes. More than you know, more than you can possibly know." I giggled awkwardly at the absurdity of my comment.

She offered a generous smile, and then, as if we had planned it well in advance, we rose in unison. The session had ended.

The woman returned my precious item. I shoved it back into my pocket, thanking her, reassuring her she'd given me what I had come for. Returning to the living room, I felt as pleased as punch, and yet . . . with each step, I felt a greater sense of loss. . . . *What am I losing? Confidence? In what? Don't I have what I came for? Only minutes ago, didn't everything make sense, seem so simple? Why isn't it simple still? Because it's complicated? Because something's off?*

At the living room entry, I stopped short, feeling my heart pound in my ears. And then . . . instinctively . . . my fingers reached into my pocket for the pinky ring, the beautiful sterling silver ring that Mom had given me for my fifteenth birthday. I slid it on and twisted the ring until the engraved initial was front and center.

There! That's better. Much better.

The Big Apple

Stu had arranged for me an entrance into the John Davidson Singers' Summer Camp on Catalina Island off the coast of Los Angeles. The night before I was to drive to Los Angeles for the four-week session with John Davidson and then pursue my career in Los Angeles, I received a call from Clark, my agent, who said, "Change of plans, kiddo. You're leaving for New York in the next couple of weeks. I'm setting up a recording session with a producer in Manhattan. He liked your demo tape. He's going to have you work with a Broadway arranger as well. They're going to start grooming you. He'll remix the tape, have you re-sing it, and then cut a 45 and ship it around to hundreds of radio stations for feedback."

I thought to myself, why remix and re-sing if he liked it the way it was? I asked what about California, and he replied, "It'll have to wait." I realized that the psychic was right. What else would she be right about?

Clark and the AKD Corp. found me a house to rent during the winter months in Southampton on Long Island while I'd be working in the city. Wendy, my friend who wanted to be my professional assistant would join me at some point.

My weekly routine was to drive my Camaro into Queens, park it, take the subway into Manhattan dragging my guitar and book of music, and walk fifteen blocks to my arranger's office. Then I'd reverse it all, hoping the car was there upon my return and no one had stolen it or, worse, stripped it. Why I didn't just take the train is a wonder to me today.

Ben Arrigo, the producer, was a short, stocky, heavyset stern Italian, a real guido type. On the day of my recording session to remix the demo tape, he arranged a practice make-up session. When I came out, I looked like a Las Vegas starlet, totally over–made-up. He said, "You have to be seen by the back row." I walked to The Stage Deli and ordered a Frank Sinatra corn beef sandwich, piled high. I ate the whole damn thing, drank an ice tea, and walked to the RCA Recording Studios. No one gave me a second glance. Everyone in New York City looks made-up, so I blended right in.

What transpired in the recording studio was agonizing. He wanted to totally change my style of singing. Dr. Tappen would have been pissed. They took my beautiful mixed arrangements of "Jas Vas Lu Blue" and "Spotlight Routine" arranged by Stu and butchered them into a new mix that lost the magic Stu and I had created.

Ben kept telling me to sing it his way. He said, "I want you to be like Jane Oliver."

I said, "Why? Let me sing it like Kim Driggs."

He said, "No, and by the way, your name doesn't work either; you need a better name." He came up with A. K. Driggs. As if I hadn't realized it already, he told me I had no rights and I was a product. "Get used to it."

This made me angry and confused. Where was Clark? I asked to have the lights dimmed in the studio, and the engineer did so. They started to play the soundtrack, and I began to sing with my eyes closed.

"Stop, Kim. Sing it this way," he said.

"Ben, that has no feeling. It doesn't feel right to me. Why are you trying to change me? The song is losing its power, its magic."

He ignored my every plea.

My emotions were rising to a point of fury. Did he know what he was doing? Should I shut up and just do it his way? After all, my investors were paying for all this. I wanted this to work and to make everyone proud of me, my parents, my corporation, my agent, and me. Where was my agent? I decided to shut up and do it his way, even though every cell of my body knew this was not right.

Ben finally said, "That's a take."

When I listened to the playback, I almost wept. It was horrible, a massacre of what Stu and I had created. I hated my performance, my style and energy in the songs. It wasn't the real me. Why Ben thought his version of my singing was better than my original, which he apparently liked otherwise, and why he would have me here in the first place were beyond me.

Ben sent the final mix to another facility to cut the 45s. He and Clark arranged to have the records shipped all over the country to forty-nine states to hundreds of radio stations to obtain airtime and feedback from the disk jockeys. I should have felt elated; my dream was coming true, wasn't it? Instead, I felt sick and depressed.

The next day, Ben asked me to come to his office in Manhattan. It was located at 157 West Fifty-seventh Street in New York City. The office was dark with only one window looking out over Manhattan. I could hear the cabs honking in the background.

He sat behind a large black desk in a huge black leather chair. He looked small and pudgy in that chair. Stern and mean looking, he pointed to a contract sitting on the desk for me to sign. "This is your contract with me. Sign it."

I thought, *Wait a minute. My corporation of lawyers should be reading this first. Did they? Did Clark? I'd like my father to read it too.*

Frankly, if it hadn't been for his big mouth and candidness, I might not have seen the light. I started reading the contract silently asking for inner help, *God, please help me. What should I do?*

"Kim, sign the contract. Once you sign, you will be part of the family," he said.

The "family"? What family? I thought. I closed my eyes and calmed myself, and then it happened, just as it had that night in my bedroom years ago when I needed to make the right decision about going back to college or moving to England. I felt that loving presence and saw the blue star again in my head and heard that little voice telling me what to do. *Don't sign.*

In that split second, I remembered the psychic telling me she saw a blue star over my head, that it has been with me all my life, and that it protected me. I opened my eyes and blurted out with confidence, "No, Ben, no. I'm not signing this contract. This doesn't feel right, none of it. I'm leaving now."

He stood up and fired back cruelly, "What do you mean you are not signing this? It you don't sign this, you will be making a catastrophic mistake with your career, young lady."

I replied my body shaking, "No, if I sign with you, I'll be making a catastrophic mistake with *my life*." I got up, tore up his contract, threw it onto his desk, and walked out into the New York day still shaking. I felt good about my decision. Walking to a nearby coffee shop, I sat down, ordered a cup of coffee, and thought about what I was going to do next and how my actions would affect everyone involved with my career. Did I just blow it with my corporation, Clark, and my career? I knew I had made the right decision. I just knew it. Why the hell hadn't Clark been there with me? What kind of manager was he not to be by my side for such an important meeting?

Taking my last sip of black coffee, I started to second-guess myself and feel insecure about my decision. I called Clark, and oddly, he picked up the phone this time. I told him what had happened. Clearly, he wasn't very pleased with me. I told him this guy was bad news and most likely Mafia and why wasn't he there with me. He continued to make up excuses. I really doubted Clark as my manager at that point, but I had no other options. My mind and soul were so confused and stressed out about the whole incident I wasn't sure about anything. I called Stu, and he said I had made the right decision and he'd try to get me into the John Davidson Singers' Summer Camp next August. I was so pissed off at Clark for abandoning me in New York. I should have fired his ass then.

After dumping Ben, I spent most of my time singing in local clubs in Southampton and at open-mike nights at some of Manhattan's most recognized places where producers frequented to discover new talent. I was bound and determined to make something of myself. I continued my weekly or biweekly reports to the investors so they would know how I was progressing. At least the record was shipped out, and if I did get a bite, we could still move forward, right?

By early December 1978, things had gone sour. With no explanation, my corporation stopped sending me money and wouldn't return my repeated phone calls to them. I was thirty days overdue on the Southampton rental house. I didn't understand what was happening, and I was getting very stressed out and depressed. My letters to the corporation were met with silence, and I felt totally abandoned in Southampton. The phantom rash had returned all over my ass and scalp.

Daily I'd sit on the beach wrapped in a blanket overlooking the dark, frantic Atlantic Ocean. This body of water didn't look anything like the beautiful Pacific, which called to me from every photo I'd gaze upon. This ocean looked foreboding.

One day when I'd ridden the rental house's bicycle to the beach, I found a large seabird with a broken wing flopping restlessly in the surf. I took the towel I had with me and flung it over the bird, picked it up carefully, and somehow managed to ride the bike with the bird tucked under one arm to the nearest vet. I begged the vet to care for it and fix its wing.

The girl at the front desk said, "Are you going to pay for this bird?"

I replied, "Yes, of course. Just fix it please."

The next day, I called the vet to see how my bird was, and the girl at the front desk said dispassionately, "Oh, we put it down."

I was speechless. I couldn't believe it. They didn't even try? Once again, I couldn't help a poor hurt bird.

My depression was intensifying. Wendy had fled weeks earlier, deciding to go back to her boyfriend in Rochester. She had had enough of show business. The psychic was right about that too. I found myself sitting on the beach on a dark, cold, cloudy winter day staring at that angry restless ocean. Miserable and alone, I wondered what it would feel like just to walk into the cold blackness and not return. I didn't know who the hell I was or what I was doing, and nothing felt right. Not wanting to upset my parents, I didn't want to tell them what was going on with me. I felt abandoned all over again.

On top of all the drama, the entire time I was in New York City, I had dreams of Mom dying in one way or another. I'd wake up in a terrified sweat and have to call to see if she was okay.

She would always reply, "Kim, I'm fine. Stop that."

"Mom, I wish I could. I don't know why I dream these horrible dreams of losing you." I even told her that I felt I needed therapy.

She just said," No, you don't. You will get over it on your own."

I was stranded on Long Island, had run out of money, and owed the landlord two months' rent, which the investors clearly had promised to pay. I always took pride on my credit and paying my bills on time. That was and always has been a very important part of my character.

My personal relationships echoed the rest of my life. I had a short affair with a guy I met in Southampton, but it didn't last long. I guess I was trying to keep my foot in the heterosexual world, still looking for Mr. Right.

After fleeing Long Island for Rochester in the middle of the night to escape the landlord locking me out of the house, I had an accident on the New York State Thruway in a blizzard. I plowed right into an exit ramp sign and flattened it. But I kept going and drove the rest of the six hours with a split frame and had to get rid of my sweet Camaro.

Failure

After being abandoned by my investors, I returned to my parents' apartment at 111 East Avenue in Rochester to start my life over again. Dad was doing consulting now for French's and moving toward full retirement trying to push aside his true feelings and disappointment of being pushed out of the company for a younger man with less experience.

During the week, Dad and I were alone in the apartment, as Mom was at the lake house. Dad would join her on the weekends. On the morning after I arrived, he was in the living room getting ready to leave for work. I woke up and came out of my room to the kitchen to get some coffee. He said, "Kimberly, tell me what happened."

I was angry, tired, and not feeling well. "Well, Dad, I guess you'd say my lovely investors blew me off and stopped supporting me. They won't pay the rent or expenses anymore, and I owe two months' rent on the house on Long Island. It appears nobody wants to follow through on their commitments but me."

Somberly he replied, "Do you have the rental agreement with you?"

"Yeah, here it is. The landlord wants to sue me," I said sarcastically.

Dad stood erect by the dining room table and started reading the lease very carefully.

"Dad, I can't believe they are doing this. I fulfilled my end of the agreement. I wrote them every week; I kept them in the loop. They knew how long this would take and there would be setbacks. We all discussed this. Why are they ignoring me? The record has being released and shipped across the country."

His brow continued to wrinkle, as his face grew very serious while continuing to read the contract. He finally lifted his head and replied, "Let me see what I can do." He shoved the agreement into his briefcase and clicked it closed. "In the meantime, you can stay here until you get back on your feet. I think the night club down stairs off the lobby could use some good entertainment."

His unemotional demeanor bothered me, but then again that was Dad. In that moment, I didn't feel he was being very understanding with my situation and was being too detached. I guess I wanted him to put his arms around me and say, "Don't worry, honey; it will all be okay, and I will ensure no one hurts you ever again." I replied by saying, "Oh great, fuck it."

He looked at me with hurt and shock in his eyes and said, "I didn't raise my daughter to talk like that. I told you I'd take care of it."

I stormed away, totally fed up with everything and everybody. But I also knew I had hurt his feelings, which only left me feeling more worthless. I did what he said, though, and landed a singing gig in the restaurant/lounge downstairs.

Dad was able to get me out of the rental agreement on Long Island. He spoke to the investors, and somehow between them and my father, the rent was paid in full. To this day, I'm not sure who all paid what.

AKD Corp. was losing interest in me yet wouldn't let me out of my contract. I was tied to them legally. I told them if they didn't want to support me any longer then dissolve the contract; I would find a way to pay them back over time. If they still believed in me, then commit and continue with the pursuit. However, leaving me in limbo wasn't right. Maybe going to LA would show them I could make it and they would continue believing in me. I told them I would write more songs and make another demo tape, and this time it would all work out. No more Ben Arrigos. Reluctantly they agreed.

I was a member of the American Society of Composers, Authors and Publishers, or ASCAP, and did receive a few checks totaling several hundred dollars for residuals of the airplay on the radio. That was very cool. I used to hear my songs being played over the radio as I'd drive around town, or I'd wake up in the morning to my voice. It was the most wonderful feeling, even though I didn't like my personal performance. One morning, my radio kicked on to wake me up, and gently pulling me from a dream was the DJ from WBBF radio. "And now, Rochester's own, A. K. Driggs singing 'Jas Vas Lu Blue.'" I thought I was dreaming it at first, and then I realized, *No, that's me on the radio.* I sat up quickly and listened to my voice ringing out through the radio thinking, *Wow, this is what I've always wanted. Here it is, me, little ole Kimmy on the radio.* I was filled with mixed emotions, excited, proud, but sad. It wasn't Stu's and my beautiful mix; it was the one by that idiot in New York who butchered the song and my performance. Well, I could only hope people listening still liked it.

They did! I had a following wherever I sang. Strangers would come up to me and tell me how I helped them through issues with their life and how my voice soothed them. At first, I'd tell them it really wasn't me but the Spirit that came through me. They'd look at me as if I was crazy. After that, I learned just to reply, "Thank you."

Los Angeles, Here I Come

Stu's career had taken him to Los Angeles by now. He contacted me and said I was in with John Davidson at his singers' summer camp for August 1979 and I could stay with him and Ann until I found a place to live.

My parents knew I wasn't happy in Rochester. They knew I had to get away and follow my dream. One day sitting on the deck of the condo overlooking the lake, Mom said, "Kim, you are a flower that needs to blossom, a bird that needs to be set free from its cage. It will kill your father and me to see you go, but we need to let you fly."

I saw the tears in her eyes. My whole life had been about my attachment to my mother and father, especially to my mother. The thought of leaving them behind and being three thousand miles away was almost unbearable to imagine. My entire life I had feared losing my parents again, especially my mother. At night after they'd fall asleep, I'd sneak into their bedroom and make sure they were still breathing. I know. Kind of weird, eh?

By now the 45 record was playing on radio stations across the country and heralded as excellent. Excellent! Really? Imagine what they would have thought if they had heard the original version, which by the way, all my closest friends and family agreed was far better. The only problem was the radio stations kept asking where was the album to follow it up? Without an album, there is no future for the singer. Unfortunately, Clark and the AKD Corporation didn't have a backup plan. Lovely!

With eyes on LA, I sold all my worldly possessions except my Martin D-18 guitar, amplifier, microphone, songs I had written, and a suitcase of clothes. I had twelve hundred dollars in my pocket.

I approached Wendy for the last time to see if she wanted to accompany me to California. She told me she was having severe problems and pain with her feet and arches and wanted to stay back with her boyfriend. I guess the psychic was right about her feet too.

I left behind thousands of memories, some wonderful and some very painful. Sue didn't want to see me leave, but she knew I had to follow my dream. My dear friend Jan, whom I'd known since grade school, supported me as well. She and Sue had gotten to be good friends by now, and both were married and had started families. I, on the other hand, was in total limbo, still having feelings for women and still looking at men, even though I didn't trust them much at that point. Sue and Jan were my best friends, and I didn't want anything to rock that relationship, so I hadn't told either of them about my confusion with my sexuality. While living at or close to home, I couldn't hide my double life any longer from my parents. I felt I had to leave to find out who and what I was. Besides, if I was really serious about my music, LA was the place to be. Leaving Rochester was the only option for me now.

Mom and Dad walked me to the gate at the Rochester Airport. I hugged them both and said, "Mom and Dad, thank you so much for everything you've done for me. I love you and will miss you horribly. I'll call all the time."

Dad was trying to be tough and hold back actual emotions. He replied, "Kimberly, just be the best you can be and always be true to yourself as we've taught you. Always be honest, and we'll stand by you, no matter what happens. We are proud of you."

Mom tearing up cupped my face in both her hands, looked me straight in the eyes with her beaming blues, and said, "Kim, sing like a bird!"

As I boarded the plane, I looked back over my shoulder at Mom and Dad waving good-bye and with a heavy heart said good-bye to the life I once knew. When the plane taxied, I felt a slight exhilaration that an exciting yet unknown journey was ahead of me, similar to the feeling I had when I left for London. The only difference was I was heading into a storm alone.

Kim singing at 111 East Avenue, Rochester, after fleeing Long Island.

"Jas Vas Lu Blue" 45 record.   *"Spotlight Routine" 45 record.*

✺ ✺ ✺ CHAPTER 15 ✺ ✺ ✺

Shaky New Start

John Davidson's Singers' Summer Camp

After Stu and Ann picked me up at the airport and took me back to their apartment off Coldwater Canyon Road in the San Fernando Valley, we quickly found a place for me to live two blocks away from them. It was an old converted motel that had been used years ago by hookers. My rental was a one-room sleeper and a real dump but within my budget. It had one window, an uncomfortable sofa bed, and a tiny bathroom. There was no kitchen, so I would have to have a hot plate and tiny tabletop refrigerator. This was a far cry from my lovely flat in Rochester, but alas, I wanted to *taste, touch, and feel life*, right?

My place wouldn't be ready for several weeks, but that was fine, as I'd be attending the John Davidson Singers' Summer Camp on Catalina Island for four weeks.

Two days after my arrival in LA, Stu dropped me off at the San Pedro docks where I boarded the boat to Catalina Island. While the students were supposed to be amateurs, I was allowed to attend, thanks to Stu, as a professional—and the only one during my session. John and Stu had become quite friendly after Stu had spent a summer at the camp as one of the arrangers. After John heard my demo tape, he was more than willing to allow me in for that August session.

On the boat trip to Catalina, I met a very talented gal named Kelley. She could dance, act, sing, draw and was a fabulous mime. We became inseparable immediately and each other's support during that grueling four weeks in August 1979. Somehow we survived the camp.

During our stay, we were taught singing, dancing, and acting. John had teachers from acting schools, dance instructors, and various musical arrangers. We had to prepare a different song every week with our assigned arranger and perform that number at the Avalon Bowl in downtown Avalon in front of the local tourists. John was very present himself. His yacht was moored off the island where he'd throw parties for us. There was quite a lot of hanky-panky going on I noticed too.

I could not tap dance worth shit. The acting classes were horrible as the teacher was cruel and did all he could to beat the students down and make even the toughest young man cry. All I cared about was the singing portion. I always received standing ovations at the Avalon Bowl from the visiting tourists.

John Davidson had a round table the last day of the camp where he gave his personal comments about all the students. When it came to me, he said, "Kim has a mystical, magical quality about her. Her voice mesmerizes me." He gave me a huge smile, and I noticed again why he had such sex appeal—that magnificent smile and those twinkling eyes.

※ ※ ※

Clark, whom I hadn't seen in months, was supposed to attend my final performance at the Avalon Bowl, pick me up, and take me back to LA. When they announced my name, "Ladies and gentlemen, A. K. Driggs," to go on, I couldn't find him in the audience. I finished with the song, "My Father's Song." After receiving my last standing ovation, I left the stage and searched frantically for Clark. No Clark.

I watched as all the students, some of whom I'd become quite close to, get picked up by their various parties and make their way to the ferry that would take them back to San Pedro or the airport to fly out. Kelly was being picked up by her dad, and they were taking the last ferry out that day.

"Kim, where is Clark?" Kelly said with worry in her eyes.

"I'm afraid he's abandoned me again, Kell." When everyone was gone and Kelly and her dad were standing with me gazing over the port area, we realized Clark was a no-show.

"Dad, we can't leave Kim here alone. We need to take her with us. Her apartment won't be ready for several days. Can she come to stay with us until then?"

Bob Wright had been the executive producer of the *Carol Burnett Show* and was the loveliest man. He replied with kindness, "Of course she can, honey. Kim, you come with us; our home is your home."

As we boarded the last ferry of the day, the sun was setting, the entertainers were gone, and the Avalon Bowl was dark and silent. The ferry made its way over the rough water heading back to San Pedro, where I'd spend the next several days with Kelly and her family at their lovely home in Palace Verdes until my apartment was ready.

The first thing I was going to do when we got to Kelly's home was phone Clark and fire his ass. This was not a good way to start my new life in California. I was twenty-five years old in Los Angeles, living out of a one-room dump, alone, and confused. I bought a 1967 white Mustang for six hundred dollars. That left me with six hundred dollars, and I needed work fast.

Doggy Love

I found a job working at a doggie hotel in the San Fernando Valley while living in North Hollywood. Every shift, I would go from kennel to kennel, do my chores of cleaning the smaller kennels and removing the little dogs. Choosing a song that seemed fitting in the moment for that little soul, I'd begin to sing to it, loving it up and reassuring the pet that its mommy and/or daddy would be back to get it. "Don't worry, sweetheart, your mommy will be back for you. Honest." For the bigger dogs that were housed in the larger walk-in kennels, I'd go inside, do my chores, and then sit down with each one for a few minutes, petting, singing, and reassuring each one. My two favorite songs, which they all seemed to enjoy, were "When You Wish upon a Star" and "Over the Rainbow."

Jeanette, the owner of the kennel, told me one day that she'd received many compliments from the owners after picking up their dogs. They'd call her a day or two after retrieving their pets, sharing an extraordinary change for the better in their pets' demeanor. "Jeanette, Daisy is so much calmer and happier this time" or "Jeannette, Max has never been so well adjusted after being kenneled when we've gone away. It's just that, well, he is so much happier." They wondered why and asked Jeanette if something different was going on there.

Jeanette would say, "That's the new girl we have working here now. She sings to the animals every day while cleaning their cages and dog runs. I think it's made a big difference in the animals while they are here."

Adrift

Desperately, I tried to get the sparkle back about my music. I was starting to lose the passion I had had for so long. While I was singing on weekends in lounges in Santa Monica and Marina Del Rey hoping someone would notice me, the whole experience was becoming more and more stressful. My relationship with my corporation didn't help. I kept trying to get AKD investors to either let me out of the contract or help me move forward. I needed to do another demo tape with the new songs I had written. They said they were on board, but still nothing came from them.

My personal relationships weren't any better. I was living a bisexual life style, knowing I could love men or women but not knowing where I belonged, so I just kept hoping one or the other would take my heart away and make the decision for me. It didn't matter to me what the body was like. It was about love. To love and be loved were the most important things, right?

I was having an affair with an African American conga player named Walter who lived below me. Walter was kind, gentle, caring, and always available. He knew about my bisexuality and didn't seem to mind. Our sex life was fantastic, and he was always there for me. In fact, he proposed to me.

The problem was, on the alternate nights I wasn't seeing Walter, I was frequenting the local ladies' gay bar called The Dummy Up, located in North Hollywood. I had a few one-night stands only to find myself more confused and frankly disgusted with myself. I was not the one-night-stand type of girl. I finally had to tell Walter I couldn't marry him if I was still looking over my shoulder. He understood, and we remained friends.

Finding Maggie

It was at The Dummy Up that I met Maggie. She was my age and adorable with a twinkle in her eye and short, light-brown hair with little streaks of premature grey. Raised by a lovely family in Minnesota, she was a true family-oriented person who loved children, music, and poetry. Maggie had a guitar of her own and would spend time writing lyrics. Her dreams of becoming a serious writer were all that consumed her, along with finding a wife. And she was a fabulous cook. One way to my heart has always been through my tummy. But it was love at first sight, before I even tasted her cooking. Maggie and I moved in together in our new place within the first month of dating. As for my parents, I told them I took a roommate on to help with the bills.

Maggie and I acquired two animals immediately—Shadow, the black cat that I rescued, and Nicki, the dog we saved from wandering Venice Beach. Our love grew, and for the first time, I felt I had found my true love. I had a family of my own and someone who truly loved me for me. The first three years with Maggie were heaven, and I didn't look at or think about men. I was fulfilled in every way.

One Saturday afternoon, we drove to The Little Brown Church on the corner of Cold Water Canyon and Ventura Boulevard in the San Fernando Valley. The church was empty. We stood before the altar and exchanged rings and commitments. Nothing was legal back then, but to us, it felt as if we were doing something special that would last a lifetime.

Second Demo

After saving up my money, I had enough to go back into the studio with Stu and record some of my other songs, a couple which Maggie and I wrote together. Stu had excellent musicians; they had recorded with some of the most well-known recording artists of the time. Walter agreed to do backup vocals and play congas on the tape. I had another backup vocalist, Leslie, who blended beautifully with Walter and me. I was very proud of this demo.

We shipped the tape out to many independent producers and record companies hoping someone would bite. Someone did.

Johnny was a fairly well-known producer in Los Angeles who thought I had what it took to make it big. He loved my voice but felt I needed a hit song. While he loved my tunes, he felt they were missing the mark for a serious commercial opportunity. He drove me to the Los Angeles Forum, empty before a game. We stood in the hall, and he pointed to the thousands of seats and said, "Do you think you can fill these?"

I replied, "Yes, with your help."

One afternoon, Johnny arrived at the house Maggie and I rented on Cartwright Street in North Hollywood. He pulled out a contract and sat close to me on the couch. Stu and Maggie were watching while seated in the kitchen. Maggie had made us each a cup of coffee.

Johnny proceeded to say, "Kim, once you sign this, you will be my property and will do as I see fit. I will own 100 percent of you and your time." Suddenly I felt his hand start rubbing my backside around my ass and then up and down my back rather sexually. He whispered in my ear, "You will be mine, sweetie, all mine." He handed me a pen and told me to sign on the dotted line.

Stu and Maggie couldn't hear him or see what he was doing. I was frozen. This couldn't be happening again, could it? Stu and Maggie thought this was my big chance to really make it in the music business. I sat for what seemed like an eternity. Stu and Maggie stared at me wondering why I was delaying signing.

Feeling a mixture of anger and misery, my stomach started to ache, and my bowels felt as if I was going to have diarrhea. I didn't know if I should scream or cry. I closed my eyes and asked for help. There it was again, that blue star in my head, that presence, that voice saying, *Do not sign. Walk away.* But wasn't this my big chance? I was confused. *Breathe,* I silently told myself. *Steady, think, listen, look at the blue star.*

My shaking hand held the pen just an inch away from the signature line on the contract. *Walk away,* the little voice in my head screamed. I moved away from Johnny, put the pen down, and pushed the coffee table away from me. Standing up shaking and holding back tears, I said, "Johnny, you can leave now. Take your contract and leave. Don't call me or come by ever again."

Stu and Maggie looked shocked. Stu started to rise and come over to me seeing I was upset. Maggie was frozen. Johnny stood up and, clearly angry, said, "What are you doing? What's wrong?"

My voice was getting louder and shakier as I replied, "Just leave now. I'm not yours and will never be yours."

He grabbed the contract and his pen and with disgust walked out and slammed the door, never to return again.

After I told Stu and Maggie what had transpired, they were shocked and disappointed in Johnny. We all sat at the kitchen table stunned and speechless.

Grabbing Nicki's leash and saying nothing to Stu or Maggie, I left the house and went for a very long walk.

Bye-Bye AKD

The AKD Corporation had ceased helping me and became a noose around my neck. I had to find a way out of it. Even though I couldn't afford an attorney, I knew I needed legal advice; after all, my corporation was a group of lawyers. After consulting an attorney, I found a loophole and got out of the contract. I sent a final letter to the investors thanking them for the past help they had given me and explained why it was the right thing to do for me to leave.

The music industry was unfriendly and lacked the integrity I brought to the art. The expectation of drugs and sex to get ahead was mandated. I was simply not willing to do this. Meanwhile, the magic had died in my voice. I no longer enjoyed singing or creating music. One day in total despair, I decided to give it all up and try to reinvent myself. I banished my beloved Martin D-18 to the closet. I was bitter and lost in LA.

Kim playing in her North Hollywood home before giving up the guitar and singing.

CHAPTER 16

NEW CAREER

In 1982, I met Gail, the wife of one of the attorneys who worked with Maggie at the law firm in Van Nuys. We all became great friends and hung out together every weekend.

The time spent with friends helped make up for the rest of my week. Trying to find myself, I was wasting my life away. I had a huge hole in my core and an emptiness that couldn't be filled by anyone. For two years, I moved from lousy job to lousy job. For a short time, I worked as a part-time courier delivering packages. That was fun. Not! Then I got a job at one of California's biggest collection agencies in Century City as office manager. That ended badly when my boss, who was a raving alcoholic, accused me of wanting to steal his job, which of course was not true. Then some of the male collectors taking his side threatened to blow up my car with me in it. He basically forced me out of the job and gave me high recommendations just to get rid of me. The best thing that came out of that job was finding a wandering female Bichon Frise in the streets near my office. I brought her home and named her Gabriel Elizabeth.

My search for a good job—or, at this point, any job—continued.

Gail worked in the natural foods industry for a local distributor. One evening while we were all drinking and making dinner together, she pulled me aside and said, "Hey, aren't you tired of working for everyone else and not being appreciated?"

I replied, "Yeah, why?"

Picking up her beer, she replied, "Well, I'm working for a distributor, but I'm not happy with my job. I don't feel appreciated at all. Why don't we start a brokerage business and get our own lines?"

I asked her to explain what a broker did in this industry of hers.

She explained that we'd represent various manufacturers' natural products, present and sell them to health food stores, and get paid a commission. We would have to obtain the business by attending trade shows and cold calling manufacturers to convince them to hire us over other brokers.

I thought about this and stared into space remembering my past sales experience. For years while growing up, I would help Mom make Christmas ornaments out of pinecones we'd gather every winter from Monroe Golf Course. We had such fun plodding through the snow-covered fairways. Mom did most of the work as I had and still have very little artistic talent when it comes to drawing and arts and crafts. I'd go door to door selling my Christmas ornaments for extra spending money. The neighbors always told Mom, "Betty, Kim is a natural-born salesman, just like Bob." Mom used to say, "Kim, you could sell glasses to a blind man."

Gail nudged my shoulder and said, "Well? Well, what do you think?"

I came back to reality, picked up my Johnny Walker Black, clinked my glass to her beer bottle, and replied, "Hell, why not? Okay, but if we are going to do this, we have to be the best brokers in this industry of yours, so let's get a plan written down. Tell me who all the players in the health industry are, and let's interview each one. We need to find out what they like and dislike about brokers, so we can be the best."

We set a date of one year to earn enough commissions from our new business that we would be able to afford a tiny office in Van Nuys and pay our personal bills. Gail quit her job at the distributor to devote all the time on our new project. My challenge was I had to be available during the day to develop the business.

Attending trade shows, developing our clients, and then spending all day driving from San Luis Obispo to the San Diego border selling consumed my days. How was I going to make money while building this business? Maggie's hours at the firm were sporadic. The pressure was on me to make this new career a success as fast as possible. I had much to learn about this new world of natural foods. My parents, while enormously supportive of this new career, were worried about me since I had decided to end my real dream of a singing career.

Making Ends Meet: Angela Is Born

One Saturday afternoon while sitting on the living room couch writing up tofu and tempeh orders I had taken from stores the day before, the phone rang. It was Kelly, my buddy from the John Davidson camp, with whom I had stayed in touch.

"Kim, sit down. I've got something to run by you. I know how you can make money and still work on your new business during the day."

I replied, "Hey, Kell, how are ya?"

"I'm great, Kim. Now listen."

I sat back into the couch and put my paperwork down. "What's up?" I said with curiosity.

"Phone sex," she stated.

"What the hell are you talking about?" I gasped.

Kelly repeated, "I'm doing live phone sex. I have to have money to pay my bills, and I need time during the day to go on auditions for acting. There's this lady named Mickey who is getting her doctorate in human sexuality. She's doing her thesis right now. She has set up a business called JJSX. She has a straight heterosexual number that guys call in on to talk to girls and a gay number for gay guys to call in on. She has several girls working for her on the heterosexual line. You work out of your home. She puts a phone line in your house with a different number than your regular house phone. You are assigned hours that you work, but if you want to earn extra money you can plug in anytime you want, and the phone just starts ringing. It rings off the hook. It's amazing."

Shocked I said, "Go on."

Kelly continued, "Okay, so Mickey advertises all over the world in those trashy sex magazines. You know the ones. The ads reads something like 'Have live phone sex with real live girls from the privacy of their homes!' The guys have to call a real 213 phone number here in LA. The recording says, "You've reached JJSX. You have to have a phone listed in your name and a credit card listed in your name in order to do a call. Tonight from four to nine is Fiona; call her at 818-555-1256. From nine to one is Ginger; call her at 213-555-6789,' and so on.

"When you plug in and the guy calls, you have to immediately get his name, address, and credit card number. Then you have to put the phone down, pick up your home phone, and call an 800 number. It goes to a local bank, and they think you are selling office supplies. You have to get a code that preauthorizes the charge on the card before you go back and pick up the other phone and start your sex call."

Shocked I replied, "But how do you know how long the call will take to get the correct preauthorization amount? You know what I mean?"

Kelly said, "Well, at first, if it is a new customer, you don't know. You have to guess. If he goes over, you lose some money; if he comes before or too soon, you've made more money. The guys don't care. All they want is to get off. Also at the end of every shift, there is a list. We call it The Bad Boy List. It has names of guys whose credit cards were declined whom you had to say no to or real perverts like child molesters calling for you to do a fantasy call with them. We give that list to the next shift, as none of us will do calls with those guys.

"You'll build up your own clients. The money is really good. I'm earning a couple hundred dollars a week. You have to choose a pseudonym, though. My name is Tiffany. So, what do you think?"

Pausing for a moment, I replied, "But is it legal?"

Kelly said, "Yep, all the way."

I thought for a moment. What would Maggie think about me doing phone sex with men? But we needed income, and I had to build my new business, my new life. Besides it would only be for a short time, right? Oh my God, I couldn't tell my parents either; they'd be appalled. Something inside told me to go for it. I was desperate, and it was a means to an end. "Well, sounds good to me. Where do I start?"

Kelly gave me Mickey's number and told me she would call Mickey to give her the heads-up and recommendation to consider me.

❋ ❋ ❋

Needing a reliable car for a change, I had bought a used blue Datsun B210 from a friend. Unfortunately, it was a stick shift, which I'd never driven before and made maneuvering the Hollywood hills a bit challenging.

Now, here I was attempting to climb the hills on my way to an appointment for a new job. "Oh shit, a stop light." Not wanting to roll back into the cars approaching close behind me, I pressed my foot firmly on the brake while trying to figure out the clutch at the same time. Rolling the window down, I uncomfortably stretched my neck to turn my head leaning out the window, looking back at the cars only a few feet from my blue bumper, and frantically waving my hands in a backward motion yelling, "Everyone get back, move back." The cars behind me gladly obeyed seeming to understand they had to protect their vehicles since I obviously had no clue as to what I was doing with mine. They could see me struggling to keep it steady as it rocked back and forth. Stressed, I was glad to see the light finally turn green as I pushed on the gas pedal and released the clutch propelling the vehicle forward. *Please, no more stop lights on hills*, I begged the Universe.

I had the radio tuned to KIIS FM listening to Dan Fogelberg sing "Leader of the Band." God, I loved that song. It always reminded me of Dad. I was singing along and thinking all I ever wanted was to be a singer, play guitar, and be happily married like my parents with a family of my own.

Hell, I'd been singing to birds, frogs, dogs, cats, and people since I was three. It was what I did. Why couldn't I make a living doing it without all the bullshit? Was that too much to ask? Having my parents be proud and approve of me had always been a major focus since I was little. The thought of disappointing them would devastate me.

Daryl Hall and John Oates came on singing "I Can't Go For That." Continuing down Sunset Boulevard watching palm trees whisk by, my memory spun back to when I was around four years old and would sing to family only if I could first hide behind something. Waiting for my audience to sit down, I'd peek out from behind the curtains or couch until they were all dutifully seated. Then springing out with arms flailing, I'd say, "Ta da! I'm going to be a singer when I grow up," and launch into some children's song Mom had taught me.

George Benson was now singing "Turn Your Love Around." As I came back to reality I thought here I was twenty-eight years old, my musical career dead, my guitar banished to the closet, my voice silent. I'm not married to a wonderful man; I'm living a secret confused lesbian lifestyle in Los Angeles three thousand miles away from my hometown, lying to my family and friends back home for fear they won't accept me.

My life assessment done for the moment, I turned into the street and found my destination. The house was tucked in-between several palm trees, ferns, and gorgeous birds of paradise. Putting the car in park and glad to have made it with no mishaps, I was reminded of Hawaiian photos from magazines I'd seen over the years. Closing my eyes for a moment, I envisioned the beautiful sunsets and rainbows of Hawaii, dreaming that I'd live there one day.

Then I shook myself back to reality. Pausing, I stared at the front door before getting out of the car. Here I was about to interview for a job doing live phone sex with men out of my house to earn a living. How the hell did I get here? I had no other choice. Trapped, I felt I had to do this. This new career was my only chance to survive and finally make something of myself. I'd be dammed if I were going to flee back to Rochester with my tail between my legs.

I opened the car door, climbed out, and hesitantly walked up the steps among the ferns and palm trees to Mickey's front door. Putting my hand on the doorbell, I thought, *Oh shit, what am I doing?* Then I pressed the bell.

Mickey answered the door and said, "Kim, right?"

"Yep, that's me. Nice to meet you, Mickey," I said as I extended my hand to hers.

"Kelly has told me so much about you and said you'd be perfect for the job."

I replied nervously, "I hope so."

Mickey motioned to a woman standing near the front entrance. "Kim, this is Sheila, our top earner." Sheila was a large, heavyset woman in her early thirties. She said nothing but gave me a somewhat disapproving look. "Kim," Mickey said, "come in and sit; let me tell you why I'm doing this." She went through the entire explanation exactly as Kelly had told me. She continued, "You can plug in more hours other than what I assign you as well. The phone will just ring. Sheila makes a great deal of money and plugs in all the time."

Sheila smirked at me.

I thought to myself, *Wow! Is this her life's passion? How pitiful.* I replied, "But is it really legal?" I had that familiar uncomfortable feeling in my gut.

"Yes, it is. I have an arrangement with the bank that we are selling office supplies so when you call to get an authorization code for the credit card amount, they think you are selling supplies, not sex."

I replied, "So it's a little misleading but still within the legal guidelines?"

Mickey said, "Yes."

I wondered how true that was, and while it bothered me, I still moved forward.

She went on, "I have professionals in once a month for seminars to teach the girls if they receive a call from someone who has a specific need or fantasy. We've had sex psychologists and even an S & M specialist. We even have a special number to hand out if you think a real sexual predator is on the line. We all refuse to do calls with anyone who wants to fantasize about a child or anything having to do with murder, rape, or mutilation.

With that, I got a sick feeling in my stomach and solar plexus and felt like dashing to the door to escape. But I didn't; I stayed.

Mickey continued, "We provide the help number and send them on their way." We try to help when we can. We have a list called Bad Boys so if someone's credit card is declined and we can't do a call, we put him on the Bad Boys List and notify the next shift. That goes for any perverts as well."

"Okay," I said somewhat reluctantly. The knot in my stomach was getting tighter. What had I gotten myself into?

Mickey said, "Kim, you'll keep a card file on every john. That way you'll be ready for the call."

"Okay," I replied nervously.

"Now, what pseudonym do you want to use? We all use fake names."

I didn't even hesitate; the name came to me instantly. "Angela. I want to use Angela."

"Okay, Angela it is," she replied.

Mickey said, "Let me do a call for you so you can see how it all works." She plugged in the hotline phone she used in her house.

I found myself getting nervous and somewhat anxious. The phone immediately rang. She answered, and it was clearly one of the johns she knew. She began, "Oh hi, babe. You know the drill. Let me authorize your card. Hold on." Then she put down the phone, picked up her real house phone, dialed the bank's toll-free number, and estimated the time it would take for him to get off. I heard her tell the bank "twenty-five dollars." She recorded the authorization number on a 3x5 index card with his name and fantasies on it and put it back in a black card-file box.

Picking up the hotline phone, Mickey said, "Hey, babe, what's happening? . . . Oh yeah really? It's that hard? . . . I bet you want me real bad, don't you, baby? . . . You are? Are you stroking it now? . . . You want to bite my nipples? . . . Oh let me take it from you and stroke it hard. I know how you like me to do that. Come on, baby; come for me; come for me, oh yeah. Oh that's a good boy. That's nice, just the way I like it." Then she said, "Okay, see ya later, baby cakes," and hung up the phone.

I was totally taken aback. Was that it? No emotion, no love? How cold and unfeeling. I felt a little disgusted but tried to be aware of my facial expressions.

Mickey removed the phone from the receiver so it wouldn't ring again. She looked at me skeptically and said, "Do you think you can do that?"

Sheila gave me a rather smug look and looked away.

"Yes, I think I can do that," I found myself saying and then suddenly realized I had just committed myself. I was not happy that I had to revert to this type of work in order to survive and build my new business. What would my parents think if they knew? They'd be outraged, as most of my friends would be. It all sounded so heartless, insensitive with no passion, no sense of caring or love of any kind. I wished I could have heard the other end of the call. Mickey had such a matter-of-fact attitude toward it.

Mickey looked at Sheila and said, "Do you want to add anything to this conversation?"

Sheila looked at me and said indignantly, "Just get them off. That's all they care about. The longer you keep them going before they come, the more money you'll make. I'm the highest earner, you know."

I replied, "Yes, so I've been told."

Mickey said, "Okay then, Angela, you take the next call. If one of my regulars calls, they know I audition new girls." Mickey plugged in another phone this time, so she and Sheila could listen in on the extension.

Within two minutes, the phone rang, and I tensed up wondering who it was, what he'd want, how I'd sound, if I'd please him, and what Mickey and Sheila would think of me. *Don't screw it up, Kim.* Then for a second I thought how odd—*I'm living with a woman as a lesbian and about to screw men on the phone. Good grief.* I felt like a loser, but I had to do this to get my new brokerage business off the ground.

Picking up the phone instinctively with my deep singing voice, I said, "Hello, this is Angela."

The voice on the other end said, "Hi, Angela; this is Tommy K."

Angela replied, "Tommy, you have to have a phone listed in your name and a credit card in your name in order to do a call."

Tommy said, "Yeah, I know the program. I'm a regular of Mickey's."

Mickey listening six feet away on the extension motioned to me that it was okay to continue with the call.

Angela said, "Okay, Tommy, hang on while I get an authorization number." Picking up the other phone, I called the bank, and Mickey motioned to me to go for thirty-five dollars. I got the authorization number, jotted it down on his card I had found while on hold, and then picked up the hotline phone again. My hands were trembling and sweating. "Hi, Tommy, what's happening?"

Tommy replied, "Hey, babe, you must be new. Tell me, what are you wearing?"

"Well for you, I'm actually just peeling off my clothes now. Do you want to help me?"

Tommy said, "Yeah."

Angela replied, "Okay, Tommy, let's start by you first unbuttoning my blouse. I'm not wearing a bra right now. Then unzip my jeans and reach into my panties and feel me. If it's wet, you can continue. If it's not, you must stop." I had turned my back slightly away from the view of Mickey and Sheila to allow me some sense of privacy so I could concentrate. *Oh my God, I can't believe I'm doing this. I feel awful, cheap, and dirty. Mom would be so disappointed in me. Just keep going, Kim. You have no other choice. This is a means to an end. Hang in there.*

Tommy went wild. He loved the challenge. He said, "Oh yeah, okay babe, I'm undoing your blouse. I'm getting hard too. It's off. Now I'm undoing your jeans, and I've got my hand inside your pants, and oh my God, you are so wet, Angela. I'm taking off your jeans and panties now."

Angela said, "Wait, baby, not yet. First I want to rub you through your jeans. That's right. How does that feel?"

Tommy was going wild. His breath was quickening, and I could almost hear his heart pound through the phone. Breathlessly he shouted, "Oh, baby, I'm gonna come. Please undo my pants."

"Not yet, Tommy. Okay, I'm unzipping you now. My blouse is off, my jeans are off, my panties are off, and I'm naked on my knees in front of you. Fuck me now, Tommy, now."

Tom screamed with pleasure and yelled out, "Oh, Angela, I can't take it; I can't hold it. I'm going to come." Tom screamed so loud on the phone both Mickey and Sheila were shocked, and Mickey had to pull the phone away from their ears. Then as fast as it got started, he was done.

All I heard next was the click of his phone hanging up on me. I was shocked by the abruptness.

Mickey said, "Don't take offense. Most of them do that." Then she added, "Well, my dear, you are a born natural. You kept him on the phone long enough to have made forty-five dollars. Pretty easy pay, eh? You start making 25 percent of every call. If you do well, you may earn a higher percentage commission. Oh yes, and if you have another girl you can have on the call with you for a threesome, you can charge double the rate. When do you want to start? I can have the phone installed by next Wednesday. Since you are the new girl, you will be on the late shift, 9:00 p.m. to 1:00 a.m., five days a week. Can you live with that?"

I replied, "Yes. I'm in." I turned and said thank-you and good-bye. I couldn't wait to get out of there.

As I was walking to the front door, I saw Sheila turn her back and walk away in a snit without saying good-bye.

Mickey smiled and said, "Yep, you're a natural."

After closing the door behind me, I stood for a moment in the front yard under the palm trees and noticed it was a beautiful spring day, seventy-eight degrees, sunny, and the sunbeams were dancing in and out of the ferns and palms fronds. In that moment, I realized this job wouldn't work for me unless I could give it 100 percent. After all, that was what Dad had taught me, no matter what job I did, right? It would have to be more than just raw emotionless sex with no heart. It needed to be a subtle learning experience for both parties.

I wanted not only the johns to get what they paid for sexually but also some of them to walk away with something more from me, something that could make them a better person, a happier individual. How happy could you be having to do phone sex all the time? I wasn't going to be just a phone-sex whore. They couldn't just hang up on me once they get off either. I'd have to have a proper thank-you and good-bye. Some mutual respect would be required. This would have to be more than just a means to a financial end; otherwise, I couldn't do this.

So I promised myself I would give it one year, as I would bring something special to this job one way or the other. After one year, I would have enough income to support Maggie and me with my new job and career. I felt better with my new strategy and walked to my Datsun B210 waiting for me out front.

Driving back to North Hollywood, I thought about the call and how easy it was for me to say all those things. Where did that come from? Why was it so effortless? I had no clue and didn't really care. I needed the money. I needed to support Maggie, Gabbie, Nicki, and our two cats, Scooter and Scamper, that we found under a tree stump in the wild. And I needed to get my new business off the ground. Plus, I had to take my attention off my bitterness for my lost musical career and dream.

Not only was Maggie fine with my new job, but also she would lean in on some calls to do three-ways so we could make double commission.

I started to develop my specific clientele. When my regulars would call, I would know how long they would take depending on what fantasy we'd do. Within two months, I started earning almost as much money in commissions as Sheila. I had quickly become the second-highest paid live phone-sex earner in the company. For working twenty hours a week, I was earning on average seven hundred dollars. Not bad for 1982. If I had been willing to plug in more hours, I would have surpassed Sheila by a landslide, but I had another career I was building.

While I had more than fifty johns, a few are worth mentioning. Each illustrates important life lessons. I have toned down the sexual dialogue; however, in order to stay true to the essence of the call, there is some sexual dialogue. Stay with me. It will be worth it in the end.

Bruce the Contractor

Bruce was thirty-five years old and worked for a family-owned contractors' business outside Hartford, Connecticut. He liked to, shall we say, make love to vegetables, especially pumpkins on Halloween, and have Angela listen to him making love to the vegetables. It was a bit comical, Angela thought, listening to sloshy, squishy suction sounds over the phone as Bruce engaged in pleasing himself while Angela spoke sultry encouraging words of wisdom.

His monthly credit card bill just for phone sex ran over five hundred dollars. He used to hang up abruptly on Angela until she told him she would not do any more calls until he said thank-you before he hung up. He finally agreed.

Martin the FBI Agent

Martin was forty-five and divorced. One evening while on duty watching a hotel for a potential suspect to show up, he pulled a trashy sex magazine from under the front seat of his car. After reading the advertisement for JJSX, he jotted down the number and decided to call after his shift ended at midnight. After doing a couple of calls with other JJSX girls, he called again and guess whom he got.

Martin was different from the other johns Angela serviced, as he liked to talk about life and his stresses with his job and wanted to know more about Angela's real life. He was always asking her what her real name was and why she did phone sex.

Of course, Angela would not divulge her real name and only stated she did phone sex as extra income in order to have time during the day to build another business.

Martin felt Angela was different from other girls he'd previously spoken with. To him, she seemed genuinely interested in listening to what he was saying and how he was feeling, letting him talk if he wanted to and not have sex; whereas the other girls only pushed him to have sex and didn't care about his emotional needs. He would pay regardless of whether he got off or just wanted to talk.

One night, however, Angela became unnerved. After she made sweet love to Martin over the phone, providing him the vision of stimulus needed for his specific needs of candles glowing by the bedside table and warmed body oil rubbed over his genitals and chest, he became suspiciously quiet. Then with a weak, cracking voice that sounded as if he had been weeping, Martin said, "Angie, I-I think I love you. I need to tell you something."

Angela replied, "What's wrong, Martin?"

He answered, "I have never felt as comfortable with any woman before as I do with you. What would you say if I showed up on your doorstep one day? You know I can find out where you live very easily in my line of work."

Terrified, she replied, "Martin, no please, do not do that. That breaks the rules, and frankly that freaks me out. I have another life, and that would be wrong of you to invade my privacy."

[Needless to say, I was shaking and horrified that he would do such a thing. What had I gotten myself into?]

He replied, "But, Angie, I know who you really are now."

Angela was silent and frightened. She didn't know what to say.

In a creepy kind of way, Martin whispered into the phone, "Ann K. Driggs is your real name, and I'd love to meet you. I know where you live. I could fly out and appear at your door anytime I wanted. What if I told you I was at your front door now?"

[Now I was totally panicked! I got up and fearfully peered out the front window anticipating some psycho stalker standing at the front door or in some black sedan in front of the house. No one was there. Maggie was in the back bedroom folding clothes from the load of laundry she had just completed. *Shit, what do I do? Hang up? No, stand strong. You can handle this.*]

Angela had to get a grip and find the words to ward off Martin. Finally she answered, "Martin, if you really love me, you will respect my privacy and my personal life."

He replied, "Just tell me, why do you do this type of work? You don't seem to be that kind of girl."

[While I didn't really feel I owed this guy an answer, my gut told me it was better to be honest and try to get a handle on the situation. I didn't want to become another LA statistic that my poor parents would have to read about in the paper.]

Angela replied, "Martin, I'm trying to start a business, and it won't generate any income for a year or so. I have to pay my bills, and I work during the day building the new business. A friend of mine told me about this gig, which I can do at night. It's only going to be for a year, I hope." Changing the subject, Angela added, "I actually used to be a singer."

Martin replied enthusiastically, "I knew it. I knew you were different, had something going for you. A singer, really? What kind of music?"

Before too long Martin and Angela were deep in conversation about her life and why she had to give up her dream in music to start a business. She didn't tell him about living with a woman, though. She inquired why the FBI?

He told her he had watched too many movies growing up and wanted to fight for justice and get the bad guys. But the reality was he was getting burned out, as the stress was so high. After over an hour on the phone, Martin promised Angela he would not show up on her doorstep and promised not to call her by her real name ever again.

Martin kept his promise.

Ricky the Slave

Ricky was a meek, twenty-four year old Italian who lived in the Bronx in a studio apartment and worked as a waiter at a local Italian restaurant. He had been living as a slave to a mistress until she abruptly moved to Florida leaving him helpless and lost. He had been totally devoted to his mistress, Cassandra. Once a week, he had actually seen her, and the rest of the time they had spoken over the phone.

Fully dependent upon Cassandra, Ricky could not function without her. She had told him what to wear, how to act, what to eat, and how to fuck. This had gone on for three years but had just been a continuation of Ricky's home life. His mother was a dominant woman never letting Ricky make his own decisions about anything when he was growing up and living under her roof. When Ricky was three years old, his father had deserted the family.

Angela didn't know how Ricky found Cassandra but knew she had dominated him in every way. Ricky had had a verbal agreement with her. Cassandra got off being a mistress and apparently had a couple of slaves in her life, Ricky being one of them. He told Angela how it had begun. Cassandra had said she would be his mistress under the following conditions:

1. He would do as he was told. If he broke the rules, she would release him.
2. He would not tell anyone about their relationship.
3. If he kept her waiting, she would release him.

4. He would always refer to her as mistress or Mistress Cassandra unless she instructed him differently. Otherwise, she would release him.
5. She would see him in person once a week only at his apartment, and the other six days she would manage him via the phone for one hour.
6. There would be no money exchanged between them.
7. She would not use written contracts of any kind, and he would not know where she lived. He would agree to these conditions of his own free will, and he could leave at any time he chose understanding she would never take him back. If he could live with these conditions, they had an agreement.

His relationship with Cassandra had been that of him pleasing her sexually as per her demands and her demanding him to live out his life as she saw fit—who his friends were, how to dress, how much time he could spend with those friends, and what time he had to be home. She had not let him have any meaningful relationships outside of her.

She had also demanded he perform sexual favors on himself per her instructions. In return, he had found peace and satisfaction both emotionally and sexually.

The day Ricky had gotten the call that Cassandra was moving away and releasing him, he had panicked. She hadn't seemed to care how he would react, and she had had no one to replace her. As Ricky told it, it had been a short, cold call: "Ricky, this is Mistress Cassandra. I'm moving to Florida tomorrow. I release you. Good-bye."

In a passing conversation one day, a friend of his told him about the sex calls he was having with various girls out in LA. He told Ricky to call sometime. Desperate, Ricky did. He happened to get Sheila. When Sheila found out he was a real slave looking for a real live mistress, she told him she could not help him and hung up on him. He tried again and got Angela.

At first when Angela spoke to Ricky, she thought he was kidding, role-playing. But when he started to cry, she realized this kid was not faking it. He really was in trouble. Angela tried to get him to call a hotline number for troubled people, but he wouldn't. He started to sound suicidal, and Angela tried to get him to call a suicide hotline, but he wouldn't do that either.

He begged Angela to be his mistress.

[I don't know what came over me, but I realized I had to try to help him move through this and live his life on his own as an independent soul. I realized the level of responsibility I would be taking on, but to say no to him could have had a catastrophic outcome, and I felt I needed to try to help this pour little bird. Then that familiar presence, that voice within me, told me to go for it.]

Angela and Ricky established their boundaries on the first call. He would call her Mistress Angela. She told him her hours of working, and they established how often he would be able to call her.

[I felt if I established certain days he wouldn't just call anytime out of panic but had to find control within his life immediately until the next call.]

Ricky shared all the things Cassandra had engaged with him, which Angela felt were demeaning. Just because you are a slave doesn't mean you have to be demeaned and persecuted sexually or emotionally. Cassandra had made him lick her boots and perform cunnilingus to her while on his knees, as she stood tall and erect wearing her S & M outfits. She had had a whip and would smack it over his back as well. He had the scars to prove it. Angela had refused to do any of this with Ricky over the phone. While she wouldn't have a face-to-face relationship with him, she had had to ensure the phone presence was powerful enough to have a positive impact. So, when Cassandra was on the phone with Ricky, she'd instructed him to place a lead pencil up into the tip of his penis, and much to Angela's horror, Ricky had complied.

Angela told Ricky he was not to do that to himself when alone ever again.

He replied, "Okay, Mistress Angela, whatever you desire."

Their initial call was to establish a new role for Ricky. He wanted to please Angela, and that was his experience in the past, so Angela allowed him to do so. She would have to give him dignity and empower him slowly.

Angela told him she was wearing black panties, a black bra with black boots. Sitting on the couch she instructed him to come to her.

[I was told intuitively to speak to him with my musical voice, a lower tone, yet authoritatively.]

"Remove your clothes and stand before me," Angela said firmly.

He did as he was told.

"Ricky, you are a fine specimen. I want you to take extra good care of your body. I want you to treat it like a piece of art. You will go buy new jeans and new shirts of your liking that extenuate your features."

Nervously he replied, "But, Mistress Angela, I don't know what to buy. Can you tell me please?"

She answered, "No, Ricky, you must decide what to buy. You will stand before the clothing racks and view each piece. You will try on as many as it takes for you to feel which one makes you feel good about yourself. Feel free to ask the employees in the store to help you. Then you will report back to me exactly what you bought and how it made you feel."

"Okay, Mistress Angela," he said shyly.

She summoned him to push her back on the couch and mount her. Angela told him to kiss her nipples and make love to her. He was shocked as he had never been talked to like this nor asked to make love to his mistress in this manner. He did as he was told. Angela gave him a gentle smack on his ass over the phone and told him he was a good boy. Then the first call ended.

[Ricky and I were together for five months and spoke between two and three times a week. He ran up quite a credit card bill, but it was probably less than professional therapy. He was changing in our calls and becoming more self-assured. I told him he could go out with his friends whenever he chose to and return home before midnight on weekdays and 2:00 a.m. on weekends. He complied. I continued with my goal to empower him into his own independent life and decision-making process. He was becoming independent but didn't realize it yet.]

On one call, Angela took a huge leap of faith. She asked him if he ever had a girlfriend other than seeing his previous mistress or her.

He replied, "Many years ago, Mistress Angela."

"Ricky, I want you to make a concerted effort to meet woman and be open to a relationship. I will not be jealous. It will make me happy and stimulate me on many levels," Angela dictated firmly.

There was a pause on the phone before he timidly replied. "If that is what you want, Mistress Angela, I will do it." He didn't sound sad, just confused.

Several weeks later on one of the calls, Angela noticed Ricky sounded cheerful, upbeat, excited, yet peaceful. She said, "Ricky, what is going on?"

He eagerly replied, "Mistress Angela, I did what you asked, and I have a new girlfriend. Her name is Lisa, and I met her at a dance club. She is a friend of my friend Joe. She and I have had several dates, but I didn't want to tell you until I knew it was real. We really like one another."

[My heart almost exploded with joy hearing this little bird so happy and healthy.]

Angela replied, "Ricky, that is good. Have you made love to her?" Shyly he replied, "Yes, Mistress Angela. We've made love to each other, and it is really good, really good. I sometimes think of you when I'm loving her."

Angela replied, "Ricky, I'm happy you have Lisa and she has you, but you do not need to think of me when you are with her. Are you happy?"

He paused for a moment and said, "Mistress Angela, I have never felt like this before. I think I am happy for the first time in my life. Are you proud of me?"

[I had a big smile on my face and a warm fuzzy feeling flowing through my body.]

Angela replied, "Ricky, of course I am. Are you proud of you?"

He said, "Ya know, I think I am."

It was then that Angela knew she could release him. She told him to call back in two days as she had something important to talk to him about.

[This gave me time to think about how I was going to release Ricky. My goal was to do phone sex for one year, to have enough money saved to open up a small office in Van Nuys for Gail's and my new brokerage business, and to be earning enough to help support Maggie and me. I had two weeks left before the year was up, and I had enough money to do just that. My goal had been met.

[It was now time to leave this job. I felt good about the last year and what I was able to achieve. Many of my johns shared with me prior to my last day what I meant to them and how our relationship had changed them for the better. I could see it, and it made all of the last year doing phone sex worthwhile. Sure, there were still some who only wanted to get off, but out of my entire card file box of johns, they were only 20 percent.

[Ricky was important to me, and I couldn't leave without knowing he was going to be okay, so I prepared for our last conversation.]

He called right on schedule. Angela did not charge his credit card for that final call.

She answered, "Hello, this is Angela."

"Hello, Mistress Angela. This is Ricky."

"Ricky, how are you feeling?"

"Great, Mistress Angela. How are you?"

She replied, "I'm wonderful, Ricky. There is something I must ask of you now. I am so proud of you and how your life is going. I want to release you. I want you to live your life and be your own man. I will always remember you and be proud of you, but it is time for you to go out on your own now and take care of others. Take care of Lisa and let her take care of you. Be happy and give to others. Take care of your body and be good to your boss as he is good to you."

[I waited. Would he be okay and accept this? There was silence on the other end of the phone for at least ten seconds, which seemed an eternity. My heart pounded with trepidation. What if he couldn't accept this?]

Angela thought she heard a sniffle.

Then Ricky replied, "Mistress Angela, are you sure I'm ready?"

Angela firmly replied, "Ricky, you were always ready. You just didn't know it until now."

He got excited and enthusiastically replied, "Okay, Mistress Angela, I will do it. I will do it."

Angela replied, "Ricky, just call me Angela."

He said, "Oh, really? Okay, Angela, thank you. Thank you. I will never forget you."

She replied, "Have a wonderful life, Ricky. I will not be available anymore on these calls as I'm retiring from this work. I too am starting a new life with new adventures. Be well and good-bye, Ricky."

He said, "Good-bye, Angela. Thank you so much, Angela. Good-bye."

⌗ ⌗ ⌗ CHAPTER 17 ⌗ ⌗ ⌗

GOOD-BYES

Dad

Early in 1981, prior to Dad retiring and my parents' moving to their dream home on Skidaway Island near Savannah, Georgia, I had visited Mom and Dad at the lake house outside Rochester. Dad and I were driving around one day doing errands when he said to me, "Kimberly, I've had a great life. I have the most wonderful wife in the world and two beautiful children. All the years I traveled for business I never once cheated on your mother."

I thought it strange his telling me all this but continued listening carefully as we drove around the beautiful countryside of Canandaigua, New York. I wondered, *What's going on? Why is he saying this stuff to me?*

"I've traveled the world multiple times and have only one regret."

"What's that, Dad?" I asked.

"That I never got to ride the Colorado rapids," he said with a little twinkle in his blue-grey eyes.

He looked tired to me, and I was worried. Was he looking at his mortality? Was he going to die? I was silent and didn't know how to respond. We sat in silence after that in the car as we finished our errands.

On that visit, I was also more open about Maggie and me. I didn't come out, but I referred to her and me as "we" all the time—"we did this" and "we did that." I was trying to get the point across gently to my family that I was in love with this woman without officially coming out.

While I was there, Chip came down to the lake house with his first wife and kids. I dropped hints to him as well about my relationship with Maggie, but he did not act as if he accepted me at all. One day, it got pretty heated when he and I were talking about love and family.

He said, "You can't possibly know what love is unless you are married and have a family as I do."

I fired back, "Of course I can. Love is love, no matter whom you love."

He replied, "No, you are wrong."

Mom was in the kitchen keeping oddly quiet, and Dad was watching me intensely as I got very uncomfortable and upset. I almost came out but didn't. I kept my mouth shut, but I think I had made my situation obvious without the exact words.

※ ※ ※

Before I got on the plane to return to Los Angeles, Dad took me aside by the gate and privately handed me a letter. "Kimberly, this is for Maggie. Please give it to her. Do not open it, as it is for her eyes only. I'm very proud of you and love you very much." He had tears in eyes, and I was holding back my own. This was an emotional side to my father that I didn't often see.

After hugging him and Mom tightly, I walked down the Jetway heading back to my bizarre life in LA.

Upon my return to LA, I quickly gave Maggie the letter. I couldn't wait to see what was inside. She opened it and read it slowly to herself first. I noticed her holding back tears. She started reading it to me. It started out with "Dear Maggie" and then proceeded with some cute joke of my father's. He was always the jokester, having all those years at sales meetings cracking up the entire R. T. French Company's sales teams.

It continued with, "While we have never met, I wanted to tell you how much I appreciate all you've done for Kim. I've never seen her so happy and fulfilled. I want you to know I accept you into our family. Thank you again for loving Kim. I hope we can meet someday. Love, Bob."

I was blown away and realized that this was Dad's way of telling me he accepted my choice of living with a woman. I also got the impression that Mom didn't know about the letter and perhaps she had not come to terms with this or even acknowledged it. I just didn't know. I had every intention of asking Dad, but . . .

⊠ ⊠ ⊠

Dad had not been well over the previous couple of years, having had several trips to the hospital. Doctors called them heart failures. Each episode left his heart with more build-up of scar tissue. Unable to kick the smoking habit, he had developed emphysema, which had killed his mother.

In July of 1982, just a couple of weeks before his sixty-first birthday, Dad had another episode after my parents' move to Skidaway. I'll never forget the phone call and the tone of Mom's voice, filled with anguish yet somehow strangely in control. "Kim, this is your mother. You need to come now. Your father is in the hospital, and I don't think he is coming out."

I distinctly remember standing by the cheap couch Maggie and I had bought at some local flea market. When Mom said, "I don't think he is coming out," I lost my balance and fell into the side of the couch. Everything stopped for me in that moment, and I went into autopilot getting the plane ticket, packing, and finding someone to drive me to LAX since Maggie didn't drive. I had to get to Mom as fast as I could.

⊠ ⊠ ⊠

The temperature was in the nineties, sticky and humid, in Savannah the day I arrived. Coming out of the Savannah airport, I felt the heat hit me as if I'd been thrown into the inferno of hell. I waited by the curb dripping with sweat, as my clothes stuck to me, for forty-five minutes on that blasted curb constantly looking at my watch.

Mom finally picked me up and apologized for being late. She had been at the hospital. "Your brother is flying in later this afternoon," she stated in a controlled voice. As she rushed me to the hospital, it was obvious Mom was trying to keep it together and just take care of business minute by minute.

Dad was not awake. He had a jaundice color about him, and his stomach was distended and full of fluid. Mom was coping, but underneath, I could see she was breaking into pieces. She motioned me to go to him.

I sat next to Dad in a chair and held his hand. "Dad, it's Kim. I'm here beside you. I love you so much, Dad." I did everything I could to hold back a fountain of tears. I did cry but not the way I needed to. In front of Mom, I needed to be her rock for a change.

There was a bad smell in the air, which I learned later is the smell of death. Mom was standing several feet away from the bed to give me space. Her hand was up over her mouth, and her eyes were wide with fear. Dad never opened his eyes again, nor do I know if he knew we were there.

※ ※ ※

After Chip arrived and had a chance to see Dad, we were all back at the house on Skidaway Island. We could barely communicate to one another, as we knew Dad was dying. Eventually, we headed for bed, but I don't know if anyone slept.

The call came at that bewitched hour, one in the morning. The head nurse said Bob had passed. Mom and I went to the hospital and let Chip sleep. That is how she wanted it. All the tubes and monitors had been disconnected. He lay there peacefully, silent.

I stood back, close to the window, to allow Mom the space to be with him. I heard her say, "Bless your heart, Bob," and she leaned over and kissed his forehead. I thought I'd die right there on the floor, as I saw her world come to an end. He had been her life and always had been, ever since he had returned from the war broken. I remembered her story of how she had gone to see him at Grandma Flossie's house and had realized then they'd be together forever . . . or until . . .

All Mom had ever wanted was to have her personal time with her beloved Bob, not shared with some demanding corporate entity hovering over them. I knew this move to Georgia was supposed to be their private time together, finally, with no obligations, just them, all them.

In that moment, a flood of pictures and memories stormed through my brain, one by one. I saw Dad holding me on his lap when I was a little girl and how he used to take me to work with him and Tiger on Saturdays and show me how the mustard was made. I can still smell the spices used in the mustard.

He had been so proud of me. When I was older, he'd have a couple of cocktails and then say, "Little Kimmy Driggs, girl singer, come here." He'd want to put me on his lap and hug me to show me how much he loved me. Whenever we'd all be out to dinner and there was a piano player, he'd ask the musician to have me go up to sing, even though that annoyed me. Every time he'd come to a gig of mine and watch me perform, the look on his face of pride and love was something I would never forget. There was always a tear in his eye. Mom was right—Dad was very sensitive; he just didn't know how to show it all the time.

More recent events whipped by in my mind—his regretting not riding the Colorado rapids, the letter he wrote to Maggie—and more distant ones, like sitting together and making the list on whether or not I should move to England with them. I remembered the story Mom had told me of how Dad had tried to stop me from crying by waving his watch back and forth the day they first saw me. Thousands of pictures flooded my brain and emotional body. I would never forget this beautiful man saving me and taking me into his heart and home and loving me as if he had created me himself.

I looked up at Mom and saw a look I'd never seen before on her face. She was crushed, lost, and hopeless. I was worried about her.

※ ※ ※

Mom had Dad cremated, rented a boat to take his ashes, and tossed them in the Inland Waterway, per his request. The service was back in Rochester. Sue and Jan came. Mom asked that I sing in the balcony "Norwegian Wood" by the Beatles. Dad had loved it when I'd sing that song for him. We had to rent a guitar, as mine was still in Los Angeles, banished to the closet. It was hard, but I pulled it off. It was the first time in a very long time I had played a guitar. It felt oddly familiar.

Mom returned to Georgia alone. I had to go back to Los Angeles, and Chip remained in Rochester.

Maggie

By 1983, three years into our relationship, Maggie and I had drifted apart. Recreational drugs played a part—or maybe they just indicated the underlying differences we weren't willing to face otherwise. I had first tried a bong when I had been still in Rochester in my early twenties. I had gotten so high I ate everything in sight and wouldn't shut up. It had burned my throat, and I hadn't liked how it had made my voice feel, so I didn't do it again. I swore I would never do drugs or smoke because they would have damaged my vocal cords and I hated the smell and energy of them.

Now in the 1980s, the drugs were everywhere, especially in Los Angeles. Uppers, downers, hash, marijuana, and cocaine ruled the world of entertainment. Despite my swearing off drugs, I allowed myself to be persuaded into trying recreational cocaine with Maggie, Gail, and her husband. After saying no for months, I finally gave in thinking I'd hate it only to find out I liked it very much.

For the next year, I found myself on Friday afternoons lined up at the ATM, along with ten other screwed-up, lost souls holding their ATM card to extract $125 cash for a small vial of cocaine for the weekend. We'd have to use hash to balance off the high, sometimes followed by booze. It was a roller coaster. I'd always feel like crap the next morning and found myself at Wendy's burgers ordering a triple cheese with everything and a container of milk.

I had my own Tweedy Bird mirror and razor to cut the cocaine on and hash pipe. I couldn't believe I was doing this. Here I was twenty-nine years old living in LA, doing drugs, and birthing a new business. What was I thinking? Who was this person? My musical career finished, my father dead, my mother alone and unhappy, and my relationship with Maggie deteriorating, I felt I was losing myself. I hated who I had become.

Maggie and I just couldn't get on the same page. She seemed lost and unhappy. I loved her very much, and I knew she adored me, but we were falling apart, and I couldn't help whatever issues she was going through at the time, nor could she help mine. I also lost the blue star inside myself and felt my spiritual connection dying. *What's happening to me? God help me.* I couldn't talk to Sue or Jan back home as I was embarrassed by who I had become. By now they knew about Maggie and had accepted me no matter whom I loved. But my doing drugs, and worse, losing myself, went beyond what I thought they could accept in me.

One unusually warm afternoon, I was sitting in the patio of our Cartwright Street rental house with Nicki and Gabbie lying next to me. I shut my eyes and prayed. *God, please help me find myself again. I'm not happy. I've lost my connection to you.* Suddenly it was as if a lightning bolt hit me, and I realized I needed to stop it all. The next day, I told Maggie I was through with all of it. I told Gail too. I tossed the Tweedy mirror and all my paraphernalia into the trash.

I heard the cute little mirror crash into a million pieces with just little Tweedy's nose showing. They all supported my decision, although I had no concern about whether or not they were quitting. All I knew is that I was! I was cleaning up my act.

Then I asked Maggie if she'd do counseling with me. She refused. We hadn't made love in months, and now we were fighting more.

I knew I had to leave. I just didn't know how.

CHAPTER 18

Opening New Doors

Love

Shannon worked at one of the health food stores I called on. Standing five feet two inches, long brown hair down to her ass, and toting a four-and-a-half-year-old son, she emanated sexuality and light. She and I fell hopelessly in love and lust. It wasn't, however, until Maggie and I broke up that Shannon and I moved into our first rental house in Burbank. I was a natural-born mommy to Kyle. We adored each other. Maggie did get to know Kyle and Shannon and, being the beautiful soul she is, understood the connection and need for me to be with them.

It all came clear to me one day when Shannon and I were sitting on the floor listening to some soft metaphysical music in my house just prior to moving in together while Maggie was at work. We got into a conversation about God, and I was sharing with her my unanswered questions that had plagued me since I was three years old. She smiled and said, "I think I can help."

She walked out to her car and came back, hair flowing from side to side, eyes beaming, and hand holding a book she had retrieved from the back seat by Paul Twitchell, called *The Flute of God.* She told me about a spiritual organization called Eckankar, the Ancient Science of

Soul Travel, and how Sri Paul had been the Living ECK Master from October 22, 1965 until September 17, 1971, when he had translated from this plane.

I told her about all the books I had read over the years attempting to seek the truth, my truth, including several by Paramahansa Yogananda (I even visited his fellowship in Los Angeles), *Music and Sound in the Healing Arts* by John Beaulieu, *90 Minutes in Heaven* (about someone who died and came back, as my mother did) by Don Piper with Cecil Murphey, *Knowledge of the Higher Worlds and Its Attainment* by Rudolf Steiner, the series of *Conversations with God* by Neale Donald Walsch, *Pets' Letters to God* translated by Mark Bricklin, *Life After Life* by Raymond Moody, *Kabbalah Month by Month: A Year of Spiritual Practice and Personal Transformation* by Mindy Ribner, and *Kahuna Healing* by Serge Kahili King. They were helpful, but none gave me all the answers I had sought for so long.

Opening *The Flute of God*, I began reading the first chapter. Looking up at Shannon with an obvious enthusiasm emanating from my being, I saw she had a gleam in her eye. I was hooked immediately. The music danced off the pages. It was written with a golden thread of truth and openness and had a cadence that grabbed my soul. I couldn't put it down. She leaned in and gave me a long, luscious, sensuous kiss. In that frozen moment in time, I knew I had found my spiritual answers in one single kiss.

Shannon continued to tell me that she was no longer a member of the Eckankar organization but of another movement born of Eckankar and of Sri Paul Twitchell's original teachings. This group was called the Ancient Teachings of the Masters, or ATOM, and it was those teachings that had resonated so strongly with me.

After Paul's death and on October 22, 1971, the rod of power, as they call it, was handed over to Darwin Gross, a student of Paul's. With "Sri" as part of his name to indicate his status as Master of the Times, Sri Darwin Gross became my spiritual master and changed my life. I quickly learned how to contemplate and still myself to allow my inner soul to travel to the various inner planes where one hears a musical instrument attached to each inner level or plane. Now I understood what the violin and flute sounds meant and where they came from when I'd shut my eyes and see that blue star. The blue star is the sign of the inner master. Wow! Had the master been with me since I was born? Is that why the psychic saw the blue star and said it was with me always?

I was finally getting answers. The more books I read by Sri Paul Twitchell and Sri Darwin Gross, the more I contemplated and the more answers I found.

※ ※ ※

I was getting more involved with the Ancient Teachings of the Masters. Shannon was heavily involved with it and worked very close to Sri Darwin. She and I attended one of its seminars in Oklahoma.

One afternoon before the evening event where Sri Darwin spoke and performed on his beautiful vibraphone, I was kneeling down outside on the grass talking and singing quietly to two little dogs that were at the event with their owners. To them, I was chanting Hu, which means God. The sound and vibration that comes from chanting Hu is of the highest and points directly to the highest level of heaven. Why chant Om or Aum, which resonates with the lower realms, when you can focus your attention on the highest?

Focusing on the dogs, I didn't realize Sri Darwin was walking up behind me. He stood there for a bit before saying, "You are very good with animals. You have a gift with your voice. You should always sing to them. Prajapati is the master over the animal kingdom. Did you know that?"

Startled at first, I looked up at him from my squatting position and nervously replied, "Yes."

"This is something you should continue doing," he said with his mesmerizing smile and twinkling brilliant blue eyes.

I wanted to tell him that I'd been singing to all living creatures since I was a child, but I just kept staring at him. He probably already knew anyway. While he looked human to me, he also had a heavenly glow around him, something I can't quite put into words. He touched my shoulder as I stood up to meet his gaze, and I felt love surge through my body as I've never experienced before. Nothing compared to that feeling. It was a God-type love.

Family

Kyle was five years old in 1985. I had just taught him how to tie his shoes, and we surprised his mom with his new talent when she got home from work.

It was December, and we had put up our first Christmas tree together. By now, Kyle and Shannon knew how important the holidays were to me. I had shared with them my endless stories of the years growing up in Pittsford and how my family celebrated the holidays—decorations, music, joy, making angels in the snow, skating at Monroe Golf Club on the frozen-over tennis courts, drinking hot chocolate in the grill room, making ornaments with Mom, and my spending endless hours listening to Johnny Mathis, Andy Williams, Perry Como, Ray Conniff, and Nat King Cole singing Christmas carols.

Underneath the activity, it was all about family. I never got from Shannon that the holidays were as important to her as they were to me, so it was hard for her to relate at first. Kyle wanted it, though, and loved that I was there to give it to him.

One evening after dinner several days later, we were sitting in the living room by the tree. The only lights on were those of the bulbs twinkling through the live Norfolk pine braches. *Oh, how I love that smell.* I was always leaning into the tree taking a big whiff of that evergreen aroma, aromatherapy at its best for sure. Shannon was lying on the couch reading poetry by Rumi, and I had Kyle sitting on my lap close to the tree. He and I had just finished our lesson on how to count to two hundred. Shannon loved the relationship Kyle and I had with each other.

I whispered to him, "Kyle, let's learn a Christmas carol."

"Okay," he said and smiled at me.

I held him tight and started singing my version of "Rudolph" with great enthusiasm.

Rudolph the red-nosed reindeer
Had a very shinny nose
And if you ever saw it
You would even say it glows
   (Like a light bulb).

. . . .

Then how the reindeer loved him,
As they shouted out with glee,
Rudolph the red-nosed reindeer
You'll go down in history
   (Like Elvis)!

Kyle burst out laughing saying over and over, "Like Elvis. Let's sing it again." This time he joined in and couldn't wait until we got to the parts for "like a light bulb" and "like Elvis."

Much earlier, at the beginning of my relationship with Shannon, I had sung to her some music we were listening to on the stereo, and I do believe it was my voice that closed the sale of our love affair. Since then I had told her of my banished musical career, and she had encouraged me to pull my guitar out of hiding. She loved music as much as I did and, oddly enough, loved to write lyrics. Willingly yet somewhat reluctantly, I had pulled the dusty blue Martin guitar case out of the closet and wiped it off. It had been the first time I'd picked up my guitar since I had banished it to the closet almost five years before. I even found myself purchasing a 1985 limited-edition Ovation. Now I was the proud owner of two guitars again. I started to get my groove back.

Now, I picked up my guitar and started to play more carols from a Christmas songbook. Shannon looked over at Kyle and me with love in her eyes. Somehow, my relationship with her, her love of music, and her encouragement to write songs with me had brought the music back into my life.

Kyle tried to join in and sing and then got up and said, "I love you Momma Two. He ran over to Shannon and said, "I love you Momma One." He ran back to me and sat down by the tree again waiting for our next song to begin. I was in heaven. I had a family.

Performing

Shannon had the role of working very closely with Sri Darwin and some of the higher initiates. This took her away from Kyle and me more than I liked. But ultimately, the time away mattered less than what Shannon was hearing from others in ATOM, and that began destroying our once beautiful love affair. A few of the other ATOM friends of ours were whispering to her that it was not okay for her to be in a relationship with a woman and still be spiritual. I could feel the wedge being painfully driven into our family and saw Shannon slowly pulling away. She was in pain, confused, and torn between her love of me, of our family, and of the teachings and whether or not they all fit together. Our love had to fit in. Didn't it?

Sri Darwin never came out and said to me that it wasn't okay for me to be in a relationship with a woman. He and I had gotten quite close, and I was given a Soul Initiation, which is considered quite an accomplishment. Sri Darwin told me, "Kim, I should have done this a long time ago for you. You earned it."

Sri Darwin wanted me to start performing with him at the seminars. I was so blown away by this and incredibly honored. Of course I accepted. This is what I was here to do, right?

At one of the ATOM seminars in Las Vegas, Sri Darwin asked me to come up and sing with him and his pianist. We opened with "Time after Time," followed by "All the Way," "You Are So Beautiful," and "When I Fall in Love." I stepped down and let the boys do instrumentals until my solo. An indescribable buzz ran through the room, filled with an extraordinary level of magic. In his low melodic voice, Sri Darwin announced, "And now I'd like to ask Kim to come back up on stage with her beautiful healing voice and sing another song for you." He and the pianist stepped down and took their seats in the audience.

A fear overwhelmed me—I was truly on my own. No backup. This was my raw voice with no instruments behind me. I chose not to use my guitar on this particular song. Instead, I was going to sing it a cappella. Pure raw spirit would be coming through me as the vehicle of IT, the Divine Spirit. I had to be on tune, and every word had to resonate the sound current provided by Divine Spirit. *Sing like a bird, honey*, I heard Mom's voice in my head say. I looked at Shannon who was sitting up close to the stage. She smiled and closed her eyes, as she knew I had rehearsed this for weeks. She was so proud.

Standing in front of the microphone, looking out over the audience, I realized that no matter what happened to my relationship with Shannon or the spiritual group, my wish of outflowing love to all living creatures had gone beyond frogs, birds, dogs, and cats. A spiritual master whom I respected and loved, no matter how he felt about my love interests, believed in my spiritual soul, my evolution, and the role my voice played. He was giving me the acknowledgment and opportunity to be that vehicle for Divine Spirit and to outflow the love to all. It didn't matter about being famous or having records; it was just about being available.

So here I was in front of all these people with no backup, no cover up, no ego. Just me. Sri Darwin sat in the back row, folded his arms over his large chest, smiled at me, and closed his eyes. In that moment, the master and I were one.

Closing my eyes, I took a deep breath and sang "Colors of the Wind" to all while singing to my mom in my mind. I heard my voice ring out every note clear and on key. Holding nothing back, I just let it all come through naturally. I never opened my eyes.

The entire time, the rainbow of colors undulated over every note in my third eye keeping me on tune. When I finished, there was a resounding standing ovation that woke me from my spell. Darwin was beaming at me, and I back at him. In that moment, I felt a love, happiness, and wholeness unlike any other kind I've felt in my entire life. It is hard to describe, but it is the kind of love that is far greater than human love. My heart was overflowing with this God love, and I knew it was the most important type of love one could feel and strive for. When you have it, when you are in it fully, everything else seems to fall into place, no matter what conflicts or challenges you are facing. I felt balanced and happy for the first time in a very long time.

Could I keep that feeling going? Could I hold onto it?

Truth

In the months after Dad's death, Mom was in agony from the loss. Moving from Georgia to Naples, Florida, she took a condo on a golf course thinking she would play golf and make new friends. She did make a concerted effort to make friends and get involved, but I could tell she was miserable. I called her every few days and could hear it in her voice.

Later that year, my mother visited Maggie and me. We had never discussed my lifestyle, and I had no clue whether Dad had discussed it with her or not. I had to tell her I was moving out from Maggie and moving in with Shannon and her little boy. How was I going to tell her? This would surely reveal that I was a living with a woman. Would she accept me? Was my purity of heart enough to keep her loving me? The last thing I wanted to do was give her more pain. I was stressed out. The phantom rash was in full bloom all over my ass and scalp.

Mom and I were sitting at my kitchen table in the house on Cartwright Street drinking coffee. Maggie was at work. I knew I had to tell Mom, and I could feel an underlying tension in the air.

"Mom, I need to tell you that I'm moving out and going to move in with a new roommate."

She looked at me with, I cringe to say it, almost hate in her eyes. With a curt, sarcastic voice, Mom replied, "What about Maggie? I thought you were happy here with her."

I got tenser. The expression on her face scared and hurt me. Who was this person? At that moment, I realized she knew. I felt like crap. My stomach was churning, and my head started to hurt in both temples across the front of my forehead. My shoulders were getting tense. I replied, "Mom, I love Maggie very much, but it isn't working anymore. I met someone I care very deeply about and realize I need to be somewhere else. Her name is Shannon, and she has a little boy named Kyle. He really loves me, and I love him. I can have a real family now, something I've always wanted."

Mom stared at me with pathetic disappointment in her eyes and blurted out those stinging words so many parents say when they realize they have a gay child, "Where did I go wrong with you? This must be my fault."

I wanted to scream. Instead, I took a deep breath and replied, "No, Mom, this isn't your fault. This is no one's fault. I learned a long time ago that I could love a man or a woman; it didn't matter what the outer shell looked like. It was the inner person. I tried to find a man that would make me feel this way, but I didn't, and even when I was with men I thought I loved, I still looked over my shoulder."

She replied angrily, "Did Bud and Earl have any influence on you?"

"No, but obviously they accepted me."

Mom said, "I blame that idiot who gave you gonorrhea. It is his fault too."

Now I was getting upset and fired back, "No, Mom, it has nothing to do with him either. I've felt this way since high school. I just tried to ignore it all these years."

She couldn't understand. I know she had wanted me to grow up and meet a wonderful guy and get married. I had too, or so I thought. I did want to be married and have a family of my own, but why did it have to be only with a man? I thought for a moment to myself but didn't share this with her. *One should be able to love whom they want with no persecution, ridicule, or judgment. If God had issues with gay people, why make them in the first place? What about those poor souls who know from the time they are tiny that they were born in the wrong body? That isn't their fault.*

Mom started to cry. I didn't know what to do. I cried too, as I felt I had disappointed the one person in the world that meant so much to me. I wished Dad had been here; he could have helped her. He would have gotten us through this. *Why did he leave? Why did God take that wonderful man away so soon?*

Clean Air

After two years working with Gail, I sold the brokerage firm to her and with Shannon started Avatar Marketing, which provided sales, marketing, and telemarketing services for manufacturers of natural products to health food stores. Avatar had barely gotten off the ground when Shannon decided to leave me to help out a friend who had lost her husband. Finding myself alone again without my newfound family, I had to survive, so survive I did. I moved to a townhouse in Reseda, continued building Avatar alone, and took on a new business partner, Barbara, who lived in Oakland, California, with her husband.

Several months later, Shannon decided to come home, and I welcomed her with open arms.

After about a year, Barbara and her husband decided to move from Oakland to Ashland, Oregon, and encouraged me to move as well. When Shannon moved out for a second time and moved to Las Vegas in 1990, the time seemed right to follow Barbara and leave wretched Los Angeles for good. The smog was killing me, and there were just too many sad memories in the City of Angels. After taking a trip to Ashland and finding a townhouse to rent that would accept my animals, I set the date.

The townhouse had two bedrooms upstairs and two full baths. Downstairs was a large kitchen, living room, den, powder room, and deck/lanai that overlooked Highway 5. In the basement was a large bonus room that would be our Avatar office. It had a two-car garage and a small backyard that sloped downhill.

Barb and Robert would be up a week after my arrival, as they had to shut down their condo in Oakland. They had bought a home in Jacksonville, thirty minutes outside Ashland.

On the set date one sunny February morning, I literally crawled out of the city, very ill with a high fever, a common occurrence for me the last four years in LA, thanks to the smog. My white 300Z sports car was packed with suitcases, two guitars, and Nicki and Gabbie. After Shannon and I broke up, I lost the voice and will to sing or write again. It was a constant reminder of my failed dream and various betrayals. Still, I couldn't part with my guitars and dragged them with me, even though I wasn't playing them.

The moving truck would arrive in Ashland three days later with all my worldly possessions.

I drove to Oakland and spent the night with Barbara and Robert. The following morning, I rose early, said good-bye, reloaded the pups in the car, and started the drive up Highway 5 to the Oregon border. I felt a little better, and the fever was finally breaking.

In LA, I also left some good memories—my dear friend Marcy whom I grew to love very much. A beautiful girl inside and out, she was married, but the marriage was floundering. After Shannon and Kyle moved out, Marcy and I got very close, and one night she said she had fallen in love with me. I was shocked. She told me she was divorcing her husband. I was still hurt and confused by Shannon and certainly not over her, yet I found myself getting intimately involved with Marcy. When I told her I was moving to Oregon for my health and well-being and to continue to build Avatar with my new partner, Marcy was crushed. She said she wanted to go too, as there was nothing keeping her in LA anymore, and a month after I arrived, she moved to Ashland too.

❋ ❋ ❋

The sun was beginning to fall low into the winter sky as I made my way deeper into Northern California. I was coming around a bend filled with large boulders and pine trees. Gabbie and Nicki smiled up at me with their adorable doggie smiles, tongues hanging out. "Girls, we will be okay; we will," I said confidently. "This is a new beginning for us. We will be okay."

Then I saw it. Swooping down, flying past our windshield, and landing on one of the pine tree branches off to the right of the car was the most magnificent bald eagle. It was staring right at us. I knew it was a sign. I smiled and said, "Thank you, oh blessed Sugmad [God]."

As I crossed over the California/Oregon border, the sun was getting closer to kissing the top of the Oregon Cascade Mountain Range. The sky had a golden-blue hue to it—or, at least to my colorblind vision, it appeared golden. I opened my window and breathed in the clean, fresh mountain air. No more smog. The cold air was cleansing and refreshing. It blew across my face and felt healing. A very special energy was coming into the car through the open window. Nicki and Gabbie perked their little heads up and gazed up at me. I reached over and petted both of their heads, "Can you smell that air, girls? This is what clean air smells like," I said. I knew now why Sri Darwin chose to live in Oregon outside Portland.

By the time I pulled up to my townhouse, it was almost dark and felt cold and eerie. The driveway was on a large slope, and I had to put the emergency brake on to ensure not sliding on the thin layer of ice that was beginning to form. First, I walked the girls into the house, and then I brought in my suitcases and guitars. I was dead tired.

The townhouse was empty, cold, and lonely. I turned on the heat. All my other possessions were in transit, so with no furniture, we slept on the floor on a blanket and pillow I had brought listening to unfamiliar sounds of a new house creaking while gazing out into the dark. All I could make out was a tiny beam of light coming from a distant street lamp through the bedroom window. Nicki and Gabbie were cuddled up close to me, a little unsure of the change in their lives. So much change and disruption had affected their little emotional bodies too.

"Girls, all will be okay. Mommy is here, and I will always be with you. This is the beginning of our new life." I kissed them both and started singing a little song I made up just for them until we all fell fast asleep.

ACT III

ON THE ROAD WITH MOM

We're coming up to Amarillo, Texas. Mom's driving, and I've been singing in my deep, sultry range when I realize she's not paying attention any longer. So I quit. She doesn't notice. What she's tuned into I've no idea.

After a period of silence, she says, "Kim? You're thirty-nine now, right?"

"Yeah," I say, wondering where this is going.

"Well," she says, "I just want you to know . . . that I can't promise to stick around much after your fortieth birthday."

"What do you mean?" I say with an odd feeling in the pit of my stomach.

"What I'm saying is I need to make sure you have your act together and you will be all right. I don't like it here anymore, how the world is becoming. It's not fun for me anymore. It's not a nice place anymore."

My colon is now feeling unsettled, and I say awkwardly, "What do you mean, 'get my act together'? Don't I have my act together?" I now feel she is not okay with me.

Mom glances over to me and sees I'm not handling the conversation well. With true love in her baby blues, she speaks lovingly, "Kim, you've already made it as a person. Anything else is icing on the cake. I'm so proud of you, and your father would be too. It's just that I need to know you will be okay if I'm not here anymore."

Over the years, I've always hated these conversations about death with my mom and when the time would come when she or Dad would be gone. Now I'm really sick to my stomach. "Mom, is something wrong? Are you sick?"

She replies half-jokingly now, "I just can't promise I will stick around much after you are forty. That's all. Get it?"

"Okay" is all I can muster up. I turn my head and peer out the window at the passing saguaro cactus.

CHAPTER 19

VIVA LAS VEGAS

My two years in Ashland were filled with much emotion and growth. I was able to heal my body and soul in many ways. I even found myself pulling out my guitar and actually wrote a song.

Shannon and I could not stop. Even though she tried a relationship with a man and I had Marcy, Shannon and I could not stop loving each other. I wanted to save our relationship and was not giving up. The pull was too strong, the karma apparently incomplete. We decided to try one more time. I told Shannon that this was the last time we would attempt this relationship and that third time's a charm. This had to work. Was she positive she was okay with our relationship and would be able to ward off any outer influences from people? She said she could. I prayed it was so. I knew she wanted it to work.

So in 1992, I arranged to move to Las Vegas. My business partner ended up working out of her home office in Jacksonville, while I packed up the office and moved to Las Vegas. I found a really cute office space off Sahara Avenue next to a charming coffee pub and café. I hired an employee.

Shannon and I found a house in The Lakes to rent. We even bought a floppy-eared bunny for Kyle. We named her Mita. Kyle was twelve and overwhelmed with joy.

I'm Okay, You're Okay

Mom on the other hand was deteriorating emotionally and physically. Her arthritis had gotten so bad she could barely walk two blocks without having to sit down. The pain was unbearable. She couldn't play golf anymore and lost all interest in bridge. She was becoming a bit of a recluse, and I was very worried.

I asked her to move out to be close to me in Vegas. She agreed, although she was not really happy I was back with Shannon. She didn't trust that this would work out seeing I had been left two times prior. Mom did try to support the relationship, though, and was kind to both Shannon and Kyle.

※ ※ ※

After Mom moved into her apartment in The Lakes in mid-1993, five minutes from my house, she was scheduled for her annual check-up, which included chest X-rays. I called her after she got home asking as I did every year for the results. They were "fine, normal," she said.

About six months later on January 17, 1994, the same day as the Northridge California earthquake, magnitude 6.7, hit, I arrived at Mom's apartment to have breakfast with her before going on to work. When I entered the kitchen, I found her hunched over the counter gasping for breath. I asked, "Mom what's wrong?"

She looked frightened and barely uttered, "I can't breathe."

I called my doctor immediately and was relieved he was there to speak with me. He told me to rush her to Valley Hospital and that due to her not being able to breathe they would take her right away.

Hurriedly, I turned off the coffee pot, grabbed my keys, and slowly helped Mom out the door, down the steps, and into my car. I tried to be calm and in control while I was driving to the hospital. Surprisingly, she didn't fight me or ask any questions. I was stupefied.

At the hospital, I rushed her into emergency telling them she couldn't breathe. The nurses put her into a wheelchair, pushed her to the back room, got her into a bed, and quickly hooked up monitors and administered oxygen. They let me sit with her.

I called the office and let my assistant, Dee, know what was happening and asked her to call Barb in Oregon. Then I called Shannon.

The hospital staff ran various tests wheeling her in and out of her room while I waited nervously. It seemed like hours waiting for the results. She looked surprisingly calm. I held her hand. I couldn't imagine what was wrong, what had suddenly struck since her tests from less than a year ago had been okay.

There was a TV attached to the wall in her room in the back of the emergency ward. We watched the disaster unfolding in Los Angeles. I was worried about my reps and their businesses. By now Avatar had taken on a larger role as an outsourced national sales management firm and had given up on telemarketing health food stores, which was how we had begun. We were thriving. I was worried about the health food stores and their businesses. I was worried about our distributors and their businesses. I was just plain worried.

Finally a young attractive male doctor came into the room. He sat down beside Mom, took her other hand, and said, "Elizabeth, I'm sorry, but I have bad news. You have inoperable lung cancer. You have two tumors in your lungs the size of baseballs. We should do a biopsy to see what protocol we can do to make you as comfortable as possible. I'm so sorry."

The doctor looked sad. Mom pulled her hand away from mine and put it on top of his. She smiled and replied, "Doctor, it is okay, really."

He looked surprised by her response and got up and said, "Elizabeth, we'll be back within the hour to take you for the biopsy." He looked at me and said, "I'm sorry, Miss Driggs," and then walked away, his white coat flowing behind him.

Frozen in time, I sat in total disbelief. This couldn't be happening.

Mom turned to me, took my hand again, and saw the horror on my face. Smiling and calm, she said the words I'd heard from her my entire life whenever someone in the family confronted challenges, "I'm okay; you're okay, right?"

What was I to say? I wasn't all right. I was far from all right. I was sick to my stomach, angry, and felt betrayed. All I could do was try to be okay, try to comfort her. I didn't really answer her but nodded my head in semi-approval.

Then it hit me like a slap in the face. This was what she had meant in the car. She must have known. Why would she lie to me? Why would she tell me she was okay if she knew she wasn't? Wouldn't she have had to know?

Just then, another doctor came in and told her they were scheduling the biopsy shortly.

Excusing myself, I left the room. I had to get myself together. All I wanted to do was scream, but I had to think. In the hall, her doctor came over and talked to me. I asked him about the X-rays she had had just a few months prior and what she had told me about them being normal.

He took my arm and said, "Kim, for these tumors to have grown so large, they would have had to be in your mother for a very long time, at least a year or more. She knew she had cancer."

So this was her way out. She had known all along. Mom wanted it this way and had manifested it. She was trying to get me ready. For twelve years, she had tried to make it without Dad, but she was miserable, and I knew it. Why should she stay if she couldn't be happy? For a moment, I felt angry and heartbroken that having her children around wasn't enough to keep her happy and here.

Then I realized something Mom had told me a long time ago. She had said all she had ever wanted was to have the time with Dad alone after retirement. That is what they had worked for, for so many years. She had said, "Kim, I feel ripped off. All those years playing the dutiful corporate wife only to have your father taken from me, I feel so betrayed and angry."

Mom also said it wasn't the responsibility of the children to take care of their parents when they get old or ill. She said she and Dad would never be a burden on Chip or me. I always told her I'd care for them, as I loved them so much. Mom wouldn't accept that. I realized she had stuck around twelve years longer than she wanted to make sure I was okay, just as when she had died and gone down the tunnel. She had come back for me then too. Who was I to keep her from her destiny?

But was I ready? Could I let this woman go?

When I returned to Mom's bedside, she said again, "I'm okay; you're okay, right?"

I looked at her, kissed her cheek, held back rivers of tears, and with moist eyes said, "Yes, Mom, I'm okay."

She smiled those baby blues and said, "All right, then."

The nurses came in and took her away to do the biopsy, and then they would take her to her room. They told me I could come back in two hours. I left and walked briskly to my car parked in the garage. With no one around, I sat in the parking garage and cried for an hour. I was never so alone. My entire life was preparing for this moment. Our time together was drawing to an end. I had to let go of this wonderful woman. How was I going to do that?

The biopsy didn't work. They attempted it twice but said her blood pressure and heart rate soared so high her body couldn't take the procedure. All they could do was make her as comfortable as possible, which wasn't much.

The doctor told me Mom would eventually suffocate. It would not be pleasant. Mom wanted no resuscitation. I contacted Chip, and he flew out immediately. It took me five days to get her affairs in order, as she had no will and had made no arrangements for her death. I was a robot just doing what I had to do, as she had done with Dad I imagined. Never letting her see me cry, I stood strong for her and showed her I was okay for her. I needed to let her go to Dad.

Five days later, I was sitting next to Mom on her bed and could see her breathing was getting harder and harder. The oxygen wasn't working. Nothing was. She mustered up that gorgeous smile and, with those baby blues now more grey than blue, said "I'm okay; you're okay, right? Now go take care of your brother."

Leave her? I wanted to be by her side till the end, but I did as I was told. When I left her room, I looked back and realized this was the last time I'd see my mom alive. *How do I walk out this door?* I thought.

I felt animosity that I had to go take care of my brother, yet this was how Mom wanted it, to go out in her own way and not to have me see her in this condition. My mother was a class act to the end.

Again, Mom said it. "Go now, honey. I'm okay; you're okay." She tried to smile at me, but her breathing was becoming very labored.

Pushing the door open, I forced myself to step out into the hall and didn't look back.

I called Shannon immediately and told her what the doctor had said about Mom's death being brutal and that she didn't want any help of any kind. I asked her to reach out to Sri Darwin and ask for help to take her quickly and peacefully if he could.

Shannon said, "If you ask, you know it will be taken care of for you. Are you sure you want this?"

I said, "Yes." Many times over the years, I had experienced on my own the power of the master, miracles, and Divine Spirit for the good of the whole being a part of the teachings. This was the last good thing I could do to help her translate.

※ ※ ※

It was again that bewitching hour, one in the morning, on January 23, 1994, my fortieth birthday, when I got the call from Valley Hospital that my mother was calling my name and I should come quickly. Kyle was spending the night at his father's house. Shannon and I sprang out of bed, dressed, left the animals in the house, and drove like crazy to the hospital. My stomach was so upset that I had to run to the bathroom with diarrhea before going up to Mom's room. *Damn it*!

When I had left Mom, she had been leaning up against the wall and had the oxygen mask and finger monitor on. If the finger monitor fell off, all the bells would ring at the nurses' station. As Shannon and I entered the hospital, all was silent. Everyone was asleep. We ran directly to Mom's room. Shannon stayed out in the hall as I entered. What I saw when I walked up to her bed I will never forget for as long as I live.

There was Mom sleeping on her side in the fetal position as she did her entire life. She was peaceful with a smile on her face and the oxygen mask and finger monitor both off. I did what I've done my entire life when I'd watch this wonderful woman sleep. Stealthily I crept up to her and listened for her breath and heartbeat. There was neither. I called her name. "Mom?" There was no reply. Then I realized true divine intervention had occurred. I kissed Mom on her cheek for the last time and left the room.

I told Shannon what I saw. She walked in with me, looked at Mom as well, and then smiled. "I told you Sri Darwin would help." I didn't question how this miracle had been done. I just accepted that it was. We ran to the nurses' station and told them my mother had passed and explained how the oxygen mask and finger monitor were off.

The head nurse said, "No, that is impossible. She was just speaking your name a few minutes ago, and all the devices were attached to her. If the oxygen mask or the finger monitor comes off, our bells go off here at the station, and none went off."

The nurse flew down the hall with us to Mom's room. She was shocked when she saw how Mom looked and said; "Your mother wasn't in that position the last time we checked on her, which was only ten minutes ago. She was lying on her back with the mask and finger monitor on. I can't understand what happened. No bells went off at our station." She looked confused and concerned that something had malfunctioned at the nurses' station.

All I said was, "Nurse, I believe there was divine intervention. You said my mother called out my name? Was she looking for me here?"

Still looking confused, she replied, "No, it seemed to me she was on the other side looking for you there. It felt good, Kim, as if she was okay."

❊ ❊ ❊

My mother died on my fortieth birthday. I had to live up to her expectation of being okay. In some ways, I was; in many other ways, I wasn't. I wrote a letter to Sri Darwin and told him how much I appreciated the help in Mom's peaceful transition.

In my mind, I kept hearing her words before she sent me out of the room, "I'm okay; you're okay, right?"

What's Taken You So Long?

After the death of Mom, both Chip and I inherited twenty thousand dollars. With that and some money from Shannon, I bought my first house. My credit was exemplary, so the house was in my name. It was my first home, built from the ground up in Summerlin, Nevada, out by the Red Rock Mountains.

One day in August 1994, Shannon had left early in the morning to go to work. She was trying to birth a new career. Kyle was off to school. I hadn't left for the office yet. The front door bell rang. Opening the door, I saw standing before me a five-foot-two- inch woman with short, curly, blond hair wearing white painter's overalls and holding a paintbrush. She was smiling profusely and had a gleam in her bright-blue eyes. Yes, another blue-eyed person in my life. What came out of my mouth to this day blows me away.

"Hello, where have you been for so long?" As soon as the words left my lips, I was dumbfounded as to where those words had come from and why.

Before I could say anything, she replied somewhat nervously and as if she too recognized me from another time and place, "I don't know, but I'm here now and to do your touch up." She looked as shocked by her reply as mine. In that moment, our eyes met, and a glimpse of soul recognition took place.

I motioned to have her come in. "Would you like some coffee first?" I said.

She replied, "Yes, that would be great."

※ ※ ※

Janet Schwartz was the customer service rep for Lewis Homes. I had to have the trusses re-done on the house, and in doing so, it required paint repair. Also when they had built the house and done the painting on the inside, they had used two different lot numbers that didn't match. I couldn't see the difference, but Janet could when she inspected the house prior to my moving in.

Every couple of days thereafter, Janet would turn up in the morning before I went to work and after Shannon had left. With all the issues my house had, Janet was responsible to make sure everything got done properly. I'd invite her in, and we'd have coffee. We'd talk for an hour each time, and then I'd have to go to work, and she'd have to get back to business. We found out quickly how much we had in common. We were both from the East Coast. Janet was from Northern New Jersey just outside New York City. Although an only child, she was also adopted. Her parents had bought her on the black market for ten thousand dollars in 1948. We loved the same kind of music and had the same tastes in food and wine. We both adored Christmas and loved animals. While her parents were Jewish, they fully celebrated the December holidays—they always had a small Christmas tree and enjoyed Hanukah.

Janet used to live in Los Angeles during the same time I did. We discovered through our morning coffee discussions that we had frequented the same places and had even been both at the Greek Theatre the night Whitney Houston had debuted. It had been raining that night, and Whitney had on a long coat and high boots. She was amazing, and we both knew she'd be a superstar. Incredibly, Janet and her friends had been sitting just two rows up from me.

There was a twinkle coming from Janet, and I knew we would be great friends. I could feel we had a bond. She was so comfortable to be around; she was at ease with herself and made me at ease. It was effortless.

Eventually we came out to each other. We even discovered we had frequented the same gay bars in Los Angeles yet never knew each other there. One day she asked me if Shannon and I were happy, as Janet had a sense that we were not. I explained our history and that we were still struggling with those same issues. Janet told me her relationship was not good either with the gal she was living with.

Shannon and Kyle loved Janet, and as Shannon was too busy with the group from ATOM, she would constantly encourage me to do things with Janet.

Burning the Past

In the summer of 1995, Shannon and I were sitting in the living room of our house in Summerlin. Kyle was at a friend's house. I was having a melancholy day missing Mom and feeling alone, fearful, and stressed about my relationship with Shannon. The intrusion of our spiritual friends about our relationship was gaining momentum again, and I felt her pulling away a little each day. I was in total conflict with all of this, as it didn't go along with anything I believed or read in the teachings.

Shannon looked me in the eye and said, "Kim, I've talked to a couple of people, and we think you need to do an exercise where you burn your newspaper article about your abandonment and see all your insecurities going up in flames. You still have abandonment issues, and until you let go of that, you'll never heal. "

Shocked, I replied, "This article means a lot to me. Mom and I found it together. It's all I have left of my past and is the only baby picture of me." Then I began rambling on. "All I've ever wanted was a home and family. I have no parents anymore, Chip and I hardly speak, and you are pulling away again. Why are you letting others interfere with our life? Why don't you fight for us? Why don't you stand up for us? I keep getting conflicting signals from you and our supposed spiritual friends. I don't believe Sri Darwin really cares whom we love as long as we love. None of this makes sense to me. What does any of this have to do with my article?"

Shannon seemed a bit confused too but said, "If you want things to get better, you should burn the article and imagine all your fears and issues going up in flames with it." She looked away and went upstairs to work on her computer. I could see she was as upset as I was. Her friends had issues with Shannon's and my lesbian relationship, yet, somehow, they thought by my doing this burning ritual, I would become a better person. I didn't see the connection, but I was willing to do anything to keep my life with Shannon and Kyle intact. I was so confused and stressed out I wasn't thinking clearly.

I found the article tucked in my bed stand, grabbed a set of matches from Caesars Palace from a drawer in the kitchen, filled a bowl of water, and sadly sauntered out to the backyard patio.

Staring at my queen palm, I imagined for a moment I was in Hawaii watching a rainbow appear after a mid-morning sun shower on Kauai. *Will I ever live there?* I remembered the first time a few years back when Shannon and I had gone to Kauai and hooked up with Sri Darwin, who was visiting. He loved Hawaii and often would visit Kauai. He even worked with a local kahuna Serge Kahili King.

I'll never forget my reaction when I set my eyes on the Hawaiian Islands for the first time in this body. We came out of Lihue Airport where I gazed upon the Sleeping Giant hillside. My knees buckled, my arms got tingly with goose bumps, my eyes filled with tears, and my heart almost exploded as I found myself saying, "Oh my God, I know this place. I'm home."

I had no such feelings now in Summerlin as I lit the match and started to cry holding the article of the abandoned child, of me, over the bowl of water. I remembered the day Mom and I had found the article at the Rochester Public Library and how happy we had been to do that together.

Will this baby ever find peace? Will the burning of this article bring contentment? Will it keep Shannon and Kyle in my life? I tried to imagine all my fears of abandonment I'd felt throughout my life—from friends in school, agents, investors, managers, boyfriends, and now spiritual friends and lovers—burning up and evaporating. All I wanted was to feel good about myself, happy and free.

I lit the right side of the page by the words "Police Seek Identity." The word "Identity" ignited, and I almost blew it out. The tears were rolling down my cheeks. Tipping the paper sideways, I let the flames quickly roll across Nurse Ruth Lyon's head and then down over the infant's face drinking the bottle offered by her. I dropped it in the bowl of water as it engulfed the remaining paper within seconds. It was over, my only copy gone in a flash.

Lost and Found in Las Vegas

By 1996, the overwhelming intrusion of supposed friends in ATOM with their private agendas was too much for Shannon and me. Third time wasn't a charm. We were through. Still loving each other but realizing we could never live together as a couple, we parted on as good terms as we could. Our final separation was extremely difficult for Kyle.

My life was in such turmoil I didn't know who or what I was any longer. Abandoned by my spiritual friends, I found my core of belief enshrouded with betrayal and confusion. I no longer was asked to sing at the events, and I pulled away from the spiritual organization I had once loved. I didn't want to be anywhere near those who didn't believe in me. The only shreds of truth I had left in me were the actual teachings themselves and my connection to the inner master. Sri Darwin and I stayed connected, and from time to time, he'd write me.

I found myself digging through massive amounts of emotions to discern what was spiritual truth for me and what part humans had played in an attempt to destroy that truth. Desperately, I tried to find the golden thread again, but it remained elusive. My huge tract house echoed with loneliness. To me it was not a home but just a building made of stucco.

Meanwhile, my beloved Gabbie had gone over the Rainbow Bridge where all animals go when they pass. Shannon and I had rescued a little shih tzu and named her Kachina. After Shannon and I broke up, I bought a beautiful golden retriever puppy named Chelsea that Kachina adored. The dogs helped ground me, as did my business, but really, I was just going through the motions. I tended to the Avatar business, kept my clients and employees happy, paid my bills, and kept my dogs loved and fed. Anything else was a blur.

One night I was so depressed I found myself driving aimlessly around Las Vegas at eight at night weeping. I pulled into a strip mall that had a 7-11 and liquor store. I don't know where I was, only that I stopped the car and called Janet. I had one of those early, large, clunky, grey Analog cell phones.

She answered and heard my voice in panic. "Kim, where are you?"

I replied sobbing, "I don't know."

"Look at the street signs," she said, "and read them to me."

I did.

She gave me directions to the Fiesta Hotel and said she'd meet me in one of the bars.

We must have talked for two hours. I called her Jae. "Jae, I don't know who I am anymore. I can't find myself. I feel I've lost my voice, my heart, my music, and my soul for good." I had stopped singing and had put my guitar back in the closet again. "I miss my parents so much, and all that I believed in feels like a betrayal. My brother doesn't talk to me either. He doesn't accept me. I miss Kyle, and I'm afraid he will forget me. I've been in his life for twelve years since he was only five.

Jae was so kind, so sweet, so real. She replied holding my hand, "Kim, there is nothing wrong with you. You are hurt." Referring to the people in ATOM, Jae said, "Those people are not worth it. It is their loss not yours."

That is something Mom would have said to me.

"You were and are a good mother to Kyle, and he will always remember and love you. You need to let go of all of it and move on. It is time to heal. I will help you. I will take care of you. You will be okay. I promise."

❈ ❈ ❈ CHAPTER 20 ❈ ❈ ❈

My One and Only

After my break-up with Shannon in January 1996, I could tell she was hurting almost as badly as I. It was still obvious how much she loved me and how our karma was inches away from completion. After a few months, she realized what really had happened and the covert plan by her supposed friends to break us up, but it was too late. She made the decision to leave, and I stuck to my agreement that if she left for the third time I wouldn't take her back. I was trying to move on.

Disgusted with the whole lesbian thing, I began looking over my shoulder at men again and had a very brief fling with a man in our industry hoping he was Mr. Right. Jae was not happy about the brief encounter and was glad to see I ended the affair almost as quickly as I began it. As always, he really wasn't interested in me, just my body.

Still unsettled in my life, I received a call one afternoon from Marion, a gal I had worked with at the employment agency in Rochester before moving to California. She told me she was gay and was coming to Las Vegas with her girlfriend and very much wanted to see me. Shocked by both the phone call from the past and her disclosure of being gay, I told her I had been with women too and would love to see her.

She wasn't totally surprised by my admittance of living with a woman since I had shared my feelings for both men and women with her while back in Rochester when we'd gotten together for dinners.

I called Jae and asked if she and her partner would be my dinner guests, as I didn't want to see Marion and her girlfriend by myself, although I wasn't sure why. Her partner in her typical detached way said, "Janet, you go alone. I don't want to." Jae was actually thrilled to be with me alone, she told me later.

I found myself struggling with what to wear so I'd look good for Jae, although, again, I didn't know why. When she arrived, I opened the back door through the garage, and Jae stood there twinkling with a big smile on her face, the same smile she had had that first day she had arrived in her painter's overalls. This time, she was wearing a Hawaiian-print shirt, opened at the chest to just slightly show off her beautiful cleavage. She wore black pants, black cowboy boots, and some fabulous men's cologne. She was adorable. I told her how fabulous she looked, and she said I looked beautiful too.

Nervously she explained how she had kept changing shirts and didn't know why. I giggled and told her I had done the very same thing. Then I did something I've never done before: I handed her the keys to my new J30 Infiniti and said, "Here, you drive."

She smiled and said, "Okay, I'd love to." Jae has a lovely female and male energy about her. Many people do. She is very much a woman but has a tad of the masculine side to her in a beautifully balanced manner. She is one of those rare people who are peaceful in their own skin. That's one of the things I love about her. I felt safe and protected when I was with her. It was effortless. I hadn't felt that way in a very long time.

※ ※ ※

Janet had worked various jobs. In New York City, she had managed a health food store, managed a sporting goods store, worked for Lord and Taylor, and worked for her uncle in the rag business. She even drove a cab in New Jersey and was robbed at gunpoint.

In Los Angeles, she had driven tour buses back and forth between LA and Vegas, driven a school bus for years, and then became a supervisor in charge of routing all the bus drivers for LA Unified School District. When she hurt her back, she had to retire early and take her pension. She had a choice of taking a larger amount all at once or a smaller monthly check with life-long health insurance. She took the health insurance. My dad would have been proud of her.

While living in LA, she developed her own successful all-women painting business, called Painting by JB. Her slogan on the pink T-shirts her crew wore was "the best man for the job is a woman." Jae is also incredibly talented with color and design.

Her last few years in LA were living in Northridge. When the big earthquake hit there, it brought down Janet's rental house around her, but by pure luck or the angels watching over, she survived. She moved to Las Vegas shortly thereafter and got the job on the construction site where I bought my first house.

Jae always loved kids and was searching for the same things I was—a family and marriage.

※ ※ ※

While driving to the Sands Hotel with Jae to meet up with Marion, I felt a strange, exciting feeling mounting in my core. There I was letting my best friend drive my new baby. I knew she was falling for me, yet she was respecting my need to heal. I was a bit confused by my feelings, as I didn't want anything to hurt this beautiful friendship, so I stuffed them down deep.

It was the last night for the Sands Hotel before they were to implode it. Everything was on sale. It was sad to see it go. Such history. During cocktails at the Sands, Marion and I reminisced about the days when we had worked together in Rochester. We'd go out to dinner and have long talks about life and love. I'd share with her my dilemma of having feelings for both men and women, talk about my spiritual quest, overall philosophy, unanswered questions about life, death, UFOs, and tell of my love of singing.

Then Marion leaned over the table and said to me, "Kim, I have to tell you something. I needed to find you. I knew you lived in Vegas. You had such a profound impact on my life and made such an impression on me. I never forgot you. You really helped me in so many ways."

I didn't know what to say about that, so I just listened. But others have made the same comment to me over the years. Some have told me how just knowing me changed their life, how I gave them a new sense of hope, or how my voice helped them when I sang. Strangers would come up to me after my performances and say my singing gave them a sense of peace or that they bought my cassette, *A Love for All Life*, and it helped them get through a divorce or illness. I'd get letters from people who had tracked down my address with similar stories of how I had impacted their lives in a positive way. Could it be this is why I was here again? Is it for the animals and to be available in some way to these people? Sri Darwin seemed to think so. I do feel I'm in some way a conduit for Divine Spirit. I don't question it anymore. I just let it be.

We had a great evening with Marion and her girlfriend. After dinner, we went to a local country gay bar, and while standing up at the bar counter, I remember moving closer to Jae and pushing my back into her. She wrapped her arms around me and tugged me closer to her chest. It felt so good. It felt right. It felt effortless and safe. It felt like home. I turned around, and we gazed into each other's eyes. Suddenly I felt as if a veil was lifted and I was seeing sunshine for the first time in years. Jae's blue eyes twinkled like stars in the night. The love that emanated from her was so thick I could have melted into it, into her—and I wanted to. I was tingly all over and was conscious of a stirring in my gut I hadn't felt since the first time I knew I was falling for Shannon. This was different, though. With Shannon, it felt like lust; with Maggie, it was a need to be loved and cared for; but with Jae, it felt like old love, someone I had found again. In time, the love attraction with Jae grew out of friendship, trust, unconditional love, and patience.

When Jae and I arrived back home, we came into the house and walked into the kitchen. Kachina and Chelsea greeted us with waggy tails and lots of kisses.

Jae leaned against the island counter in the middle of the kitchen. I was facing her. She pulled me close, and our eyes studied each other. I remember feeling my life was about to change again and would finally have meaning and peace. Then we leaned in and kissed for the first time since I had opened up that door on that hot summer morning and felt I knew her from before. I felt as if my prince had slipped on my missing glass slipper and it fit perfectly. The kiss I will never forget. Our mouths melted into one long, luxurious, wet, passionate moment. It was filled with hope, love, security, patience, and intimacy, an intimacy I'd never felt before. My best friend was about to become my lover. We talked about our friendship and of my concern that if we shifted into lovers, could and would it destroy us? Jae assured me it wouldn't and that our foundation of unconditional friendship would be our foundation for life. I believed her, and it has been. We also decided we would not consummate our relationship until she moved out from her partner.

Once Jae announced to her partner she was leaving, Jae and I spent the most amazing evening together. The love that radiated between us was indescribable. She took me from a lost, lonely, confused woman to a secure, loved, solid human being. For the first time in my life, I felt I had found my soul mate. From that day forward, I never looked over my shoulder again. I was finally home with my sexuality.

Bringing My Music Back

Jae's father was a professional pianist and had his own band for years when he was younger. Jae adored music and was instrumental in getting me to pull that blasted guitar out of the closet again and sing.

In December, I had the opportunity to do a gig at the theater in the Debbie Reynolds Hotel in Las Vegas with a pianist named Mike. He and I were the opening act for the play, *A Christmas Carol*. This was opening night of a three-night stint. Mike had beautifully arranged three Christmas songs in his electric piano with full orchestra, and we were to sing harmony together. The music would be played out from the theater's sound system. In addition to the songs I'd sing with Mike, I was to do two solos, one on my guitar singing an original song I had written in honor of Park City, Utah, and the other was singing "Merry Christmas, Darling," a Carpenters' song to Mike's arrangement. This was the first time since England when I had performed with the Ivy Benson group that I would be on a stage of this magnitude. I was terrified.

I started to feel that familiar upset colon again and spent the hour before I had to go on in the bathroom with diarrhea. I was so nervous and fearful that I'd forget my lyrics or my voice would quiver. I kept asking myself why, why after all these years of performing in clubs, did I still have this fear and trepidation? I'd look into the mirror in the bathroom when I was alone and talk to myself out loud. "Kim, what is wrong? What do you fear? Why can't you just get over this crap? Stop it. Just stop it!" The harder I tried to analyze it, the more upset I got.

Janet was behind stage with me before I went on. She whispered, "Kim, just focus on the song. Remember, sing like a bird."

I hugged her.

When the emcee announced us, Mike and I walked out together. There were probably two hundred people in the audience. All my friends were there. All I could see were the first and second rows, but the theater felt huge. The sound system was fantastic. I was shaking and terrified; I didn't want to screw it up in front of my friends.

We opened with "Chestnuts Roasting on an Open Fire," and harmonized beautifully. It brought back memories of me singing with Richard Bennet, the Aussie in England. The crowd loved it.

Then we went into my solo, "Merry Christmas, Darling." I closed my eyes and remembered everything Dr. Tappen had told me, "Just focus on the music, Kim." This song was always one of Mom's and my favorites. When I lived in California, I'd call her up on the phone at Christmas time and sing it to her. Now, when I started to sing the lyrics, "Merry Christmas Darling/We're apart that's true/But I can dream and in my dreams/I'm Christmasing with you," I thought of Mom and Dad and all the wonderful Christmases I'd had with them. My voice started to quiver, but I could hear Mom saying to me, *Sing like a bird, Kim.* When I finished, the crowd went wild, and everyone stood up applauding and whistling.

Janet, who was sitting in the sound booth in the back, said when I started singing the words "Merry Christmas, Darling," a gentlemen sitting down front gasped with joy and said, "Wow," and you could hear a pin drop.

I thought all was good until I picked up my Martin D-35 to play the Park City song alone on stage in the spotlight. *Holy shit.* As I strapped on the guitar and stepped up to the microphone, my stomach started to hurt, and I felt my colon gnawing at me again. My hands were sweating. I started playing the riff on the guitar and then opened my mouth to sing. The first verse came out fine, and then it happened. I forgot the lyrics to my own song. I sang the first verse twice, forgot the second, sang the last verse next, and the third verse last.

All my immediate friends and Mike knew the song and knew I blew it. No one else noticed. I kept going like a pro and ended the tune in a big way. The applause was great, and I received a standing ovation. I bowed, left the stage, and ran into Mike backstage.

I was so pissed with myself for screwing up my own song, my own lyrics. Why did this happen to me? My mind had gone blank. It didn't matter to me that Barbra Streisand has to have monitors on when she performs, as the same thing happens to her. I didn't want it to keep happening to me. Mike tried to calm me down. Janet came back stage and tried to calm me down. Nothing worked. I was mortified and fed up. I promised myself I wouldn't let it happen again, so I created a cheat sheet stuck to my guitar where no one could see it but me when I was playing for the remaining two nights.

Janet said, "Kim, you are expecting perfection from yourself all the time. You always beat yourself up when you do something wrong or something you feel isn't up to par with what you set. You can't keep doing that to yourself. So what? You forgot your lyrics. Lots of artists do. Don't you remember when we went to see Wynonna Judd at the MGM and she forgot her lyrics to her own songs?"

I answered, "Yeah, I know, but I'm tired of it."

Janet replied, "Kim, they loved you. You sounded beautiful. You got a standing ovation. You and Mike were great. Focus on that."

Janet and I packed up my guitar and started out the back door of the theater. Before I exited, I stopped and peeked into the back stage area. I could hear the dialogue of Ebenezer Scrooge from center stage. I love that play.

Pausing, I reflected on the best parts of the evening's performance. I closed my eyes and saw the rainbow of seven colors dancing off each musical note and could hear our vocal harmonies echoing in my ears. While I can't see the colors of the rainbow with my physical eyes, my mind holds them strong, and my ears still hear the harmonies. I could hear the roar of the applause and knew that Divine Spirit did use us to move the audience. That was all that mattered, really. I smiled. It shouldn't be about my ego forgetting the lyrics or how that made me feel. It was and has always been about the outflow to all living creatures. That is why I've always sung to the birds, frogs, dogs, cats, and people. Awareness flowed through my body of peace and tranquility, like the answers to so many of my questions finally beginning to make sense to me. My frustration dissolved, and I followed Janet out the door to our Isuzu Trooper waiting for us in the parking lot.

Mauied on Maui

In December of 1996, Janet proposed marriage to me. Yep, on her hands and knees no less. "Will you be my one and only?" Of course I accepted. Experiencing a real true engagement period was just like an MGM movie and how I had envisioned it all my life. She moved in with me about four months after that. Then and only then did my empty cold stucco house finally become a home.

The biggest challenge was being introduced to her closest friends who serve as her family—Dan, Nancy, Tara, Adam, and Nushka. She's known them since she was five years old. Janet's parents had passed away a very long time ago, and she had no siblings. Thank God I was accepted and they loved me as they do her. They became my family as well. In fact, from the start, it felt as if they've always been in my life. The unconditional love and support is so strong it causes my heart to expand with every year they are in my life.

I had turned Janet onto Hawaii, and on our first trip there together, she fell in love with the islands. So when we set our wedding date for October 19, 1997, naturally, we chose the ceremony to take place on the island of Maui at Poipu Beach.

We rented a condo there, and on the day of the wedding, an hour before leaving for the ceremony, Janet and I stood on the lanai with a glass of champagne in our hands, looking into each other's eyes. I said, "Jae, you are the love of my life. I have no doubts. I know this is it. I adore you. I will always love you. I no longer look over my shoulder. You saved me, *mahalo* [thank you in Hawaiian] for loving me. I only wish Mom and Dad could have known you."

Kissing my lips, she replied, "I wish my parents could have known you too. I adore you and will always be by your side. Soon you will be my wife. Now let's go get married."

The ceremony was beyond beautiful. Janet and I wrote our own ceremony while a gay woman minister added the required expressions to make it official. (Well not totally. Hawaii had recently passed a law legalizing gay marriage and then overturned it just before we married in 1997.) Janet wore a flowered Hawaiian shirt of blue, green, white, and black with hibiscus flowers on it, black shorts, and sandals. A white tuberose lei was draped around her neck. I wore a Hawaiian sleeveless dress that complemented her shirt, and I too wore a white tuberose lei gently draped in the traditional Hawaiian fashion around my neck. The rings that we exchanged were her mother's and father's thick gold bands with diamonds set elegantly throughout the band.

Our vows touched on several points—accepting each other for who we are, having patience during challenging times, supporting each other through illness, personal goals, and dreams, and most important, allowing each other the space to grow individually.

❈ ❈ ❈

For years Janet and I prospered. I asked her to join Avatar after Barbara retired from the business since Janet had skills I didn't have but the company needed. With two employees, Janet and I could have the same vacation time off. Our life was wonderful. Twice a year, every six months, we visited Hawaii and stayed for seventeen days. We always took our laptops and worked from wherever we were.

Janet was instrumental in bringing the music back into my life. With help from a friend, we built a little recording studio in the garage.

I was a lousy engineer and couldn't play the piano or read music well, so it took me months to record the instrumental backings for my songs, pecking away at each note on the keyboards. Oh how I loved singing to the tracks, creating the strings and brass sections to my songs. My whole body would tingle with divine energy. It brought back the beautiful memories of Stu and me in Boston and Los Angeles laying down the tracks to his gorgeous arrangements. I was singing, creating, and outflowing again. That's all that mattered. Life was good.

Janet, left, *and Kim,* right, *in marriage ceremony on Maui, October 19, 1997.*

❈ ❈ ❈ CHAPTER 21 ❈ ❈ ❈

DOWNERS

Chip

I had looked up to Chip in so many ways and had such fond memories of when we were kids. After all, he was my big brother. When I was little, he'd watch over me. If kids bothered me or threatened me, he'd come to my rescue. Being almost seven years my senior made it tough, though, to have the kind of closeness I wanted with my brother. When I was going through my preteen and teen years, he was mostly out of the house, then was on his own, and wasn't around much.

Unfortunately, after several attempts to have the kind of meaningful relationship I wanted with Chip, I realized it just wasn't meant to be. We tried. We both did. I don't fully understand what the issues are, other than we simply do not resonate on the same plane. I think about him from time to time and always inwardly send him Divine Love and blessings.

Breast Cancer

Every year I got mammograms, and every year the radiologist had a hard time viewing them due to my dense breasts. What they thought looked suspicious always turned out to be watery cysts. For this reason, they recommended I see a breast specialist. It was then that I found a renowned—and gorgeous—breast surgeon in Vegas who could have passed as Celine Dion's older sister. Dr. Josette Spotts wanted to see me every six months, regardless of whether it was time for my annual mammogram. Each time she ended up having to aspirate watery cysts and then sent me on my way with a clean bill of health.

In 2003, a week before my forty-ninth birthday, the mammogram had gone as before. The radiologist's report was normal. I also had my biannual standard appointment with Dr. Spotts to go over the films and to do her normal exam.

Jae, who usually accompanied me on these appointments, was reading cooking magazines as we waited for Dr. Spotts. The nurse called us in.

Dr. Spotts entered the room looking radiant as always. "Hello, Kim and Janet. How are you?"

"We're great, thank you. How are you?" I replied with a big smile. I was perched on top of the exam table gently kicking my legs to and fro while Jae sat with legs crossed in a chair in the corner.

Dr. Spotts put the films up on the lighted wall screen reviewing them carefully, no real change in her expression.

I blurted out, "The radiologist said the report was all normal."

She replied, "Okay, looks good, but let's have a feel."

Her nurse assistant came in. She laid me back onto the table, opened up my gown, and began the physical breast exam using her hands as she always did. First she did the right breast, and all was fine. Then she commenced squeezing the left breast and feeling around. Suddenly I felt a sharp pain and winced. She looked at me and then at the nurse standing next to me on my right. Taking my right hand, she moved it over to the left breast and placed it on the outside area saying, "Can you feel this?"

I replied nervously, "Yes. What is it?" I couldn't see Jae's expression, as I was fixated on Dr. Spotts's change in facial expression and her obvious sudden concern.

Dr. Spotts glanced at the nurse with a serious expression and said, "Go get the ultrasound." Then to me, she said, "Kim, this is a lump, and we need a closer look."

The nurse brought in the familiar machine, which had always found watery, non-worrisome cysts before. They look like black round circles on the ultrasound screen, and when you watch them aspirate, they shrink into nothingness. I knew what they looked like. I wanted to see that again.

Putting the gel on the device, Dr. Spotts slowly moved it around my left breast until she found the lump. My head cocked around as far right as I could turn it to observe the procedure on the ultrasound machine's screen. It was not a black round circle of liquid; it was most definitely a round brownish/beige (to me) colored, dense, ugly blob.

I watched the expression on Dr. Spotts's face turn to concern as her eyes glanced at the nurse. Following her gaze, I noticed the expression on the nurse's face as well change to concern. I lifted my head slightly to look over at Jae, who looked stonefaced in the chair in the small room.

Then I heard the words I didn't want to hear, "We need to get this biopsied immediately so we know what we are dealing with. It may not be malignant, but we need to know. I'm going to schedule the biopsy for next week."

Jae and I left the building in silence and walked to my dream car, a bright-blue 325i convertible BMW, which I had just bought but now no longer felt so exciting. We sat in the car with the top down for forty-five minutes trying to process Dr. Spotts's words.

Then Jae drove us home, as she usually did. We talked about how it could be nothing and that we shouldn't get upset. I kept telling Jae that the cyst looked totally different and the expression on Dr. Spotts's face was not good. Jae didn't want to worry me, but she knew it probably wasn't going to be good news.

⊠ ⊠ ⊠

It was the longest week waiting for the biopsy and then waiting for the results. My birthday came and went without fanfare. Always on my birthday, I think of the day Mom died. It never changes year after year.

The day we drove back to Dr. Spotts's office for the results, I felt I was in a slow-motion movie. Janet had our family back East—Dan,

Nancy, and the gang—rooting for us. And our Avatar family knew, but we'd told no one else. We were keeping it quiet for now.

The nurse called us into the little room. We waited for what seemed felt like an eternity. Jae sat in the chair staring at me sitting on the table with my clothes on. I was kicking my feet up and down in a nervous motion.

Dr. Spotts entered the room looking as always radiant and stoic. In that second as she walked in, I wondered how doctors deal with telling bad news to patients they've grown to care about. Do they prepare for it? Is it second nature?

She didn't mince words. "It's a cancer."

My immediate reaction was wanting to dash from the room, buy a ticket to Hawaii, and disappear into the night. Instead I replied, "No. Are you sure?"

"Yes," Dr. Spotts replied, "it is a stage I, invasive estrogen positive cancer."

I went numb. *What does that mean?*

The expression on Jae's face was surreal, as if a new role was to begin in her life. A role she didn't want to play again. At age seventeen, Jae had lost her mother to a long drawn-out cancer. Seeing me suddenly shut down, Jae came alive and took charge.

Dr. Spotts started rambling on about a recommendation for an oncologist, a sentinel node biopsy that had to be done to remove some lymph nodes to make sure there was no lymph invasion, clean margins, radiation, and the dreaded word "chemotherapy."

I was in a daze-like state until I heard "chemotherapy." My head perked up, and I immediately came back to life saying, "No way. I'm not putting that poison in my body." Jae tried to calm me down. I got emotional and fired back, "I'm in the natural products industry. I know what that does to you. Isn't there any other way?"

Dr. Spotts proceeded to explain to us the various modalities with treating breast cancer and the statistics behind each. With an invasive cancer, you want to throw all you can at it. She kept telling me the good news was we caught it early.

I said, "Dr. Spotts, how could the mammogram have missed that when it was so obvious on the ultrasound?"

She replied, "With dense breasts, that can happen, and mammograms are not 100 percent accurate. Were you not doing your own breast exams, Kim?"

I thought to myself, *Not as often as I should have.* The lump was obvious to me when Dr. Spotts put my hand on it. I said, "I guess I haven't been doing it as often or as thoroughly as I should have. Dr. Spotts, I'm so grateful to you for catching this."

She kept talking, and I was missing half of what she said. All I could hear was the word "chemotherapy." It terrified me on every level. Then I heard her say, "You will be scheduled in one week to do the sentinel node biopsy. We will know more about what we are dealing with then."

Dr. Spotts gave us the name of a highly recommended oncologist, Dr. Michael, who ran the cancer center in Green Valley. She recommended we set up an appointment immediately.

As Jae and I walked out of Dr. Spotts's office, I saw several women sitting nervously in the waiting room reading *People* magazine, *Vogue*, and various breast health publications. I moved quickly so they wouldn't see the terror on my face. Jae and I said nothing as we hit the elevator button and waited to be transported to the lobby.

I remember feeling the sun on my face as we walked to my beautiful new BMW. I leaned over the stick shift and cried in Janet's arms. She held me tight.

"We will get through this, babe," Jae told me. "We will. You will be okay. We will get two other opinions. We will make sure the protocol is correct. Don't worry. I will take care of everything."

"I don't want chemo, Jae. I'm afraid it will weaken my body in some other way. I'm terrified of it, and I'll lose all my hair too. I've heard so many horrible things about it. Is there no other way?"

In the softest, most assuring way, she replied, "Honey, we will make sure we get all the right information so we can make the best decision for you. Don't worry."

❈ ❈ ❈

The day of the sentinel node biopsy, I had a screaming headache. Janet sat by my side in the hospital and asked the nurse if they could please give me something for the excruciating pain. The nurse injected some wonderful drug to help dull the pain.

Dr. Spotts came to chat with us before taking me in reminding us that while I was under they would do two major procedures: one, to clean the margins around where the tumor was and, two, to remove a few lymph nodes and test them for cancer while I was under. If they were invaded, she would remove many more nodes, and I'd wake up with a nasty drainage system tucked under my arm. If they were clean, I wouldn't. I remember thinking as they wheeled me into surgery, *Please God, angels who watch over us, and great beings, please let me wake up with no tubes under my armpit.* Just before they put me out, I said what I always say when I have to have some kind of surgery. I looked up into the eyes of the anesthesiologist and nurses and said, "Thank you for taking such good care of me."

After the surgery, Dr. Spotts came out and talked to Jae. "Janet, the surgery went well, and I feel I got good clean margins, but it is for sure cancer. The good news is there was no lymph invasion."

Janet was relieved.

When I woke up in recovery, the first slurry words out of my mouth to the nurse hovering over me were, "Is there a tube there?"

She said, "No, honey, there isn't. You are fine. Now rest."

※ ※ ※

Dan and Nancy had a contact at Memorial Sloan Kettering Cancer Center in New York City, so we sent my records there for review and to get another opinion. Janet and I also made an appointment with a woman oncologist at Cedars-Sinai Medical Center in Los Angeles who was recommended to us as well. We drove from Las Vegas to Los Angeles for the appointment. Both sources came back with the same protocol, as did the Las Vegas oncologist Dr. Michael. I would need four sessions of heavy chemo, followed by seven weeks of localized radiation five days a week. I did not need any type of mastectomy. The protocol was clear—throw the arsenal at it and cure it.

※ ※ ※

Dr. Robert Milne was a highly gifted and recognized medical doctor in Las Vegas who also believed in alternative medicine in conjunction with Western medicine. He was our primary physician. Even he told me to do the chemo. "Kim, I will put you on an alternative protocol while you are undergoing the chemo and radiation treatment. This will keep you healthier and help offset the side effects on your body from the chemo,"

Jae added, "Honey, all that I have read and all that we have heard do justify the use of chemo. You really need to embrace it. I want you to think of it as little Pac-Men eating up the bad cells. You love that game. Just visualize it; you can do it."

The entire protocol would take six long months from the first chemo treatment till the end of radiation. I was told my hair would begin to fall out after the first chemo treatment and I would stop my period forever by the second treatment.

We alerted my hairdresser, Michael, to get ready to cut off my hair, as I didn't want to go through the agonizing experience of clumps falling out daily. The protocol would start right after Expo West in Anaheim in March 2003, and we scheduled the chemo treatments on Fridays to allow me the weekend to recover in the hope I could work on Monday. The chemo center was located five minutes from our house. Janet went with me almost every time. It was very hard for me to see women in the later stages of treatment, as they showed me how I was going to look soon. Some ladies wanted to talk constantly about what they were going through, but I didn't. Still in shock, I just needed to get through it. I didn't want to focus on it, didn't want to go to support groups, and didn't want to add attention to it. My belief always has been "energy flows where attention goes." That is, what you give energy to will manifest more.

The first treatment was terrifying. I wasn't sure what I was going to feel like afterwards as some women said they didn't get real sick and others got very ill. I have always been sensitive to drugs of any kind. Painkillers usually knock me out, and the only ones I can tolerate are the common over-the-counter varieties—aspirin, ibuprofen, and acetaminophen.

Janet sat next to me, brought me snacks, earphones, and Hawaiian music to listen to. The nurse who administered the chemo was very kind and gentle. I sat in a comfortable chair, and she administered the solution in my right arm since the surgery and lump were on the left.

The chemo was red and had a sweet berry smell to it. When the nurse inserted the needle and began the flow of pink liquid, I immediately noticed a weird metallic taste in my mouth.

Janet told me to close my eyes and envision little Pac-Men eating up all the bad cells. I tried. I really did. But I was so frightened thinking, *There is no turning back. I can't run away. Oh please, help me handle this. I can do it. I'm strong!* Still, I kept envisioning the Pacific Ocean and Hawaii.

On the way home after my first treatment, I noticed I didn't feel so bad. Maybe all I'd heard wasn't true, at least for me. While resting on the couch watching TV, I heard a knock on the door. Janet opened it, and there stood Dan and Nancy. They had been at their second home in Park City, Utah, skiing and had driven six hours to Vegas just to be with us and give us moral support. I can't tell you how happy that made both of us feel. Janet had known they were coming but wanted it to be a surprise for me. Such powerful feelings of love, kindness, and support came over me. This was my new family, my real family now. Oh, how I love them both. In Hawaiian we call this *hanai ohana*, or extended family or adopted family. There is a wonderful saying, "friends are the family we choose for ourselves."

On the second day after my first chemo treatment, I started to get sick. Real sick. My body couldn't tolerate it. By the second treatment, I threw up almost immediately after the infusion and continued on and off for hours until having the dry heaves. Chelsea, my golden retriever, stayed by my side licking my face to comfort me and lying on the floor beside the toilet. I was cold all the time. Janet bought me scarves in various colors for my head to warm me, as well as cover my balding head.

I lost my healthy appetite for most foods, as they didn't taste the same. Needing to drink lots of water, I found I couldn't without putting fresh lemon juice and ice into it. Worried about my red blood count staying at healthy levels, Janet fed me lots of steak and baked potatoes; those seemed to go down well. That was pretty much my diet, plus puttanesca pasta from the local Italian restaurant. I no longer could tolerate anything that remotely smelled or tasted like berries. That included Paradise ice tea. Just a whiff and I'd start gagging. It was too similar to the drug in the chemo. It would be four years until I could eat berries or drink Paradise ice tea again.

Our goal was to keep me on track with my treatments and not have to stop due to lowered red or white blood cells. Having previously bought tickets for a seventeen-day trip to the Big Island of Hawaii in July 2003, nothing was going to stop us from getting on that plane. Nothing! *Keep your eye on the prize*, I'd say to myself.

By treatment number three, I was gagging just at the sight of the building as we drove up. Once I was dropped off, I rushed into the building and started throwing up in the elevator. On one of my visits, I ran from the elevator through the chemo room to the bathroom, and just as I opened up the door, I vomited. So humiliating.

As the fourth and last chemo treatment approached, I resisted. I'd had enough. The chemo made me so ill that I felt as if I had entered the dark night of soul from the liquid surging through my veins. Depressed, I couldn't find my spiritual spark. The battle between good Pac-Men fighting off the evil cancer took a toll on this warrior, and on the day of my last treatment, I told Janet, "I'm not going. I can't take it anymore."

"Yes, you are. You are almost done. You have to go. You can do it," Jae said abruptly.

"No, I can't. I just can't," I argued. I was so emotionally spent I couldn't see how much this had also affected my beloved caregiver.

Cleary pissed off, Jae replied, "Yes, you are going. Get up and get in the car now!"

I could see she was upset and worn out. With my head down, I obeyed and sauntered to the car.

After my fourth treatment in May of 2003, Jae and I looked at each other and said, "Okay, we are done. Now on to radiation for seven weeks."

For the Love of Jae and Her Danny Boy

Jae sat me down one evening and told me she needed to go to Danny's party. He was turning sixty in June of 2003, and they were having a huge party back in New Jersey; everyone was flying in from all over the country. Jae needed to go, to take a break from all the stress. Her nerves were frayed along with her emotions. More than anything, she needed to be by her closest friends/family. Dan was like a big brother to Jae; their parents even knew each other, all coming from small Northern New Jersey townships.

She wanted me to go and had carefully planned it all out. We'd leave right after my radiation treatment on Friday on an overnight flight arriving Saturday at seven in the morning. Tara, Dan and Nancy's daughter, would pick us up at the Newark airport, and we'd stay with her at her house so we could rest up. Then covertly, she'd sneak us into Dan and Nancy's house in the late afternoon. No one knew we were coming except Tara. We'd fly back on Monday and be home in plenty of time for my next radiation treatment.

It all sounded doable.

I still had no hair, I was weak and thin, and my skin was a greyish tone. Through it all, I hadn't missed one day of work. We had set up a cot in my office for me to rest if needed. The natural supplements did help, along with the hydrogen peroxide drips I received from Dr. Milne a couple of days after each chemo treatment to revitalize me.

But compared to chemo, radiation was a walk in the park. I was not having any negative side effects from the radiation. The entire time I was having treatments, I had not gotten the flu or a cold, which commonly happens. I attribute keeping my immune system up to all the natural products I was taking in-between the chemo and the infallible care by Janet and Dr. Milne.

Jae told me she would take every precaution to keep me safe, warm, and healthy. At first I was terrified about the idea of traveling, but then I knew not only was it imperative that Janet go, but it would do me good too. I looked bad, but nobody would care.

"Okay," I said.

※ ※ ※

As we stealthily drove to Dan and Nancy's house the afternoon of the party, I remember gazing out into the miles of beautiful green wooded acres surrounding the highway. Northern New Jersey is so gorgeous with all the trees and woods. It reminds me of Pittsford,

New York, where I grew up. As we were traveling through Jefferson Township, I started reciting out load that famous poem my father made up and said every time he'd hit a golf ball into the woods, "Trees and leaves, leaves and trees, woodsy, woodsy, woodsy." Janet knew the poem, and we all laughed hysterically. It was the first time we had laughed in over five months.

Jae and I snuck into the house and made sure the few family members who had arrived earlier that day stayed quiet in the living room when they saw us appear. Still, they all gasped when they saw us walk through the dining room towards Dan and Nancy's bedroom door. No one expected us to be there. Dan and Nance were tucked away in their bedroom getting ready for the big event.

Jae and I stood outside their bedroom door as she called the house phone from her cell.

Dan recognized her number, picked up the phone, and said, "Hey, Schwartz."

Jae replied, "Happy birthday, Dan. Hope you guys have a great party. So sorry we can't make it. You know we would be there if we could."

He replied, "I know you would."

Before he could get another word out, Jae knocked on the door.

Dan said, "Hang on, Schwartz; someone's at my door."

Jae replied, "Okay, go answer it. I'll hang on."

Danny proceeded to open the bedroom door in his underwear, and the moment he saw Jae, he let go of the door handle in shock as it closed in her face. He opened it again, and this time, he saw me standing by her side, both of us with elated smiles on our faces.

"Happy birthday, Dan," we said in unison.

His eyes opened as big as saucers. Laughing, he yelled, "No way. No way. Nance, come here. It's Schwartz and Kimmy." He kept gasping and laughing as tears welled up in his eyes. He couldn't believe it.

Nancy had just stepped out of the shower and was dripping wet. She couldn't hear Dan's words, only noise from him. "What Dan?"

"You won't believe this. It's Schwartz and Kimmy."

Nancy still couldn't hear anything he was saying. She threw a towel around her petite body and ran to the door. Sounding a little annoyed with Dan's ranting, she said again, "Dan, what is it?" At that moment the door was wide open, and she saw us both standing there. Her arms rising high into the air and the towel almost falling off, she gasped, "Oh my God, I can't believe it. It's Kimmy and Jae."

We all hugged, cried a little, and Janet said to her closest and oldest friends, "We wouldn't have missed it."

Follow-up

Since 2003, I've been cancer free. A year doesn't go by that I don't get a little apprehensive each time my annual mammogram, blood work, and bilateral breast MRI come due. I know in my heart it is over, but the nervousness is there every time I'm waiting for the "all clear." I find this is very common with many others who have gone through a similar experience.

The main thing always to remember is not to give it much thought or energy. Acknowledge the emotion, and then be done with it. Move on. Don't dwell on it.

❈ ❈ ❈ CHAPTER 22 ❈ ❈ ❈

LIFE IS TOO PRECIOUS

"Kim, you are cancer free. You are cured. I don't say that always, but I'm sure of it." So said my oncologist, Dr. Michael in July 2003. And five days later, as his words repeated in Jae's and my heads, we sat in a plane pushing back from the gate at McCarran International Airport in Las Vegas. We were on our way to Kailua Kona on the Big Island of Hawaii for another seventeen-day vacation.

My body was tired from the previous seven arduous months of fear, stress, shots, tests, treatments, and inner turmoil. I was totally bald, and my skin looked dull and greyish. But my spirit was overflowing with happiness, and my smile beamed with joy. I was going to Hawaii.

❈ ❈ ❈

One morning while Janet was still sleeping, I got up to go outside and listen to the Hawaiian mourning doves. I took a yellow pad of paper and sat on the grass overlooking the ocean. Closing my eyes, I thanked God, the angels, and the great beings who watch over us for saving my life and giving me another chance. I realized in that moment that life is short, is precious, and can change in a heartbeat. Although Jae and I had talked of moving someday to Hawaii, I no longer wanted to wait so long. I asked them please to show me a way to manifest how Jae and I could move now, not five or ten years from now, to the islands.

As I began my contemplation, I started to sing the Hu quietly, as I didn't want to wake Janet or anyone else in the condos.

Every time I'd sing the Hu around animals or birds, I would notice their reaction. Animals would come closer or, if they were sleeping, oftentimes wake up. Birds would stop singing for a moment and then start again singing back to me. Dogs that were agitated would become calm. One time when I was in Florida visiting Mom, she took me to an alligator farm. I pushed my body up against the fence where over forty of them were sound asleep, one on top of the other. I started to sing the Hu at them. It was amazing. They started to stir, and their bodies began to move. Mom asked me what I was doing. I told her I was talking to them and sending them love. While she may not have totally understood it all, she knew this was my religion, not the dogma of a church, and always supported me in my spiritual path, as it gave me a sense of happiness and oneness with my God.

I must have sat in contemplation for about fifteen minutes. Then I saw it, that blue star shining between my inner brows, and heard that celestial sound of violins again. Keeping my breath steady, I could hear the doves in the background, mixed with a faint sound of the violins. A gentle trade wind came up, and I felt it whisk across my face. The sun was creeping around the front of a fan palm and covered my face with light. I could feel its healing rays enter every cell of my body and felt it was put there for a purpose to heal me.

About five minutes later, I found myself writing on the pad their answers for how Janet and I could make our move to Hawaii now.

1. You need to manifest three new clients. The income from them will be put into an Avatar saving account exclusively to pay for the move.
2. You need to sell both houses, the one you live in and the one you work out of. The sales of both of these houses will help with the down payment of the new house and for the move.
3. You need to sell the two acres of land in Bryce Woodland in southern Utah. [We had bought the land with the idea of someday building a cabin on it.]

4. You need to find a house to buy in which you will live and conduct work for Avatar. It will need a totally separate area for the business so as not to interfere with your living space. It will need a separate entrance for an employee to come and go. It will need to be ready to move in and not require any build out.

5. Due to the Hawaii laws on keeping rabies out of the state, you will have to prepare the dogs for immediate release, a six-month process, and not make any mistakes in doing so, so they don't have to go into quarantine.

When Janet woke up, I made her 100 percent Kona coffee with a little half-and-half, just as she likes it, and asked her to come outside with me as I had the solution on how to make our dream move to Hawaii work. I showed her the list and the process I went through. "Honey, I feel life is too short to put off doing what we want. Why are we waiting to make our dream come true? The ten-year plan won't work. The five-year plan won't work. Let's make our dream come true now. We can manifest this; I know we can," I said with confidence.

"Kim, this is a lot to manifest, but I don't want to wait either. I only have one thing to say: If we do this, I will not live in a dump."

"Fair enough. Let's start today looking at houses and doing the necessary research," I replied.

With a new focus in our lives, we set out to make our dream come true. At that very moment, I remembered the postcard my mother had sent to me when I was young and she and Dad were in Hawaii on vacation, the one with a photo of a humpback whale breaching out of the water and Mom's words on the back, "Another GD beautiful day in paradise." It was the day after viewing that postcard that I got the calling to live in Hawaii and knew it was home to me.

※ ※ ※

We returned to Vegas empty-handed, unable to find an affordable place to house both Avatar and us that wasn't a dump. I found myself depressed, but we weren't done. While in Kona, we'd met two lesbians, Sharon and Nancy. They'd been together for over thirty years. We became friends immediately, and they said they'd be on the lookout for houses for us as well.

About one week after we returned from Hawaii, the Avatar phone rang. It was Sharon. She said they had found our house in the paper. It was perfect but was a hundred thousand dollars more than we wanted to spend. After doing a walk-through with the owner, Ed, they took fifty photos and emailed them to Janet.

It was in downtown Kona at five hundred feet above sea level and three minutes to town and the ocean. The lot was 8,583 square feet, had over thirty palm trees, and my very own twin queen palms. It had 1,500 square feet downstairs to house Avatar with a covered lanai and a private entrance and 1,700 square feet upstairs with a 300-square-foot, covered lanai for us. It even had an ocean view, koi pond, and pool. Sweet! We flew back to Kona, closed the deal, and told ourselves we would manifest all else that was on that list.

And we did just that.

The Big Move

I had my fiftieth birthday bash in our empty house in Vegas in January 2004. Everyone came—the New Jersey clan, friends from Los Angeles and Vegas, and even some clients of Avatar's. The celebration was three-fold—for my birthday, for my being cancer free, and for our big move to paradise.

My brother had no idea I had had breast cancer or that I was moving to Hawaii, as we were still not communicating. Bud and Earl were thrilled by our decision to move. I knew Mom and Dad were in heaven smiling down as well.

Janet had been in charge of the coordination and logistics of moving the house and office. I was in charge of getting the animals, Chelsea and Kachina, ready for the immediate release through the quarantine center in Honolulu and then on to the inner island flight with me. I was also in charge of all matters regarding the sale of all properties and purchase of the new house in Kona.

We shipped the BMW over first so Janet would have a vehicle upon her arrival one week ahead of mine. Her job was to get the office ready so we could be up and running immediately. Phone and cable had to be finalized and turned on. Sharon and Nancy were kind enough to pick up the Beemer for her in advance. The Trooper was the last vehicle shipped just before I left.

❈ ❈ ❈

I had coordinated my exit of the house with the new owner who had bought much of my furniture, including my noble fir I had raised as a baby in a pot in the living room that now stood nine feet tall.

February 13, the night before I left Las Vegas, I sat in the backyard on the steps of the hot tub gazing up at the stars thinking about my life, my loves, my losses, Mom, Dad, and my brother. Thinking about my last twelve years in Vegas, I felt happy that Shannon and I remained friends, that I stayed connected to Kyle, that Maggie and I remained friends.

Looking at the night sky took me back to an extraordinary experience a few years before. I had just finished cleaning up the dishes from dinner when a sudden urge to go out into the patio overcame me. Feeling compelled to look up into the night sky, I saw to my surprise a huge diamond-shaped machine hovering very close to the roof. It was beautiful with just four blinking lights of various colors located at each corner of the diamond. No sound came from it.

After realizing what it was, I ran into the house and yelled for Janet to come quickly. I grabbed her by the arm, rushed out the front door, and caught it coming over our roof into the front yard. After she took in what was happening and what we were seeing, it dashed away over the Red Rock Mountains.

My thoughts moved to more recent events. Even after replaying the last year of my diagnosis, treatment process, the emotions, fears, and anxieties that came with it all, I reflected how so much of what I'd asked for over the years had been given to me. I sent a huge wave of love and appreciation to all of the doctors, nurses, and friends who had stood by us and helped me through that dark night of the soul and to keep my eye on my true desires at all times, Hawaii. I had made it; I was almost home.

Then I smiled when I recalled the day Janet had rung my bell and changed my life forever, and a warm sensation traveled through my heart chakra.

※ ※ ※

The Lincoln Town Car picked up Jean (our employee who was helping me with the move), Chelsea, Kachina, and me around four thirty in the morning. It was going to be a very long day for the girls. I had copies of all the paperwork taped to the inside of their kennels, as well as the originals with me.

At the airport, as I pushed their kennels up to the United Airlines counter, I pulled out the necessary travel documents for them. United then required I remove the dogs from the kennels while they checked for bombs within them. This was the new protocol since 9/11.

Chelsea got very excited when I removed her. She thought she was free and pushed her sweet golden retriever face into my neck licking me. My heart sank, as I knew she didn't want to go back into the kennel. I reassured her it would be okay and in a short time we'd all be reunited as a family and that Jae was waiting for us across the pond. "It's okay, sweetie. Mommy loves you. We will see Janet soon. Be patient. We will be to your new home soon," I whispered to her as I closed the door to her kennel. I kissed her nose through the grate door and sang a few notes of her favorite lullaby.

Kachina had that familiar look on her face, very much like the one she had the day Shannon and I brought her home from the pet store in Flagstaff. Her overbite was protruding and her expression seemed to say, "Make my day." She was tough, and I told her to take care of Chelsea and that we would be together soon. Providing numerous kisses, I gently placed her back in the kennel. Watching the crates slowly move down the conveyor belt into the abyss of McCarran International Airport brought back the memories of moving Gigi and Tiger to England. I knew my kids would be okay but felt sad that they had to go through this scary and uncomfortable experience.

In the background, the sounds of the slot machines were ringing, even at five in the morning. Don't people ever sleep in this city?

Jean and I had to fly to Los Angeles to change planes. As we boarded the plane in Vegas, I didn't look back. I did what I always do, pat the plane with one hand as I embark through the door, say a quick blessing, and take my seat. As the plane started down the runway, I began to feel exhilarated and filled with wonder.

Throughout the flight, my main concern was making sure the dogs were with me all the way and that they were okay. At the gate in Los Angeles, the crew was gathered waiting to board. I walked up to the captain and introduced myself. "Captain, sir, my name is Kim Driggs, and I'm moving to Kona on the Big Island today. I have my two children with me, two dogs, Chelsea and Kachina. Can you please make sure the temperature is controlled for them down below and that they are okay? And can you kindly verify they are on the plane with me? We just flew in from Las Vegas."

He smiled, tipped his hat, and said, "Certainly, Ms. Driggs."

While I was seated on the plane, I heard the flight attendant say, "Flight attendants, close doors and cross check." Just then a woman flight attendant approached and handed me two little orange cards. One read, "Hi, I'm Chelsea, and I'm flying on this flight." The other read, "Hi, I'm Kachina, and I'm flying on this flight." She smiled at me, and it was then I started to relax.

❊ ❊ ❊

Sharon and Nancy picked us up in their big white van that normally held their two Great Danes, Dolly and Puden. They were so excited to see us, and the first thing out of their mouths giggling was, "Yeah right, the five-year plan."

At our house, workers were well underway unloading the container with Janet supervising every step. The entire upstairs and downstairs lanais were filled with boxes. All of Avatar was downstairs, and all personal items upstairs. Janet ran over to greet us, and the minute the girls saw Jae, they started wiggling and panting with delight.

I attached their leashes and let them hop out of the crates for the first time in twelve hours. Then I opened the front gate and walked them into their new backyard. As I removed the leashes, both Chelsea and Kachina bounded off by the pool, up the rock steps, to the back of the property, and by the shed smelling every inch of the ground and peeing everywhere to mark it theirs. Tails wagging and tongues hanging from their mouths, they had never looked so happy. Nuzzling each other in acknowledgment of their survival of the ordeal, they clearly relished having a piece of property so big to call their own. They were home, and so was I.

The Rainbow Bridge

One year into living in paradise, we lost Chelsea to cancer. Losing an animal, which is a child to you, is beyond words. Dr. Beth, the vet, said, "First, I will administer the shot to relax her. Then, I will administer the other that will stop her heart. There will be no pain. She will go to sleep." Oh, how many times I've heard those words. Gigi, Tiger, Nicki, Gabbie, Sly Boy, Rosie, Max, and now Chelsea. I hate those words, yet it is the most humane and respectful way to die. Why can't they have those two wonderful shots for humans? It isn't fair.

Almost immediately after the first shot entered her vein, Chelsea's eyes closed, and her entire body relaxed to a state of no movement. My hands were still holding her head. Jae and I kissed her, and Dr. Beth pushed the last syringe into her vein while the tears rolled down her face. Within ten seconds, we could feel the life leaving her sweet body. I started to sing to her the best I could through sobbing. I asked Prajapati, the master of the animal kingdom, to help her as she passed over the Rainbow Bridge. Dr. Beth and the technician were crying as well.

Dr. Beth took her stethoscope and listened for Chelsea's heartbeat. She looked at us and said, choking back tears, "She's gone now in peace."

I whispered in Chelsea's ear, "Go over the Rainbow Bridge now, sweetie." But I wanted to scream—I couldn't leave her. I didn't know how to say good-bye. These sweet creatures enter our life and wrap a string of lights around our heart that never stops glowing, even when they are gone. The unconditional love they bestow upon us is more than any human or spiritual love I've ever known. It's different. It just is!

Jae and I looked at each other, speechless. Chelsea had been my savior during chemo and sat next to me when I hugged that toilet throwing up incessantly. She'd lick my face and lie next to me on the couch never leaving my side. Janet had her own things she needed to say to Chelsea; I didn't want to leave the room, but I forced myself to do so.

I wanted to run from the vet's but, instead, walked briskly to the front desk where they told me I could pay another day. If I hadn't had my spiritual beliefs and answers I found regarding life after death, this would have been even harder on me, but knowing what I know now gives me more peace.

The Rainbow Bridge
Author Unknown

Just this side of heaven is a place called Rainbow Bridge. When an animal dies that has been especially close to someone here, that pet goes to Rainbow Bridge. There are meadows and hills for all of our special friends, so they can run and play together. There is plenty of food, water, and sunshine, and our friends are warm and comfortable.

All the animals that had been ill and old are restored to health and vigor; those that were hurt or maimed are made whole and strong again, just as we remember them in our dreams of days and times gone by. The animals are happy and content, except for one small thing; they each miss someone very special to them, who had to be left behind.

They all run and play together, but the day comes when one suddenly stops and looks into the distance. His bright eyes are intent; his eager body quivers. Suddenly he begins to run from the group, flying over the green grass, his legs carrying him faster and faster.

You have been spotted, and when you and your special friend finally meet, you cling together in joyous reunion, never to be parted again. The happy kisses rain upon your face, your hands again caress the beloved head, and you look once more into the trusting eyes of your pet, so long gone from your life but never absent from your heart.

Then you cross Rainbow Bridge together.

Our Hanai Ohana Grows

After Chelsea passed away, it was obvious we needed a companion for Kachina, who was heartbroken, and so were we. This is when Emma Nani, a purebred black English Labrador retriever and my animal soul mate, entered my life. *Nani* means "beautiful" in Hawaiian.

I've always known Emma, and she and I have a remarkable spiritual connection. This became verified one day eight years later when I had a phone session with a recommended pet psychic. Pam told me that Emma spoke to her inwardly and told her that she has known me before in another time and place. She added that Emma said when she is no longer on this physical plane she will wait for me on the other side because I am her forever soul mate. This astounded me and confirmed my original feelings of her when we met for the first time. Emma and I are connected in a way that I can't explain. It simply takes my breath away.

In September 2008, we lost our beloved Kachina to dementia. Both Janet and I were crushed, as was Emma, who was now three years old. We had to see another child go over the Rainbow Bridge. This was a hard one, as she was with us almost fifteen years. She was our pride and joy. Oh how I loved that sweet little soul.

TO THOSE I LOVE AND THOSE WHO LOVE ME
Author Unknown

When I am gone, release me. Let me go.
I have so many things to see and do.
You mustn't tie yourself to me with tears.
Be happy that we had so many years.

I gave you my love. You can only guess
How much you gave me in happiness.
I thank you for the love you each have shown,
But now it's time I traveled on alone.

So grieve a while for me, if grieve you must;
Then let your grief be comforted by trust.
It's only for a while that we must part,
So bless the memories within your heart.

I won't be far away, for life goes on.
So if you need me, call and I will come.
Though you can't see or touch me, I'll be near
With all my love around you, soft and clear.

And then, when you must come this way alone,
I'll greet you with a smile and say, "Welcome
Home."

In October, we found a little boy shih tzu to be the brother for a grieving Emma, Janet, and me. Makonu Noa (Mak) was born August 2, 2008, and became the newest member of our hanai ohana. Emma now paying it forward would become his momma, and he our new son.

Our family now complete again, Janet and I continued on our Hawaiian journey learning how to scuba dive and volunteering annually for the Hawaiian Islands Humpback Whale National Marine Sanctuary. Every year the last Saturday of January, February, and

March we partake in the Sanctuary Ocean Count project. This offers the community a chance to monitor whales from the shores of Hawaii Island, Kauai, Maui, and Oahu. The whale count, as we call it, helps bring real-time data to the number of whales that come back every year. It has brought us such joy, and we have learned so much about the migration of these gentle giants who swim from Alaska to the warm Hawaiian waters, where annually many birth their babies and find new mates.

❋ ❋ ❋

But our family was not quite complete. We had others to add.

Newlyweds Karly and Matt had moved from Montana to Kona in late 2009. Matt, a handsome, kind, gentle man works as a finished carpenter and supervisor building multi-million dollar homes and resorts on the Big Island and neighbor islands in Hawaii. Karly, his wife, is a stunning five feet seven inches tall with long naturally blond hair and is as gorgeous inside as she is outside.

We met them when we hired Karly as our administrative assistant after their arrival. The four of us bonded immediately: They felt like our own children, and they felt similarly, as if we were their parents. We knew these wonderful young people would be in our lives forever, even after Karly was offered a better job opportunity and we encouraged her to take it.

Early in 2010, Karly called us announcing in shock she was pregnant. She and Matt were not ready for a child. She had never missed a day on the pill, but this soul wanted in. Janet and I helped them through the difficult process to prepare for a life-altering change. Then in September 2010, Hailie Lynn was born, the newest member of our hanai ohana. Friends are the family we choose for ourselves.

Their first stop on the way home from Kona Community Hospital was our house where Karly and daughter were in the back seat and droopy-eyed Matt was behind the wheel. What a sight to behold. Even though exhausted and in pain from sutures from the cesarean, Karly radiated a beautiful new glow. The baby was amazing and looked just like Matt. We were the first ones outside the hospital community to see her.

Standing in the driveway and leaning into their car, we gazed into the barely opened eyes of this child of the rainbow. Janet looked at me, and we both knew our lives were about to change for the better. In that moment, I realized that there was another hole inside me that had remained empty since moving to my beloved Hawaii. Jae and I had often talked about how, if we had met each other when we were younger, we could have adopted a child. Now, this child would more than fill that gaping hole.

As Matt put the car in gear to drive his family home, Karly's words struck me and will ring in my memory forever, "Hailie, look, this is your Auntie Kim and Auntie Jae. They will be with you and in your life now forever. This is your family. Can you hear the dogs barking? They're Emma and Mak. They will be your dogs too." Choked up, Jae and I kissed Hailie and Karly's forehead and leaned in to kiss a frightened daddy Matt good-bye.

Hand in hand, Jae and I walked back into the house and sat down in silence staring at each other. I know we were both thinking how our life would be changing.

I said, "Did you see her eyes? She is a child of the rainbow. I'm so excited."

Jae responded, "Yep. This is going to be amazing. We get to be with her every step of her life. Sweet."

And it has been—amazing and sweet. As Karly had said, our dogs became Hailie's dogs, and they wholeheartedly returned the love she lavished on them. At two, Hailie talked constantly and always referred to Janet and me as her aunts. One day, we drove Hailie to the playground. Upon getting out of her car seat and commencing walking through the parking lot, she took my hand and said, "Auntie Kim, I la lu." Janet came around the corner of the car to reach out for Hailie's other hand, and out from her mouth came "Auntie Jae, I la lu." With both of us walking through the parking lot, we lifted her high into the air bringing her back down on the pavement. She giggled, "Do it again, Auntie Kim and Jae."

Janet sat on the picnic table taking photos and videos with her iPhone while I climbed on the jungle gym and slides with Hailie.

"Auntie, come here; climb with me," she yelled to me.

I happily accommodated her. All the other moms, aunties, and grandmas at the park smiled at me, as it must have been obvious we were new enthusiastic aunties. I watched how good she was with other children, kind and helpful.

On to the slide, Hailie went. "Auntie, climb with me. Slide now," she said.

I wasn't so sure. The massive, towering slide went through a hidden tunnel section. *What might be hidden in there?* When I was a little bit older than Hailie, I was sliding into a kiddie pool. As I went down, I wrapped my arms around the slide. My flesh caught on a screw, and it ripped my arm open to expose the muscle hanging down bleeding. Feeling very protective of Hailie, I looked wide-eyed and frightened at Janet. *What if I can't see her in the section that is covered?*

Janet motioned and yelled, "It's okay. Go ahead, Kim. She's waiting."

Hailie running in front of me athletically assaulted the ladder up to the top of the big slide and said, "Come, Auntie Kim."

I replied, "Right behind ya, buddy." I got to the top, and she had already launched herself into the dark tube. Luckily, the tube was large enough to hold me if I lay back. I cautiously launched myself, only to have the sickening memory of my slide into the kiddie pool shoot into my head. Shaking off that image, I slid down the abyss to the light at the end of the tunnel. Glad to be out and into the bright Hawaiian sunlight, I could hear the next child right behind me screaming all the way, but I couldn't find Hailie. I started to panic. I looked everywhere and looked back at Jae.

She was shaking her head back and forth smiling and pointing, "Over there," she said laughingly.

Hailie had immediately run about twenty feet away to the teeter-totter swing yelling, "Auntie Kim, Auntie Kim, hurry."

Climbing onto the teeter-totter and showing her how to hold on and push off lasted only thirty seconds, as she hopped off sending me to the dirt. Running to the area of the playground meant clearly for older children, she jumped into the air several times to try to grab the metal bars that were too high to reach.

"Hailie, wait for me," I yelled as I ran to meet up with her.

She was reaching as high as she could into the air. "Auntie, Auntie," she yelled. Clearly she wanted me to hoist her up to the bars, which were five feet off the ground.

"Okay, Hailie, now grab on tight; don't let go. I'll hold you."

Determined, this tiny athletic child grabbed the metal bars while I loosely held her in place giving her the sense of freedom, as if she was hanging by herself, yet ready to grab her if she let go. Looking back over my shoulder for a moment to see if Jae could see what this kid was attempting, I saw Jae had repositioned herself on another table in the playground and was videoing the whole thing.

Hailie was holding on so tight I could see she was strong. Letting go of her, I kept my arms in position underneath her. "Hailie, look you are doing it all by yourself. You are hanging by yourself."

She beamed.

I put my arms around her and said, "Ready to get down now?"

"Yes, Auntie".

As Hailie and I walked hand in hand back to where Jae was sitting, I recalled Karly saying to Jae and me, "I am so happy that you are not only in our lives but also in Hailie's. She can learn so much from you. You are our family. We look forward to years of birthdays, holidays, and recitals with you both." I remembered, too, the day Karly told me something Hailie said that just blew our minds. Karly and Matt had to explain to Hailie that her best friend, Isla, was moving to the mainland and, while Hailie would miss her friend, Isla would always be in Hailie's heart. Hailie understood that and put her hand to her heart and said, "Momma, Isla is in my heart, but Auntie Jae and Auntie Kim are in my heart too."

When we got back to Jae waiting for us with all the other parents, aunties, and grandparents, I said, "Hey, how about going to Petco to learn about the animals?"

Hailie said, "Peco, yeah, let's go."

Jae put her back in her car seat, and off we went to Peco singing "The Wheels on the Bus."

The joy and love that rushed through my body and soul was indescribable. The love of a child is the most amazing and fulfilling experience. It is allowing me to pay it forward and to give her all the joy, love, lessons, and wisdom that I received from my parents.

That includes sharing my love of the big holiday. On Christmas Eve, the three always come for a family dinner at our house, and then on Christmas morning, we go to their house for present openings and brunch. The Christmas of 2013 after all the gifts were opened, Karly reached over and pulled Hailie close to her. "Hailie, what is Christmas all about?"

Three-year-old Hailie bowed her head slightly and in the most loving voice whispered, "Love and family."

I said, "What, Hailie?"

She replied again louder, "Christmas is love and family."

All the adults looked at each other at once, and I knew that if it were possible we'd all melt into a puddle of liquid love right there on the carpet in their living room.

When we were ready to leave, Hailie came up to Jae and me providing multiple hugs and kisses and said, "Thank you, Auntie Jae and Auntie Kim. I la lu." Even though she can now properly say "love you," our family ritual is always to say "la lu."

❊ ❊ ❊

A few weeks before in early December, Jae and I had picked Hailie up at preschool. At three years old, she had graduated to the middle room. She was having dinner with us that evening as her mom and dad wanted to have a date night.

After an afternoon of doing puzzles, reading, and watching Mickey Mouse, we had dinner together at the table as always. Then it was bath time for forty-five minutes with light-up toys in the tub and Emma keeping watch over Hailie. Clean and dried off, we stuffed Hailie into her Doc McStuffins PJ's and watched a Berenstain Bears DVD.

When Karly and Matt arrived to pick her up, she was still watching Berenstain Bears on our bed with Emma and Mak by her side. After a few minutes of visiting, the family headed to the front door to leave.

As we walked, Hailie and I played our special game where we make up a song adding new lyrics each time we see one another. It's all about bears and buffaloes because the game started one day when we picked her up from preschool and she was talking about bears and buffalos.

"Bears and buffalos sitting in a tree," Hailie sang.

"Bears and buffalos sitting in your ear," I added.

Giggling, Hailie sang back, "Bears and buffalos sitting on the couch."

"Bears and buffalos sitting at the table."

And so we continued. As Janet, Matt, and Karly were going out the front door giving their good-byes, hugs, and la lu's, Hailie was still in the kitchen hugging me good-bye. "Goodnight, sweet princess," I said to her. "Dream of bears and buffalos."

Hailie paused, stared deep into my eyes, and replied, "No, Auntie Kim, I'm going to dream of rainbows."

Finally

Janet and I decided to make some magic for ourselves. Since the state of New York had passed a law in July 2011 to allow same-sex marriage, we decided after being together for seventeen years and having to be on the East Coast in October for a trade show that we'd get legally married in New York City.

Dan and Nancy were delighted as were all our hanai ohana in Hawaii. Uncle Bud and Earl had passed away by now, and Chip and I were still not talking to one another.

We asked a wonderful gay rabbi to perform the ceremony. Rabbi Shai was a spiritual man and interviewed both Janet and me prior to our getting married. I told him about my spiritual path over the years and that I had read the Kabbala and how my feelings of God and Divine Spirit were all about the temple within. He knew exactly what I was talking about. He was the perfect person to do our ceremony.

Janet and I were married on the West Side in the apartment of Rabbi Shai and his lover. Dan, Nancy, Tara, Adam, and his wife, Jane, were present the day we pledged our lives again to each other. Neighbor and good friend Sylvia, who performs hula beautifully, had made a CD of her dancing on her lanai to a gorgeous Hawaiian song as a surprise to open up our ceremony. She, Chuck, Mary Jane, and Larry, our other close friends, were watching the ceremony on their iPad from the kitchen of Sylvia and Chuck's house in Kona.

Rabbi Shai asked Janet and me to share why we wanted to marry each other. He then performed the most beautiful spiritual ceremony. I cried through the whole thing, just as I had in Maui in 1997, only this time it was for real. Janet had that incredible smile she gets when she is beaming with happiness. I could see Dan and Nancy tearing up as well during the entire ceremony. They've known Jae almost forever, and all they ever wanted was for her to find the right person and be happy. She had, and they knew it. To have that acknowledged after all these years by the state of New York, giving us the same rights they have, just put the icing on the cake.

Nancy read our *ketubah* out loud before she, Dan, and the rabbi signed it. In ancient times, a ketubah was a special type of Jewish prenuptial agreement. Our ketubah included a painting of two palm trees entwined on a beach overlooking an ocean.

Nancy read these words:

> On the first day of the week, the fourth day of Tisheri, in the year 5772, which corresponds to the second day of October in the year 2011, in New York, New York, the partners, Kimberly Driggs and Janet Schwartz, joined each other before family and friends to enter into the mutual covenant of marriage, and with love and compassion each vowed to the other: "Who would I be without you? Without you, I stand on my own. But with you, I stand tall, I have confidence, and I am assured. Without you, I merely exist. But with you, my life has meaning, my years have joy, and my days have happiness. Without you, I am a good person. But with you, I am special, I am inspired, and I am better than I knew I could be. I did not know I could love this deeply and now, I do not know how not to. I cannot express how much I love you with just simple words. You are the sun in my days and the moon in my darkest nights. You are the brightness in my universe. You are beauty itself. I believe in you, I trust in you, and I have faith that you will always be there for me. You are my champion, you are my counselor,

and you are my friend. I pledge myself to you today and all of my tomorrows. I will be with you through times of joy and times of sorrow. I will try to always be understanding and forgiving. You are always in my thoughts and my dreams. My commitment to you and yours to me bind us together and seal this document.

❊ ❊ ❊

While here on this Earth in this body, I discovered the choice I have been given— to accept and embrace what makes me who I am or to abandon that truth by choosing to live out the rest of my days and nights as though I weren't me at all. It's that simple. And it's that complicated.

Janet, left, *and Kim,* right, *legally married by Rabbi Shai,* center, *in New York City on October 2, 2011.*

Hailie and Kim, 2012.

CHAPTER 23

Filling the Last Holes

My Guitar

Soon after Jae and I moved to Hawaii, we become dear friends with Sylvia and Chuck, animals lovers up the street from us, who have two beautiful golden retrievers, Ted and Stella, along with two sweet cats.

Growing up, Sylvia was classically trained on the piano. One day, she and I decided to try playing and singing together. We both fell in love with the process. Getting together a couple of times a month allowed us to build up quite a repertoire of show tunes, Christmas songs, ballads, and standards. We would sing for friends at dinner parties at their house, which everyone loved. I was back. Well, my voice was back.

Sylvia would beg me to pick up my guitar and start playing again, but every time I tried, my hands were slow, they would hurt with a little arthritis, and the guitar felt uncomfortable. With no calluses, it was just too painful both physically and emotionally. I felt I had lost it. Without my guitar, I felt part of me was missing, as if there was a big hole inside me, and I just couldn't face it.

Jae had tried for years to get me to start playing again.

Every New Year's, I'd make a resolution, "Honey, this year I'm going to start playing my guitar again."

Jae would say, "Yeah, I'll believe it when I see it."

As the years went by, the guitars continued to sit alone and abandoned in the closet.

Then in early August 2013 while I was writing this book, it hit me. I'm a fraud. How could I talk about being a singer and playing the guitar if I wasn't playing it, at least for my own pleasure? Not that I wanted to be a professional entertainer anymore. I didn't have any desire to perform in front of crowds, although I would love to make music in the studio.

My not playing haunted me daily, woke me up at that bewitched hour of one in the morning for months. I had to play my guitar again. I felt this pull like never before. It was like the loss of an old love.

Finally, one day in the middle of August, I pulled out my 1995 Limited Edition, signed, and numbered Martin D-35 Dreadnought. I hadn't touched it in years. I tried to play it. *What's this?* I thought. *It's too big now. I can't wrap my arms around it comfortably. Also the sound doesn't seem right. Out of tune. What's wrong with it?* I took it to the local music shop, and they attempted to fix the issue by adjusting the neck. No good. It still sounded out of tune. I tried new strings. Still no good. I called Martin and found out I had never registered it so it wasn't under warranty. *Crap.* They gave me the name of a registered Martin repairman who miraculously was here on the Big Island one and a half hours away. I called him, and we made an appointment.

Dennis Lake was able to repair it, but it was just too big for me. I put it up on Craigslist and found a buyer on Maui. That left me with my 1985 Limited Edition Ovation. I had to be focused, had to try. *Don't give up,* I told myself. *Don't have ego.*

Every day I'd practice in my little writing room. My fingers almost bled, and my voice was not up to par due to growing older. But vog made it worse. Vog (combining "volcanic" and "fog") is a form of air pollution that results when sulfur dioxide and other gases and particles emitted by an erupting volcano, such as Kilauea on Hawaii, react with oxygen and moisture in the presence of sunlight. Vog is hard on the vocal cords, eyes, and people with asthma on those heavier days when the wind brings it up the western side of the Big Island.

In the meantime, my calluses were back, my hands were getting used to the neck of the guitar again, and the clumsiness in moving from chord to chord was getting replaced with more precision. I was starting to find myself, coming alive again. When I'd play and sing my old tunes Stu had arranged for me when I was living with Maggie, I'd close my eyes and feel totally at peace and happy again. I could feel Divine Spirit rushing through my veins filled with love and joy. I knew I had to have a new guitar to make this process complete.

One Saturday afternoon after rehearsing for an hour and a half, I walked upstairs and said to Janet, "Jae, I've decided to buy a new guitar. Dennis, the Martin repairman, turned me on to a place on Staten Island called Mandolin Brothers. You should see their online virtual tour. It's like guitar heaven, hundreds of guitars lining the walls. Since we'll be back in New Jersey the end of September for the show, can we go?"

Jae perked up and said, "Absolutely. Staten Island is forty-five minutes from Tara's house. Kim, I'm so excited. Are you going to get another Martin?"

I replied, "Well, I'm open to it, but I'm also open to any other guitar that speaks to me. We'll have to see. It has to be smaller, something I can get my arms around. I've been told I will most likely have to give up the big sound my Dreadnought made for a smaller guitar, but being able to play it is the key, right?"

Jae nodded her head and said, "Yes."

❊ ❊ ❊

I emailed Stan, the owner of Mandolin Brothers, and his son, Eric, that I would be arriving on September 22 at 10:00 a.m. when they opened. Then I spent weeks researching guitars online.

On the appointed day, Janet and I parked the car and walked into an old house at the given address on Staten Island. The door opened into a tiny administrative office.

"Oh, I'm sorry. Did we come in the wrong door?" I said in embarrassment.

The young gal sitting in front of a computer screen replied sweetly, "Nope. You are in the right place. Just keep walking forward, and you'll enter the showroom."

As we walked in, our eyes gazed upon literally hundreds of guitars of all makes hanging from the walls. There were many rooms in the house, and each room represented a different cost and quality of instruments. There was the $500-$1,000 room, $1,000-$1,800 room, $1,800-$3,000 room, $3,000-$6,000 room, and so on. In one of the rooms, I saw a vintage $60,000 Martin hanging on the wall. Also displayed were mandolins, banjos, and electric guitars. I thought I had died and gone to guitar heaven.

Stan and Eric were there and greeted Janet and me as we entered. "Aloha" we both said as we shook their hands.

I had let them know I couldn't spend more than $3,000 on a guitar. Eric brought me everything from a $1,800 Martin to a $2,800 Martin to a Taylor guitar. I always kept going back to the Martins, but still not the right one spoke to me. Then Eric brought me a custom guitar Stan had designed for Martin to produce. I fell in love with it. There I was playing and singing softly in a guitar shop as I used to. Janet was taking a video on her iPhone and posting it to Facebook. She was beaming, and I was so happy. I felt like the old Kim again when I was young and in love with my music.

Then I saw Stan whisper something in Eric's ear, and Eric disappeared into one of the other rooms out of sight where the special, more expensive guitars were. Eric reappeared holding the most exquisite smaller guitar. He said, "Kim, try this. It's an OOO-18 Golden Era 1937."

My eyes got huge as did Janet's, and I replied, "Oh wow! That is gorgeous. Look, it's a sunburst."

Janet sitting a few feet away on a stool said, "Oh, Kim, that's awesome."

I hit a chord, and it rang out with this huge round sound, so close to my D-35 I almost fell off the stool. "Oh my God, why is the sound so huge for this little guitar?" I asked.

Stan peered around the corner from the other room smiling. "That is due to the Adirondack spruce top and mahogany back sides. The Adirondack wood gives a nice big sound," he said with pride.

I couldn't stop playing it. That little sunburst spoke to me, grabbed my very core, and wrapped its ever-loving strings around my heart. This was it, my new baby. I started to play and sing a bit louder. Janet was crying a little on her stool, as she hadn't seen that side of me in twenty years. We had been there for only one and a half hours, and

I had found my new baby. It cost $3,600 list, but they sold it to me for $3,100 and gave me a brand new state-of-the-art Martin case and one of their T-shirts, which I proudly wore home on the plane.

As I was handing my credit card to Eric, a beautiful memory cascaded through my brain and into my heart—the day Mom and I bought my first Kent acoustic guitar from The Music Lovers Shoppe in Pittsford with the strings too high off the neck. I felt the same exhilaration and joy, as if this was my first time. I could even feel Mom looking down on me with happiness that I had found my way back home to my music.

I shook both Eric's and Stan's hands and thanked them so much for all the time and effort they had spent with me to help me find my new baby. I picked up the beautiful case with my guitar safely tucked inside, and while Janet and I started out the door of Mandolin Brothers, I looked back and enthusiastically said, "Mahalo and aloha."

The Rainbow

Prior to flying to the East Coast and buying my new guitar, I was playing my Ovation, practicing in my writing room. My eyes were closed. The colors of the rainbow appeared, and then it happened. Lyrics started coming; chords started playing. I grabbed a yellow legal pad and started writing furiously. Lyrics, chords, the story, it all spilled out; I couldn't stop. It kept flowing.

> I've been chasing rainbows, year after year,
> Searching for the answers, and fighting back the tears.
> Can't see all the colors with my eyes open.
> All I see are shades, which make me feel broken.
> Will they all accept me if I come out true?
> Will my purity of heart be enough for you?

There it was, the first verse. Then came the second verse, the bridge; the third and fourth followed. Within fifteen minutes, the song was done. It was rough, but it was basically done. I had to record it. I had to find my way back into the recording studio, for this song was my life's story.

I called up to Janet to come down. She listened. As I played, the room filled with divine love. Her eyes wept with joy. I hadn't written a song since 1998 when I'd composed a lullaby for Sarah Rose, a newborn baby of our friends Marty and Leslie.

The Article

My life was complete—I had my music, my guitar, my voice, my spiritual answers, my Janet, my children both human and four-legged, and my beloved hanai ohana, family and friends whom I had chosen. I was complete. Or was I?

No, I'm not. I don't have my article anymore.

I had to find the article.

I decided to contact the Rochester Public Library and see if they could locate it. Had too many years gone by since 1954? I dialed the number. "Hello, this is Kim Driggs. I'm needing to talk to someone about finding an article from January 1954."

The woman said, "Let me connect you."

A minute later, a serious man picked up the phone and said, "Hello, my name is Robert Scheffel. How may I help you?"

I explained to him who I was, the article I was looking for, and the date would be somewhere between January 20 and 30, 1954.

With no real emotion, he replied, "You need to pay in advance fifteen dollars for the fee. Then I can start the process to see if we have records that go that far back. I'm not sure."

"Oh, Mr. Scheffel," I said, "I can't thank you enough. I'll put the check in the mail today and call you next week."

All week I worried whether he'd be able to find my beloved article. Then a week later before I could call him, the phone rang in my office,

"Ms. Driggs," Mr. Scheffel said, "I have located your article and will be emailing it to you. It is a bit damaged due to the old microfilm, but most of it is readable. What is your email address?"

I couldn't believe my ears. Elated, I gave him my email and waited anxiously by the computer continuing to hit "Get Mail" until I saw it arrive in my inbox. There it was, a PDF of the original article. I printed it, ran with it into Janet's office, and showed it to her.

She had never seen it and was quite moved by the story. I walked into my writing room and sat quietly reading it over and over again, staring at the photo of me being fed a bottle by this kind nurse who no longer is alive to read this story. I remembered the day Mom and I found it for the first time. It still amazes me that I was the child they adopted after reading the article in the paper that morning in 1954.

The Recording

A little more than a year after getting my Golden Era guitar, I walked into Lava Tracks Recording Studio in Waimea. Grammy Award winning producer/musician Charles Michael Brotman greeted me with a tantalizing smile. It was the first time I'd been in a professional recording studio since the 1980s, and it felt like home.

The twenty-four-track board and Apple computers dominated the control booth. Hundreds of wires protruded from behind the huge mixing board. I set up in the main studio behind two microphones, one for my voice and one for the guitar.

Jae watched through a large glass window from the control room.

I was nervous, and my voice was not in great shape that day, despite hot tea and lemon attempts to soothe it. Even with the singing I did from time to time with Sylvia, my voice went through rough stages. The speech therapist in England had told me after the vocal cord strip not to do anything where I used my voice often because my sensitive vocal cords couldn't take it. How could I avoid talking? I continued my work at Avatar that required talking all the time. Also I have allergies with lots of phlegm that play havoc with my voice. Yet, there were also days when my voice was absolutely perfect. While my range has gotten lower and I can't hit the high As anymore, who cares? It's all about outflowing to all living creatures.

Today we were laying down the guitar tracks for "I Found the Rainbow" and a rough vocal track to use as a baseline for the other musicians who would be brought in. Like riding a bike after a long absence, all involved in the recording came back to me. It was effortless. Strumming to the click track. Punching in when a do-over was needed. Charles was amazed at how consistent I was after so many years. I was in heaven.

Two weeks later, I returned to the studio to work with a live drummer, Michael. He was a gem. Janet and I watched through that glass window while he finished the set-up of his drums in the main studio. Michael listened to my song a couple of times, and it was as if he had connected inwardly with me a week prior when I had been lying on my bed imagining the future session with him and thinking what the drums should do in each section.

As we sat back and listened to Charles turn the prerecorded guitar track and rough vocal on, we could see Michael focusing hard on the song as he listened to the tracts in his head sets. Then he got serious and started to play, and the magic began. It was perfect. We only had one change. He was one with the rainbow and me.

After Karl, the pianist, laid down the piano and strings two weeks after that, it was time for my final vocal performance and harmonies. Before I started singing the final tracks, Jae said loud and proud, "Kim, sing like a bird."

Charles helped me identify some new harmonies, and the joy of hearing my voice harmonize with myself again after so many years made my heart explode with ecstasy. The time I shared with Charles and the guys was some of the happiest moments ever. I loved the process of working in the studio and could spend the rest of my days doing it.

My mother was right. I have always had a deeply passionate nature. A workaholic and tending towards perfectionism like my dad, I give my work my all, my best. What is so incredibly magical, however, is that whenever I create my music, the experience feels nothing at all like work. It is as though a loving spirit works through me. All I have to do is be myself, be in the music, exactly as I am, just as Dr. Tappen advised me.

That I'd done in the recording studio.

On the final mix day, I said my mahalos and good-byes to Charles, and Jae and I walked out of the studio in Waimea. It was beginning to mist while the sun was out, not uncommon for Waimea. As we continued to our car holding my final mixed CD, a beautiful double rainbow appeared over the mountains.

But of course!

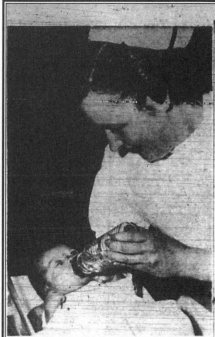

Police Seek Identity Of Foundling's Mother

Nameless and abandoned, a days-old foundling girl last night cried lustily in Genesee Hospital while police and children's welfare authorities tried to find the woman who left her wrapped in a paper bag in a restaurant washroom earlier in the day.

The infant was found in the rest room of Saeger's Grill, 218 Clinton Ave. N., about 11 a. m., minutes after a mystery woman in black entered the place. Mrs. Charles Slora, wife of the grill operator, found the baby.

Mrs. Slora, who told police she had seen a tired-looking young woman enter the rest room three or four minutes earlier, rushed to the door after the discovery. But she could see no sign of the mysterious visitors' appearance.

She called police, who turned the baby over to the Society for the Prevention of Cruelty to Children. An investigator rushed the child to Genesee Hospital where doctors pronounced her in apparent good health. They added the opinion that the girl was between two and five days old.

Mrs. Slora told Det. Sgt. I. James Martin that she saw a strange woman, between 25 and 30, come to the restaurant through a side door and go straight to the rest room. She got a close look at the visitor, she said, because she looked at first glance like an acquaintance.

The woman, Mrs. Slora added, wore a black coat, a flowered kerchief around her head and carried a paper bag. The oper-ator's wife said she went about her business, but a few minutes later went to the rest room to see if the guest needed help.

The woman had vanished when Mrs. Slora opened the door, she said, but on the lid of the toilet seat was the paper bag. Investigation showed the sack contained the baby, sleeping peacefully.

While the SPCC took charge of the child, Martin went about tracking down the mother. His investigation was continuing last night. He said he had at least one promising lead.

Guy D. Harris, director of SPCC, said his agency was joining police in the effort to identify the foundling. The child will be kept in the hospital for a few days, and then probably will be placed into a foster home.

War 2 Vet Serves With Army in Italy

A World War II veteran of Rochester's 209th Antiaircraft Artillery Battalion is now personnel officer at an Army camp in Leghorn, Italy. He is Chief Warrant Officer George Ruedenauer, 35, of 485 Oxford St. Since 1940 Ruedenauer has been in service. With the 209th he served in Northern Ireland, North Africa and Italy.

WHOSE? — Foundling girl, abandoned in rest room, finds solace in bottle offered by Nurse Ruth Lyon in Genesee Hospital. Investigators seek baby's mother.

Article in the Democrat and Chronicle *newspaper, January 26, 1956, of Kim as a newborn left in a washroom.*

Kim in Lava Tracks studio recording "I Found the Rainbow," 2014.

Kim's new Martin 000-18 Golden Era 1937 guitar, 2013.

Christmas with hanai ohana, counterclockwise from bottom left:
Janet holding Mak, Karly, Matt holding Hailie, Kim, and Emma.

⊠ ⊠ ⊠ CHAPTER 24 ⊠ ⊠ ⊠

OUTFLOWING TO ALL
LIVING CREATURES

I put on my blue volunteer's apron, which is required when you arrive to work with the animals at the Hawaii Island Humane Society as a volunteer. After signing in and filling my apron pocket with a bountiful amount of dog cookies, I walked through the door into the adoption area. Sanitizing my hands, I started visiting the older cats and kittens. Sitting with the older cats in the cat room, I sang some made up on the spot, sweet songs for just them. They rubbed their bodies against me purring with delight.

Re-sanitizing my hands, I made my way to the kittens allowed to be held that are kept in smaller crates, opened each crate, and loved every one until it purred, reassuring each little soul that it would have a home of its own soon.

Again re-sanitizing my hands and before entering Adoption Row, I stepped firmly on the two mats that contain a wet bleach-water solution to sanitize my shoes. Walking slowly, I stopped at each dog run, knelt down, and spoke to each little soul by name through the bars of the kennel door. If they had been taken out for a walk by another volunteer within the last two hours, I slowly opened their door, entered, knelt down, spoke softly, and sang while administering cookies. The idea here is to help socialize these often abandoned, rejected, unloved, and sometimes abused children. They needed reassurance. The background barking I imagined as translated simply to "Me too. Pick me. Pick me." I repeated this task with every sweet dog along the way.

On this particular day, I came upon a sweetheart named Cadence, who hadn't been taken out yet that day. I grabbed a leash from the wall, slowly opened her kennel door, and entered. Kneeling down, I administered cookies and words of love and encouragement until shy Cadence approached and accepted me with tail wagging. This was the first time she had met me. I slipped the leash over her head, and together we walked out of her kennel and out the back door of Adoption Row onto the property.

The sky had turned dark over Hualalai Mountain, and it had rained a little while I had been inside loving the animals. Now the air was clean, and the scent of pikake flowers filled the air. Cadence and I walked slowly toward the small, enclosed doggie park situated off the main driveway. If there were no other animals inside, she and I could enter and I could let her off leash to get some exercise. Good news. No dogs.

We entered, and I removed the leash from her neck and said, "Go run, Cadence. I'll be right here."

She cocked her head sideways and looked at me as if she was saying, "Really?"

"Yep. Go, honey. Have fun."

She ran around and smelled every corner of the small park area. I sat on the ground and watched her. My heart was bursting with love and joy. I tried to get her to come to me, but she was too excited. After about ten minutes, I approached her and, displaying the cookie in my hand, said, "Cadence, come get a cookie." She ran to me. I slipped the leash around her neck, gave her the cookie, and practiced heeling and walking on a leash properly now that some of her energy was eliminated. *Boy, all that training I had with Emma sure paid off.*

Opening the door of the park, we walked through the parking lot towards the back of the kennels. I started to sing a special song to her.

> When you wish upon a star
> Makes no difference who you are
> Anything your heart desires
> Will come to you

> If your heart is in your dream
> No request is too extreme . . .
> When you wish upon a star
> Your dreams come true

As I sang, she raised her head, tilted it, and looked directly into my eyes. We stopped for a moment so she and I could have that special connection.

Just then, I heard a voice yelling in the distance, "Kim? Where're Kim and Cadence?"

"Over here," I yelled back.

One of the staff members came running, smiling from ear to ear, all excited. I couldn't imagine what was going on. She ran up to Cadence and me and shouted out, "Guess what! We just got a call from a lady who saw Cadence a couple of days ago. She is going to adopt her. She picks her up tomorrow. Come on. We have to get her ready. Cadence is getting adopted!"

As the volunteer ran back to the administrative office to get the papers ready, Cadence's sweet eyes looked up to me, and her tail began to wag. I started to sing again but this time louder and with more enthusiasm.

> If your heart is in your dream
> No request is too extreme . . .
> When you wish upon a star
> Your dreams come true

My energy and emotions must have flowed down that leash into her body, for Cadence started to jump up and down, tail wagging, mouth open, smiling. Up and down she jumped with enthusiasm. I understood perfectly. *Hi, Judge. Hi, Judge. I'm getting adopted!*

Then it happened. Over Hualalai Mountain, the clouds parted, and a full-spectrum rainbow appeared above Cadence and me. Tingling with emotion, I leaned over and took her sweet white face in my hands. Kissing her nose, I whispered, "See, Cadence, your dreams *can* come true!" And she licked me back.

⌗ ⌗ ⌗

Life, by its very nature, is always in a state of flux. Sometimes you get all gooey inside, sometimes you roar with disgust—all because of what's happening at the time. Life can make you jump up and down with such glee that you might reach the top of the world. Sometimes, you run for the toilet, praying only that you'll get to it in time. Other times, you have to let go of something or someone you treasure. So you part from your lover. Or you place your newborn in a paper bag somewhere you know she'll be found.

But sometimes you can't let go. So you come back. You stick around until you believe your beloved child has finally gotten her act together.

> Now when I close my eyes
> The colors all appear.
> In perfect harmony
> My answers are clear.
> With my eyes finally open,
> And now I can see.
> For I found the rainbow
> And the rainbow is . . . ME.

"I Found the Rainbow" by A. K. Driggs

A Note from the Author

Within and between the pages of my story, perhaps you've come to recognize and rediscover yourself, your passions, and the joy of doing what you love, sharing it with others, and having only to be exactly who you are.

That's the gift.

That's the harmony.

That's the rainbow.